Robust Computer Vision

Computational Imaging and Vision

Managing Editor

MAX A. VIERGEVER
Utrecht University, Utrecht, The Netherlands

Editorial Board
GUNILLA BORGEFORS, *Centre for Image Analysis, SLU, Uppsala, Sweden*
THOMAS S. HUANG, *University of Illinois, Urbana, USA*
SABURO TSUJI, *Wakayama University, Wakayama, Japan*

Volume 26

Robust Computer Vision

Theory and Applications

by

Nicu Sebe

LIACS Media Lab,
Leiden University,
Leiden, The Netherlands

and

Michael S. Lew

LIACS Media Lab,
Leiden University,
Leiden, The Netherlands

KLUWER ACADEMIC PUBLISHERS

DORDRECHT / BOSTON / LONDON

A C.I.P. Catalogue record for this book is available from the Library of Congress.

ISBN 978-90-481-6290-1

Published by Kluwer Academic Publishers,
P.O. Box 17, 3300 AA Dordrecht, The Netherlands.

Sold and distributed in North, Central and South America
by Kluwer Academic Publishers,
101 Philip Drive, Norwell, MA 02061, U.S.A.

In all other countries, sold and distributed
by Kluwer Academic Publishers,
P.O. Box 322, 3300 AH Dordrecht, The Netherlands.

Printed on acid-free paper

To Dafina and my parents
Nicu

To Hyowon
Michael

Contents

Foreword

The field of computer vision is both intellectually stimulating and full of important applications. As the field approaches maturity and commercial products start to appear, one of the most challenging problems is: How to make algorithms robust? Computer vision algorithms are notoriously brittle. This timely book presents a Maximum Likelihood framework to deal with robustness. To paraphrase Kendall and Buckland: "An algorithm is robust if it is not very sensitive to departure from the assumptions on which it depends."

During the past decade, researchers in computer vision have found that probabilistic machine learning methods are extremely powerful. This book describes some of these methods. In addition to the Maximum Likelihood framework, Bayesian Networks, and Hidden Markov models are also used. Three aspects are stressed: features, similarity metric, and models. Many interesting and important new results, based on research by the authors and their collaborators, are presented. To single out one result: Experiments after experiments have shown that in many applications the empirical noise/error can be fitted better with a Cauchy rather than a Gaussian model. This reminds me of an analytical result I derived many years ago when I was working on the compression of two-tone images: The differences between corresponding runlengths of two successive scan lines obey a Cauchy distribution if we assume the directions of the boundaries between black and white is uniformly distributed. Why does the Cauchy distribution pop up so often in real-life data? Are there theoretical results for the Cauchy distribution, akin to the Central Limit Theorem for Gaussian?

Although this book contains many new results, it is written in a style that suits both experts and novices in computer vision. To quote one of my more junior graduate students, who carefully read the manuscript of the book, "It is very clear and easy to understand even for a non-computer vision expert like me."

Finally, a personal note. Michael Lew was my Ph.D. student at Illinois. Nicu Sebe was Michael's Ph.D. student at Leiden, and thus my grand-student. Nicu has also spent time at Illinois, collaborating with my students and me. I am extremely proud to see my student and grand-student produce such a wonderful book.

Thomas S. Huang
Urbana, Illinois
U.S.A.
February 9, 2003

Preface

Computer vision is the enterprise of automating and integrating a wide range of processes and representations used for vision perception. It includes many techniques that are useful by themselves, such as image processing (transforming, encoding, and transmitting images) and statistical pattern classification (statistical decision theory applied to general patterns, visual or otherwise). Moreover, it also includes techniques for geometric modeling and cognitive processing. The field of computer vision may be best understood by considering different types of applications. Many of these applications involve tasks that require either work in a hostile environment, a high rate of processing, access and use of large databases of information, or are tedious for people to perform. Computer vision systems are used in many and various types of environments - from manufacturing plants, to hospital surgical suits, and to the surface of Mars. For example, in manufacturing systems, computer vision is often used for quality control. In this application, the computer vision system scans manufactured items for defects and provides control signals to a robotic manipulator to remove defective parts automatically. Current examples of medical systems being developed include: systems to diagnose skin tumors automatically, systems to aid neurosurgeons during brain surgery, systems to perform clinical tests automatically, etc. The field of law enforcement and security is also an active area for computer vision system development with applications ranging from automatic identification of fingerprints to DNA analysis.

In a standard approach, statistical techniques in computer vision applications must estimate accurate model parameters despite small-scale noise in the data, occasional large-scale measurement errors (outliers), and measurements from multiple populations in the same data set. Increasingly, robust estimation techniques from statistics are being used to solve these parameter estimation problems. Ideally, these techniques should effectively ignore the outliers when estimating the parameters of a single population. In our approach, we consider applications that involve similarity where the ground truth is provided. The goal is to find the probability density function which maximizes the similarity probability. Furthermore, we derive the corresponding metric from the probability density function by using the maximum likelihood paradigm and we use it in the experiments.

The goal of this book is to describe and illuminate some fundamental principles of robust approaches. Consequently, the intention is to introduce basic concepts and techniques of a robust approach and to develop a foundation, which can be used in a wide variety of computer vision algorithms. Chapter 1 introduces the reader to the paradigms, issues, and important applications involving visual similarity, followed by an in-depth chapter (Chapter 2) which discusses the most influential robust framework - maximum likelihood.

In recent years, the vision community has generalized beyond grayscale algorithms toward color techniques which prompts the third chapter on color based retrieval of images and objects. The other primary features which are frequently discussed in the vision literature are texture and shape which are covered in the fourth chapter and in the fifth chapter, respectively.

Beyond classification algorithms, the computer vision area has been interested in finding correspondences between pairs of images which have been taken from different spatial positions (stereo matching) or different moments in time (motion tracking). Our analysis extends to both of these with respect to recent developments in robust techniques in Chapter 5.

Images containing faces are essential to intelligent vision-based human computer interaction. The rapidly expanding research in face processing is based on the premise that information about the user's identity, state, and intent can be extracted from images and that computers can then react accordingly, e.g., by observing a person's facial expression. The area of facial emotion recognition is covered in Chapter 7.

In each of the chapters we show how the literature has introduced robust techniques into the particular topic area, discuss comparative experiments made by us, and conclude with comments and recommendations. Furthermore, we survey the topic area and describe the representative work done.

Acknowledgments

This book would not have existed without the assistance of Nies Huijsmans, Ira Cohen, Ashutosh Garg, Etienne Loupias, and Larry Chen whose technical contributions are directly reflected within the chapters. We would like to thank Frans Peters, Arnold Smeulders, Erwin Bakker, Harry Wijshoff, Joost Kok, and our colleagues from the Leiden Institute of Advanced Computer Science and the IFP group at University of Illinois at Urbana-Champaign who gave us valuable suggestions, discussions, and critical comments. Beyond technical contributions, we would like to thank our families for years of patience, support, and encouragement. Furthermore, we are grateful to the Leiden Institute of Advanced Computer Science for providing an excellent scientific environment.

We would also like to acknowledge the profound influence of Thomas Huang on our scientific work and on this book in particular.

Chapter 1

INTRODUCTION

Computer vision has grown rapidly within the past decade, producing tools that enable the understanding of visual information, especially for scenes with no accompanying structural, administrative, or descriptive text information. The Internet, more specifically the Web, has become a common channel for the transmission of graphical information, thus moving visual information retrieval rapidly from stand-alone workstations and databases into a networked environment. Practicality has begun to dictate that the indexing of huge collections of images by hand is a task that is both labor intensive and expensive - in many cases more than can be afforded to provide some method of intellectual access to digital image collections. In the world of text retrieval, text "speaks for itself" whereas image analysis requires a combination of high-level concept creation as well as the processing and interpretation of inherent visual features. Examples of visual features include color, texture, shape, motion, etc. In the area of intellectual access to visual information, the interplay between human and machine image indexing methods has begun to influence the development of computer vision systems. Research and application by the image understanding (IU) community suggests that the most fruitful approaches to IU involve analysis of the type of information being sought, the domain in which it will be used, and systematic testing to identify optimal methods.

The field of computer vision may be best understood by considering different types of applications. Many of these applications involve tasks that either are tedious for people to perform, require work in a hostile environment, require a high rate of processing, or require access and use of large databases of information. Computer vision systems are used in many and various types of environments - from manufacturing plants, to hospital surgical suits, and to the surface of Mars. For example, in manufacturing systems, computer vision is often used for quality control. There, the computer vision system will scan manufactured items for defects and provide control signals to a robotic manipulator to remove defective parts automatically. Current examples of medical systems being developed include: systems to diagnose skin tumors automatically, systems to aid neurosurgeons during brain surgery, systems to perform clinical tests automatically, etc. The field of law enforcement and security is also an active area for computer vision system development with applications ranging from automatic identification of fingerprints to DNA analysis.

1. Visual Similarity

Similarity has been a research topic in the psychology field for decades, for example, early researchers were Wallach [Wallach, 1958], and Tversky and Krantz [Tversky and Krantz, 1977]. Recently there has been a huge resurgence in the topic. Similarity judgments are considered to be a valuable tool in the study of human perception and cognition, and play a central role in theories of human knowledge representation, behavior, and problem solving. Tversky [Tversky, 1977] describes the similarity concept as "an organizing principle by which individuals classify objects, form concepts, and make generalizations."

Retrieval of images by similarity, i.e. retrieving images which are similar to an already retrieved image (retrieval by example) or to a model or schema, is a relatively old idea. Some might date it to antiquity, but more seriously it appeared in specialized geographical information systems databases around 1980, in particular in the Query by Pictorial Example system of IMAID [Chang and Fu, 1980]. From the start it was clear that retrieval by similarity called for specific definitions of what it means to be similar. In the mapping system, a satellite image was matched to existing map images from the point of view of similarity of road and river networks, easily extracted from images by edge detection. Apart from theoretical models [Aigrain, 1987], it was only in the beginning of the 90s that researchers started to look at retrieval by similarity in large sets of heterogeneous images with no specific model of their semantic contents. The prototype systems of Kato [Kato, 1992], followed by the availability of the QBIC commercial system using several types of similarities [Flicker et al., 1995], contributed to making this idea more and more popular.

Typically, a system for retrieval by similarity rest on three components:

- Extraction of features or image signatures from the images, and an efficient representation and storage strategy for this precomputed data.

- A set of similarity measures, each of which captures some perceptively meaningful definition of similarity, and which should be efficiently computable when matching an example with the whole database.

- A user interface for the choice of which definition of similarity should be applied for retrieval, presentation of retrieved images, and for supporting relevance feedback.

The research in the area has made evident that:

- A large number of meaningful types of similarity can be defined. Only part of these definitions are associated with efficient feature extraction mechanisms and (dis)similarity measures.

- Since there are many definitions of similarity and the discriminating power of each of the measures is likely to degrade significantly for large image databases, the user interaction and the feature storage strategy components of the systems will play an important role.

- Visual content based retrieval is best used when combined with the traditional search, both at user interface and at the system level. The basic reason for this is that content based retrieval is not seen as a replacement of parametric (SQL), text, and keywords search. The key is to apply content based retrieval where appropriate, which is typically where the use of text and keywords is suboptimal. Examples of such applications are where visual appearance (e.g. color, texture, motion) is the primary attribute as in stock photo/video, art, etc.

A concept of similarity is inherently present in stereo matching. In a stereo matching setup, shots of a given static scene are captured from different viewpoints and the resulting images differ slightly due to the effect of perspective projection. Features that distinguish stereo matching from image matching in general are the following:

- The important differences in the stereo images result from the different viewpoints, and not, for example from changes in the scene. We therefore seek a match between two images, as opposed to a match between an image and an abstract model (although the latter may be an important step in determining the former).

- Most of the significant changes will occur in the appearance of nearby objects and in occlusions. Additional changes in both geometry and photometry can be introduced in the film development and scanning steps, but can usually be avoided by careful processing. If the images are recorded at very different times, there may by significant lighting effects.

- Modeling based on stereo matching generally requires that, ultimately, dense grids of points are matched.

Ideally, we would like to find the correspondences (i.e., matched locations) of every individual pixel in both images of a stereo pair. However, it is obvious that the information content in the intensity value of a single pixel is too low for unambiguous matching. In practice, therefore, coherent collections of pixels are matched.

Matching is complicated by several factors related to the geometry of the stereo images. Some areas that are visible in one image may be occluded in the other, for instance, and this can lead to incorrect matches. Periodic structures in the scene can cause a stereo matcher to confuse a feature in one image with features from nearby parts of the structure in the other image, especially if the image features generated by these structures are close together compared with the disparity of the features. If there is a large amount of relief in the scene (e.g., a vertical obstruction that projects above the ground plane in an aerial view), the corresponding features may be reversed in their positions in the two stereo images.

Similarity is also present in a video sequence where motion is the main characterizing element. Here the frames differ slightly due to a change in the relative position of spatial entities in the sequence or to a camera movement. Methods that compute an approximate estimation of motion follow two approaches. One method takes into account temporal changes of gray level primitives, from one frame to the following one, and computes a dense flow usually at every pixel of the image. The other one is based on the extraction of a set of sparse characteristic features of the objects, such as corners or salient points, and their tracking in subsequent frames. Once interframe correspondence is established, and constraints are formulated on object rigidity, motion components are obtained by solving a set of non-linear equations [Aggarwal and Nandhakumar, 1988].

Gudivada [Gudivada and Raghavan, 1995] has listed different possible types of similarity for retrieval: color similarity, texture similarity, shape similarity, spatial similarity, etc. Some of these types can be considered in all or only part of one image, can be considered independently of scale or angle or not, depending on whether one is interested in the scene represented by the image or in the image itself.

Representation of features of images - like color, texture, shape, motion, etc. - is a fundamental problem in visual information retrieval. Image analysis and pattern recognition algorithms provide the means to extract numeric descriptors which give a quantitative measure of these features. Computer vision enables object and motion identification by comparing extracted patterns with predefined models. In this section we discuss specific issues regarding the representation of the visual content in applications involving color, texture, shape, stereo matching, motion tracking, and facial emotion recognition. A more elaborate discussion is presented in Chapters 3, 4, 5, 6, and 7.

1.1   Color

Color is an important attribute of visual information. Not only does color add beauty to objects but it also gives information about objects as well. Furthermore, color information facilitates our daily life, e.g. in traffic when reading a stop light or in identification of a favorite team in a sport event. Color is related to chromatic attributes of images. Human color perception is concerned with physical phenomena, neurophysiological effects, and psychological behavior [Boynton, 1990].

Color distribution similarity has been one of the first choices for retrieval because if one chooses a proper representation and measure, it can be reliable even in the presence of changes in lighting, view angle, and scale. However, the recorded color varies considerably with the surface orientation, position and spectrum of the illuminant, the viewpoint of the camera. Moreover, the human perception of color is an intricate problem and many attempts have been made to capture color perceptual similarity.

From the physical point of view, color perception derives from the spectral energy distribution of the electromagnetic radiation that strikes the retina. This is usually expressed as a function of wavelength $E(\lambda)$ in the visible range of 380-780nm. Spectral energy distribution can be expressed as:

$$E(\lambda) = S(\lambda)R(\lambda) \tag{1.1}$$

where $S(\lambda)$ is the spectral distribution of the light source when light strikes the observed object and $R(\lambda)$ is the spectral reflectance characteristics of the object surface.

The response of the human visual system to differences in $E(\lambda)$ originates from three distinct types of photoreceptor cells in the retina, called cones, which have long, medium, and short wavelength sensitivity $S_i(\lambda)$.

Spectral energy distribution of a colored light $C(\lambda)$ produces signals which are described by a spectral response $\alpha_i(C)$

$$\alpha_i(C) = \int_{\lambda_{\min}}^{\lambda_{\max}} S_i(\lambda)C(\lambda)d\lambda \qquad i = 1, 2, 3 \tag{1.2}$$

These signals are transformed in order to produce output signals that provoke color sensation in the brain.

On the other hand, from the psychological point of view, perception of a color is related to several factors including color attributes (brightness, chromaticity, and saturation), surrounding colors, color spatial organization, the observer's memory, knowledge, or experience.

Color indexing is one of the most prevalent retrieval methods in content based image retrieval. Given a query image, the goal is to retrieve all the images whose color compositions are similar to the color composition of the query image. Typically, the color content is described using a histogram [Swain and Ballard, 1991]. A color histogram is obtained by discretizing image colors and counting how many pixels belong to each color. The fundamental elements of the color histogram based approach include the selection of a

color feature space [Sebe and Lew, 2000a] together with the associated quantization scheme [Sebe and Lew, 2000b], and the histogram distance metric [Sebe
and Lew, 2001a].

There has been no consensus about which color feature space is most suitable for color histogram based image retrieval. The problem is a result of
the fact that there does not exist a universally accepted color space, and color
perception is significantly subjective [Wyszecki and Stiles, 1982]. As a consequence, a large variety of color spaces is used in practice.

RGB representations are widely used [Flicker et al., 1995][Jain and
Vailaya, 1996], however, the RGB color representation is a good choice only
when there is no variation in recording or in the perception because this representation was designed to match the input channel of the eye. An image
expressed in RGB makes most sense when it is recorded in frontal view under
standard conditions.

A significant improvement over the RGB can be obtained if the brightness information is separated from the chrominance. A solution is to use the
opponent color representation which uses the opponent color axes $R - G$,
$2B - R - G$, $R + G + B$ [Swain and Ballard, 1991]. With this solution, the
first two chromaticity axes can be down-sampled as humans are more sensitive
to brightness than they are to chroma. This color representation is invariant to
changes in illumination intensity and shadows.

The HSV representation is also often selected for its invariant properties
[Stricker and Orengo, 1995]. The hue is invariant under the orientation of the
object with respect to the illumination and camera direction and hence is more
suited for object retrieval [Gevers and Smeulders, 1999].

Other approaches use the Munsell or the $L^*a^*b^*$ color spaces [Sebe and
Lew, 1999a] because of their relative perceptual uniformity. The $L^*a^*b^*$ representation is designed so that the Euclidean distance between two colors models the human perception of color differences. A wide variety of photometric
color invariants for object retrieval were derived in [Gevers and Smeulders,
2000] from an analysis of Schafer's model of object reflection.

Typically a histogram intersection criterion is used to compare color histograms. Different approaches introduced sophisticated methods of comparing histograms which more correspond to human judgment of color similarity
[Sawhney and Hafner, 1994][Hafner et al., 1995]. Hafner et al. [Hafner et al.,
1995] suggest the usage of a quadratic form of distance measure which tries
to capture the perceptual similarity between any two colors. Observing the
fact that the color histograms lack information about how color is spatially distributed, Huang et al. [Huang et al., 1997] introduced the color correlogram as
a color feature for image retrieval. This feature characterizes how the spatial
correlation of pairs of color changes with distance in an image.

In all of these works, most of the attention has been focused on the color models as well as on finding better features. However, little or no consideration was paid for investigating the noise models and finding better metrics. Even when different metrics were presented as in [Kelly et al., 1995] and [Kelly et al., 1996], there was no discussion how and why these metrics influence the retrieval results.

Color representations and color based retrieval are addressed in detail in Chapter 3.

1.2 Texture

Texture is a broad term used in pattern recognition to identify image patches (of any size) that are characterized by differences in brightness. Generally speaking, a texture has to do with repeated patterns in the image. Smoothed images are usually not considered as textured images. The size of the image patch, the number of distinguishable gray levels primitives, and the spatial relationship between these primitives, are all interrelated elements which characterize a texture [Brodatz, 1966]. A scale of reference must be decided in order to analyze a texture. It is conventional in the texture analysis literature to investigate texture at the pixel resolution scale; that is, the texture which has significant variation at the pixel level of resolution, but which is homogeneous at a level of resolution about an order of magnitude coarser. From the psychological point of view, texture features that strike the human observer are granularity, directionality, and repetitiveness [Tamura et al., 1978][Liu and Picard, 1996].

Interest in visual texture was triggered by the phenomenon of texture discrimination which occurs when a shape is defined purely by its texture, with no associated change in color or brightness: color alone cannot distinguish between tigers and cheetahs! This phenomenon gives clear justification for texture features to be used in content based retrieval together with color and shape. Several systems have been developed to search through image databases using a combination of texture, color, and shape attributes (QBIC [Flicker et al., 1995], Photobook [Pentland et al., 1996], Chabot [Ogle and Stonebracker, 1995], VisualSEEk [Smith and Chang, 1996], etc.). However, texture alone can be used for content based retrieval [Ma and Manjunath, 1998][Ramsey et al., 1999][Smith and Chang, 1994].

In practice, there are two different approaches in which texture is used as the main feature for content based retrieval. In the first approach, texture features are extracted from the images and then are used for finding similar images in the database [Ma and Manjunath, 1998][Gorkani and Picard, 1994] [Smith and Chang, 1994]. Texture queries can be formulated in a similar manner to color queries by selecting examples of desired textures from a palette, or by supplying an example query image. The system then retrieves images with texture measures most similar in value to the query. The systems using this approach may use previously segmented textures as in the applications with Brodatz database [Picard et al., 1993], or they first have a segmentation stage after which the extracted features in different regions are used as queries [Ma and Manjunath, 1998]. The segmentation algorithm used in this case may be crucial for the content based retrieval. In the second approach, texture is used for annotating the image [Picard and Minka, 1995]. Here, vision based annotation assists the user in attaching descriptions to large sets of images. The user is asked to label a piece of an image and a texture model can be used to propagate this label to other visually similar regions.

The method of texture analysis chosen for feature extraction is critical to the success of the texture classification. However, the metric used in comparing the feature vectors is also clearly critical. Many methods have been proposed to extract texture features either directly from the image statistics, e.g. co-occurrence matrix [Haralick et al., 1973], or from the spatial frequency domain [Van Gool et al., 1985]. Ohanian and Dubes [Ohanian and Dubes, 1992] studied the performance of four types of features: Markov Random Fields parameters, Gabor multi-channel features, fractal based features, and co-occurrence features. Comparative studies to evaluate the performance of some texture features were made in [Reed and Du Buf, 1993], [Ojala et al., 1996], [Sebe and Lew, 2000d], and [Sebe and Lew, 2000c].

Recently multiscale approaches applied to the texture problem have received wide attention. Wavelets have often been considered for their locality and compression efficiency. Smith and Chang [Smith and Chang, 1994] used the statistics (mean and variance) extracted from the wavelet subbands as the texture representation. To explore the middle-band characteristics, tree-structured wavelet transform was used by Chang and Kuo [Chang and Kuo, 1993]. Ma and Manjunath [Ma and Manjunath, 1995] evaluated the texture image annotation by various wavelet transform representations, including the orthogonal and bi-orthogonal wavelet transforms, the tree-structured wavelet transform, and the Gabor wavelet transform (GWT). They found out that the Gabor transform was the best among the tested candidates, which matched the human vision study results [Beck et al., 1987].

A texture is usually represented through a numerical vector, holding measures of texture features. Image processing operators, operating in either the space or frequency domain, are used to derive measures of texture features [Sebe and Lew, 2001b][Tuceryan and Jain, 1998]. A texture is therefore modeled as a point in a suitable multidimensional feature space. Standard mathematical distances like L_2 or L_1 are used to measure the distance between two points in the texture feature space. Most of the previous studies have focused on the features, but not on the metric, nor on modeling the similarity distribution.

Texture modeling and retrieval by texture similarity are discussed in detail in Chapter 4.

1.3 Shape

Shape is a concept which is widely understood yet difficult to define formally. For human beings perception of shape is a high-level concept whereas mathematical definitions tend to describe shape with low-level attributes. Therefore, there exists no uniform theory of shape. However, the word shape can be defined in some specific frameworks. For object recognition purposes Marshall [Marshall, 1989] defined shape as a function of position and direction of a simply connected curve within a two-dimensional field. Clearly, this definition is not general, nor even sufficient for general pattern recognition.

In pattern recognition, the definition suggested by Marshall [Marshall, 1989] is suitable for two dimensional image objects whose boundaries or pixels inside the boundaries can be identified. It must be pointed out that this kind of definition requires that there are some objects in the image and, in order to code or describe the shape, the objects must be identified by segmentation. Therefore, either manual or automatic segmentation is usually performed before shape description.

To humans, a few selected signs are not only sufficient for identification but also determine the impression of a complete and real representation of the object. On the other hand, computer vision research has provided many different solutions for shape representation and measurement of the difference of two shapes. For the purposes of retrieval by shape similarity, representations are preferred such that the salient perceptual aspects of a shape are captured and the human notion of closeness between shapes corresponds to the topological closeness in the representation space.

A proper definition of shape similarity calls for the distinctions between shape similarity in images (similarity between actual geometrical shapes appearing in the images) and shape similarity between the objects depicted by the images, i.e. similarity modulo a number of geometrical transformations corresponding to changes in view angle, optical parameters, and scale. In some cases, one wants to include even deformation of non-rigid bodies. The first type of similarity has attracted research work only for calibrated image databases of special types of objects, such as ceramic plates. Even, in this case, the researchers have tried to define shape representations which are scale independent, resting on curvature, angle statistics, and contour complexity. Systems such as QBIC [Flicker et al., 1995] use circularity, eccentricity, major axis orientation (not angle-independent), and algebraic moment. It should be noted that in some cases the user of a retrieval system will want a definition of shape similarity which is dependent on view angle (for instance will want to retrieve trapezoids with an horizontal basis and not the other trapezoids).

In the general case, a promising approach has been proposed by Sclaroff and Pentland [Sclaroff and Pentland, 1995] in which shapes are represented as canonical deformations of prototype objects. In this approach, a "physical" model of the 2D-shape is built using a new form of Galerkin's interpolation method (finite-element discretization). The possible deformation modes are analyzed using the Karhunen-Loeve transform. This yields an ordered list of deformation modes corresponding to rigid body modes (translation, rotation), low-frequency non-rigid modes associated to global deformations, and higher-frequency modes associated to localized deformations.

As for color and texture, the present schemes for shape similarity modeling are faced with serious difficulties when images include several objects or background. A preliminary segmentation as well as modeling of spatial relationships between shapes is then necessary (are we interested in finding images where one region represent a shape similar to a given prototype or to some spatial organization of several shapes?).

A promising approach toward shape segmentation is using active contours. Active contours were first introduced by Kass et al. [Kass et al., 1988], and were termed snakes by the nature of their movement. They are a sophisticated approach to contour extraction and image interpretation. Active contours are defined as energy-minimizing splines under the influence of internal and external forces. The internal forces of the active contour serve as a smoothness constraint designed to hold the active contour together (elasticity forces) and to keep it from bending too much (bending forces). The external forces guide the active contour towards image features such as high intensity gradients. The optimal contour position is computed such that the total energy is minimized. The contour can hence be viewed as a reasonable balance between geometrical smoothness properties and local correspondence with the intensity function of the reference image. The principal advantage of using an active contour approach is that the image data, the initial estimate, the desired contour properties, and the knowledge-based constraints are integrated into a single extraction process.

Perhaps the most popular method for shape description is the use of invariant moments [Hu, 1962] which are invariant to affine transformations. When gross structural features are characterized by the invariant moments, the global (region) properties provide a firm common base for similarity measure between shapes silhouettes. In the cases where there is no occlusion, the invariance to position, size, and orientation, and the low dimensionality of the feature vector represent good reasons for using the invariant moments in matching shapes.

Shape based retrieval issues are discussed in detail in Chapter 5.

1.4 Stereo

Because our eyes are placed some distance apart, they do not see the exact same image. However, the two different impressions on the retina are united in one single image representation in the brain. Although the eyes actually record two images, we have the sensation of viewing the scene from one spot, as if we had only one eye in the center of the forehead. The process is called stereopsis, and we talk of the stereoscopic or cyclopean image. Recognition of this surprising fact is the starting point in stereoscopy.

More generally, stereopsis refers to the capability of determining the depth of a three-dimensional point by observing the point on two perspective projection images taken from different positions. The common area appearing in both images of the stereo pair is usually 40% to 80% of the total image area.

Stereo imaging offers an intuitive way to reconstruct the lost depth information. It relies on one fundamental finding: if two shots of a given scene are captured from two different viewpoints, then the resulting images will differ slightly due to the effect of perspective projection. Stereo matching implies finding correspondences between these images. If the correspondences can be found accurately and the camera geometry is known, then a 3D model of the environment can be reconstructed [Marr and Poggio, 1979][Barnard and Fischler, 1982]. Stated more simply, stereo matching is the process of finding a pair of image points produced by the same object point in a stereo arrangement. The distance that one of the points has shifted with respect to the second one - relative to its local coordinate system - is termed disparity and is the fundamental measure required to reconstruct a scene.

Several algorithms have been developed to compute the disparity between images, e.g. the correlation based methods [Luo and Maitre, 1990] or feature based methods [Grimson, 1985].

In correlation based stereo [Luo and Maitre, 1990][Mori et al., 1973] [Kanade and Okutomi, 1994] disparity is computed by fixing a small window around a pixel in the left image, then measuring the Sum-of-Squared-difference (SSD) error between intensities in that window and those in similar windows placed at different locations in the right image. The placement that yields the lowest error gives the disparity estimate. However, as Barnard and Fischler [Barnard and Fischler, 1987] pointed out, "a problem with correlation (or SSD) matching is that the patch (window) size should be large enough to include enough intensity variation for matching but small enough to avoid the effects of projective distortion." If the window is too small and does not cover enough intensity variation, it gives poor disparity estimate, because the signal (intensity variation) to noise ratio is low. If, on the other hand, the window is too large and covers a region in which the depth of scene points (i.e., disparity) varies, then the position of maximum correlation or minimum SSD may not represent correct matching due to different projective distortions in the left and right images. For this reason, a window size should be selected adaptively depending on local variations of intensity and disparity. For doing this a statistical model of the disparity distribution within the window is proposed by Kanade and Okutomi [Kanade and Okutomi, 1994]. Another solution is given by Fusiello et al. [Fusiello et al., 1997]. They implemented an algorithm that is the extension of the simple SSD match in the sense that nine windows were used instead of one. The reference and matching image points were placed at pre-defined locations within the windows in order to find the best area-correlation amongst them.

In feature based stereo [Grimson, 1985][Matthies, 1989] semantic features (with known physical properties and/or spatial geometry) or intensity anomaly features (isolated anomalous intensity patterns not necessarily having any physical significance) are the basic units that are matched. Semantic features of the generic types include occlusion edges, vertices of linear structures, and prominent surface markings; domain specific semantic features may include such features as the corner or peak of a building, or a road surface marking. Intensity anomaly features include zero crossings or salient points [Sebe et al., 2000b]. Methods used for feature matching often include symbolic classification techniques, as well as correlation.

Cox et al. [Cox et al., 1996] presented a stereo algorithm that performs matching on the individual pixel intensity, instead of using an adaptive window as in the correlation based methods. Their algorithm optimizes a maximum likelihood cost function which assumes that corresponding features in the left and right images are normally distributed about a common true value. However, the authors [Cox et al., 1996] noticed that the normal distribution assumption used to compare corresponding intensity values is violated for some of their test sets and therefore they decided to alter the stereo pair so that the noise distribution would be closer to a Gaussian.

Most of the efforts mentioned above were concentrated on finding a better algorithm or feature that can provide a more accurate and dense disparity map. Some of them use a simple SSD (L_2) or SAD (L_1) metric in matching correspondences or make assumptions about the corresponding features in the left and right stereo images. Recent research by Bhat and Nayar [Bhat and Nayar, 1998] concluded that the SSD used in a stereo matching procedure is sensitive to outliers and therefore robust M-estimators should be used for stereo matching. However, the authors [Bhat and Nayar, 1998] did not consider metrics based on similarity distributions. They considered ordinal metrics, where an ordinal metric is based on relative ordering of intensity values in windows - rank permutations.

1.5 Motion

Motion is the main characterizing element in a sequence of frames. It is directly related to a change in the relative position of spatial entities or to a camera movement. The measurement of object or camera motion from video sequences is an important component in many applications. For example, in computer vision systems it enables the identification and tracking of the objects that make up a scene; while in video data compression it provides a means of reducing redundancy - knowing the motion of an object allows its position in successive frames to be predicted, removing the need to retransmit identical frame data and leading to a reduction in the bit rate required to transmit the video. Other applications include the generation of high resolution and panoramic images from video and the automated building of virtual reality environments. In the case of video sequences the differences in two images result mainly from the changes in scene and not from the different viewpoint positions as in stereo matching.

An important issue is to track moving feature points on human faces in order to analyze human facial movement. The motion parameters of these feature points can be used to reconstruct the original motion (e.g., human expression synthesis [Tang and Huang, 1994]) or for further analysis (e.g., computerized lipreading [Bregler et al., 1993] and expression recognition [Black and Yacoob, 1995; Cohen et al., 2003]).

There are two classical methods for tracking feature points, namely optical flow and block correlation (template matching). The former method tries to find the correspondence between two images by calculating the velocity (displacement vector) at which a point in the first image has moved in the second image [Barron et al., 1994]. The latter tracks a specific point by finding the maximum similarity between two pixel patterns of images containing this point [Tang et al., 1994]. This approach is very similar to the correlation based approach in stereo matching.

Stereo matching and motion tracking issues are addressed in detail in Chapter 6.

1.6 Facial expression

Human face-to-face communication is an ideal model for designing a multimodal/media human-computer interface. The terms "face-to-face" and "interface" indicate that the face plays an essential role in interpersonal communication. The face is used to identify other people, to interpret what has been said by the means of lipreading, and to understand someone's emotional state and intentions on the basis of the shown facial expression. Personality, attractiveness, age, and gender can also be seen from someone's face. Considerable research in social psychology has also shown that facial expressions help coordinate conversation [Boyle et al., 1994; Stephenson et al., 1976] and have considerably more effect on whether a listener feels liked or disliked than the speaker's spoken words [Mehrabian, 1968]. Mehrabian [Mehrabian, 1968] indicated that the verbal part (i.e., spoken words) of a message contributes only for 7 percent to the effect of the message as a whole, the vocal part (e.g., voice intonation) contributes for 38 percent, while facial expression of the speaker contributes for 55 percent to the effect of the spoken message. This implies that the facial expressions form the major modality in human communication.

Recent advances in image analysis and pattern recognition open up the possibility of automatic detection and classification of emotional and conversational facial signals. Automatic facial expression analysis could bring facial expressions into man-machine interaction as a new modality and could make the interaction tighter and more efficient. Such a system could also make classification of facial expressions widely accessible as a tool for research in behavioral science and medicine.

Ekman and Friesen [Ekman and Friesen, 1978] developed the Facial Action Coding System (FACS) to code facial expressions where movements on the face are described by a set of action units (AUs) (each AU has some related muscular basis). This system has been developed to facilitate objective measurement of facial activity for behavioral science investigations of the face. Most of the studies on automated expression analysis perform an emotional classification. The most commonly used study on emotional classification of facial expressions is the cross-cultural study on existence of "universal categories of emotional expressions." Ekman [Ekman, 1994] defined six such categories, referred to as the *basic emotions*: happiness, sadness, surprise, fear, anger, and disgust. He described each basic emotion in terms of a facial expression that uniquely characterizes that emotion. In the past years, many questions arose around this study. Are the basic emotional expressions indeed universal [Ekman, 1982; Ekman, 1994], or are they merely a stressing of the verbal communication and have no relation with an actual emotional state [Fridlund, 1991; Russell, 1994]? Also, it is not at all certain that each facial expression that is displayed on the face can be classified under the six basic emotion categories. Nevertheless, most of the studies on vision-based facial expression analysis rely on Ekman's emotional characterization of facial expressions.

An important step in facial expression analysis is to classify (interpret, identify) the facial display conveyed by the face. Therefore, the design of the classifiers used for emotion recognition is of crucial importance. There are basically, two types of settings for emotion classification from video sequences: dynamic and static classification.

The 'static' classifiers classify a frame in the video to one of the facial expression categories based on the tracking results of that frame. The most commonly used classifiers for this approach are the Bayesian network classifiers [Sebe et al., 2002; Cohen et al., 2002]. Typically, Bayesian network classifiers are learned with a fixed structure – the paradigmatic example is the Naive Bayes classifier. More flexible learning methods allow Bayesian network classifiers to be selected from a small subset of possible structures – for example, the Tree-Augmented-Naive-Bayes structures [Friedman et al., 1997]. After a structure is selected, the parameters of the classifier are usually learned using maximum likelihood estimation.

Dynamic classifiers take into account the temporal pattern in displaying facial expression. Hidden Markov model (HMM) based classifiers are commonly used in this case [Otsuka and Ohya, 1997a; Oliver et al., 1997; Lien, 1998]. One possibility is to use a multi-level HMM classifier [Cohen et al., 2003]. In this case, combining the temporal information allows not only to perform the classification of a video segment to the corresponding facial expression, as in the previous works on HMM based classifiers, but also to automatically segment an arbitrary long video sequence to the different expressions segments without resorting to heuristic methods of segmentation.

An important aspect is that while the static classifiers are easier to train and implement, the dynamic classifiers require more training samples and many more parameters to learn.

Details on facial expression recognition studies and experiments are given in Chapter 7.

1.7 Summary

In conclusion, several major problems need to be addressed for the visual similarity techniques:

- Study of the distribution of measures for various feature spaces on large real-world sets of image. In particular, how well is the perceptive similarity order preserved by the measure when the number of images/videos grows?

- Study of ranking visual items that correspond to human perception.

- Definition of methods for the segmentation of images in homogeneous regions for various feature spaces, and definition of models of this spatial organization which could be robustly combined with the similarity of the local features.

- Detection of salient features to a type of images or objects, so that to free the user from specifying a particular set of features in query process.

- Combination of multiple visual features in image query and search.

- Developing efficient indexing schemes based on image similarity features for managing large databases. It has been shown that traditional database indexing techniques such as using R-trees fail in the context of content based image search. Therefore, ideas from statistical clustering, multi-dimensional indexing, and dimensionality reduction are extremely useful in this area.

Apart from these issues, extraction and matching of higher (semantic) level image/video attributes (such as recognition of object, human faces, and actions) are perhaps the most challenging tasks. Only when the features extracted at both these levels are combined, can similarity-based indexes be built.

In addition, to the success of the field, formalization of the whole paradigm of visual similarity is essential. Without this formalism it will be hard to develop sufficient reliable and mission critical applications that are easy to program and evaluate. Some early applications may be implemented without such a rigorous formalism, but the progress in the field will require full understanding of the basic requirements in visual similarity.

2. Evaluation of Computer Vision Algorithms

Most of the research in the computer vision and pattern recognition community is focussed on developing solutions to vision problems. With three decades of research behind current efforts and the availability of powerful and inexpensive computers, there is a common belief that computer vision is poised to deliver reliable solutions. Unfortunately, for some applications there are no methods available to test whether computer vision algorithms can live up to their claims. Nor is there any way to measure performance among algorithms, or to reliably determine the state-of-the-art of solutions to a particular problem.

How do you evaluate the work of others when you do not have their programs? What does it mean when a reimplementation does not work? Who failed, the algorithm or the implementation? How do you compare results? These problems are nicely presented by Price in his article "Anything You Can Do, I Can Do Better (No You Can't)..." [Price, 1986]: "A graduate student determines that an operator, called the Homer Operator (HO for short), can be used to determine stereo disparities. She writes her thesis and publishes several papers with all the details that seem relevant ... A professor tells a new graduate student to reimplement the algorithm described in the original thesis and papers. Disparities which seem reasonable, are generated by the program, and the student proceeds with research in motion, forgetting stereo. Eventually, another student tries the programs on completely new data and the programs fail to produce meaningful results. This student, being adept of symbolic computation, discovers that the original algorithm works properly only under extremely specific conditions, which were never explicitly discussed, but which often occur in practice."

The evaluation work can be divided in three basic categories. As is the risk with any classification, the categories will not necessarily be clean divisions. Evaluation work could fit into more than one category, or not neatly fit into any category.

The first category is evaluations that are independently administered. In the prototypical independent evaluation, one group collects a set of images, designs the evaluation protocol, provides images to the users, and evaluates the test results. This method allows for a high degree of standardization in the evaluation, since all algorithms are tested on the same images and scored by the same method. Thus, independent evaluations usually allow for a direct comparison between competing approaches to a problem. The competing approaches are usually state-of-the-art algorithms and the individual competitors are often the original developers of the algorithms. Independent evaluation by a non-competitor gives a greater sense of impartiality and objectivity to the results. The major drawback to this form of evaluation is the level of ongoing effort required by the group administering the evaluation. Ideally, the evaluation mechanism needs to evolve and be refined over time.

The second category is evaluations of a set of classification algorithms by one group. The group wanting to do the evaluation will often not be able to get access to original implementations of all of the algorithms of interest, and so will have to implement some of the algorithms based on information in the literature. This introduces the possibility that the version of the algorithm evaluated will not be identical to that used by the original developers of the algorithm. However, implementation and evaluation of a set algorithms by one group can at least establish performance for baseline algorithms.

An important theoretical aspect of the first two categories is that ground truth is not fuzzy and can be determined accurately. Classification problems often exhibit this property. For example, the identity of a person in a face image is not fuzzy, and the particular character that is written in a certain location is known. As long as provision for recording ground truth is made at data collection time, it should be possible to get reliable and accurate ground truth. However, in practice things are sometimes not so simple.

The third category is problems where the ground truth is not self evident and a major component of the evaluation process is to develop a method of obtaining the ground truth.

Our effort fits best in the second category. We implemented several sophisticated algorithms from the computer vision literature and evaluated their results in the presence of ground truth [Sebe et al., 1998][Sebe et al., 2000a] [Lew et al., 2000]. For some of the algorithms we used the original source code (when it was available) and we modified only the part of the code where the information given by the ground truth was used. For our image retrieval experiments we considered the applications of printer-scanner copy location and object recognition by color invariance. In the printer-scanner application, an image was printed to paper and then scanned back into the computer. This task involved noise due to the dithering patterns of the printer and scanner noise. In object recognition, multiple pictures were taken of a single object at different orientations. In these applications, the correct match (ground truth) for an image was known at the moment of the creation of the database. In our texture classification experiments the ground truth was implicitly given from the procedure the texture database was created. We considered the Brodatz texture database [Brodatz, 1966] and random samples from the original textures were extracted and stored in the database. When presenting a texture sample as query, the goal was to retrieve as many as possible samples from the same original texture. Also, in the case of shape retrieval the ground truth was obtained from the procedure the database was created. We used the Coil-20 database [Murase and Nayar, 1995] which consists of 1,440 images of common household objects. Each object was placed on a turntable and photographed every $5°$ for a total of 72 views per object. In stereo matching and motion tracking, the ground truth is typically generated manually. A set of reference points are defined in the images and then a person finds the correspondences for the stereo pair or video sequence. In our experiments the ground truth was provided by the laboratories where the images were taken. For the facial expression recognition experiments we used two databases of subjects that were instructed to display facial expressions corresponding to different emotions. In this case, the ground truth was consisted of the known labeled emotions.

As noted before, the presence of ground truth is very important in the evaluation and comparison of different algorithms. Additionally, the ground truth may also provide some extra information for improving the results of an algorithm. How can one use the information provided by the ground truth? This is exactly one of the questions we try to answer in this book. Typically, in a computer vision application involving similarity, feature vectors are extracted from the images and a comparison metric is used to compare these feature vectors. The ground truth contains the definition of similarity for that particular application. In an ideal case, the similar images (or features) would be identical and then the retrieval or matching would be an easy problem to solve. However, in real cases, the similar images are not identical and therefore when comparing these images a certain distortion between them, called similarity noise, will be present. If one can accurately model the similarity noise distribution, then the retrieval or matching results can be significantly improved by using a suitable metric. The link between the similarity noise distribution and the comparison metric is given by the maximum likelihood theory. For example, according to the maximum likelihood theory, if the similarity noise distribution is Gaussian then the corresponding comparison metric is L_2. In summary, having the ground truth in an application involving similarity, our goal is to find the probability density function which maximizes the similarity probability. Furthermore, applying the maximum likelihood procedure we determine the corresponding metric and use it in the experiments.

There were some efforts in the literature to model the noise that appears in the images. Boie and Cox [Boie and Cox, 1992] model the noise that appears in the images due to the cameras used to record the images. Machine vision cameras rely on the correspondence between the optical intensity distribution that is imaged on a sensor surface and the photoionization distribution produced in the sensor. Photoelectric effect devices were used, but the majority of modern cameras are based on internal ionization sensors such as silicon target vidicons and charge coupled devices (CCD's). The conversion of optical photons to electrical signal charge is a Poisson process in all cases, and, hence, introduces a probabilistic measurement error due to the statistics of the process. Second, these sensors are capacitive sources of signal charge and, hence, are limited by two important electronic noise sources. Third, the serial method of sensor "readout" produces direction-dependent correlations in the electronic noises. Summarizing, camera noise is comprised of stationary direction-dependent electronic noises combined with fluctuations due to signal statistics. These fluctuations enter as a multiplicative noise and are non-stationary and vary over the scene. The authors [Boie and Cox, 1992] show that a substantial simplification appears if the noise is modeled as Gaussian distributed and stationary.

This work is complementary to ours. They try to model the imaging noise. We try to model the noise between two images which are different due to varying orientation, random sampling, motion, or printer noise.

3. Overview of the Book

We introduce and expose a maximum likelihood framework to be used in computer vision applications when ground truth is available. Chapter 2 describes the mathematical support for the maximum likelihood approach, together with the setup of our experiments. In Chapter 3 we apply the theoretical results from Chapter 2 to determine the influence of the similarity noise model on the accuracy of retrieval methods in color image databases. Maximum likelihood framework in texture classification and retrieval is addressed in Chapter 4. Shape-based retrieval issues are presented in Chapter 5. In Chapter 6 we study the similarity noise model to be chosen in stereo matching applications. The same approach is then applied on a video sequence. Finally, a classification-based framework for facial expression recognition is discussed in detail in Chapter 7.

Chapter 2 formulates a framework for a maximum likelihood approach in computer vision applications. It begins by introducing the robust estimation procedure together with some historical examples where this procedure was applied (Section 2.1). In Section 2.2, we provide basic information regarding the statistical distributions that are used across the book. We consider the Gaussian distribution (Section 2.2.1), the exponential and the double exponential distributions (Section 2.2.2), and finally the Cauchy distribution (Section 2.2.3). Further, we introduce the basic concepts from robust statistics including the outliers generation mechanisms (Section 2.3) and the classical robust estimation procedure (Section 2.4) with an emphasis on Hampel's approach [Hampel et al., 1986] based on influence functions. The maximum likelihood relation with other approaches is investigated in Section 2.5. We draw on the ideas of robust estimation and influence functions in formulating problems in which similarity is provided by a ground truth. Furthermore, in Section 2.6 we illustrate our approach based on maximum likelihood which consists of finding the best metric to be used in an application when the ground truth is provided. The experimental setup is presented in Section 2.7.

Color based retrieval issues are discussed in Chapter 3. The chapter starts with a historical introduction regarding the first color experiments, including the famous debate between Newton and Goethe about the physical and perceptual color analysis (Section 3.1). Physical aspects of light and color formation are presented in Section 3.2. Color models are discussed in Section 3.3, with details regarding two of the most commonly used color models in content based retrieval (RGB and HSV) and a color model introduced by Gevers and Smeulders [Gevers and Smeulders, 1999] suitable for object retrieval and recognition applications. Color based retrieval principles and applications are investigated in Section 3.4. Color histograms and the metrics used in color indexing are presented in Section 3.4.1. We examine two applications from computer vision which involve distortions derived from changes in viewpoint and the process of printing and scanning. The first application was finding copies of images which had been printed and then scanned. For this application we used the Corel stock photo database and a color histogram method for finding the copies (Section 3.5). The second application (Section 3.6) dealt with finding all images of an object in a database where the images were taken from different viewpoints. Both the ground truth and the algorithm came from the work by Gevers and Smeulders [Gevers and Smeulders, 1999]. Furthermore, for both applications, we implemented Hafner's quadratic perceptual similarity measure [Hafner et al., 1995] and Huang's correlogram [Huang et al., 1997] as benchmarks (introduced in Section 3.4.1).

Texture classification and retrieval from a maximum likelihood perspective are presented in Chapter 4. Section 4.1 suggests some of the possible definitions that can be applied for texture. It emphasizes the fact that texture should always be defined relative to a scale of reference. Human perception of texture is investigated in Section 4.2. It presents the pioneering work of Julesz [Julesz et al., 1973; Julesz, 1975] regarding the texture perception in the context of texture discrimination. We also present some psychophysical experiments that suggest the brain performs a multi-channel, frequency, and orientation analysis of the visual image formed on the retina. The approaches in which texture is used as a main feature for content based retrieval are presented in Section 4.3. Additionally, different texture features presented in the literature are discussed. We focus on texture distribution models (Section 4.3.1) and on multi-scale texture representations using Gabor and Wavelet texture models (Section 4.3.2). In the first experiments (Section 4.4) nine classes of texture taken from the Brodatz's album [Brodatz, 1966] were used. There were random samples extracted from each original texture (class) and the classification of a sample was based on comparing the sample distribution of feature values to several pre-defined model distributions of feature values with known true-class labels. The samples were assigned the label of the model that was found to be more similar. In the last experiments (Section 4.5) all the 112 Brodatz textures were used in a texture retrieval application. Random samples were extracted from the original textures and the goal was to retrieve as many samples as possible from the same original texture as the query sample.

Shape based retrieval issues are addressed in Chapter 5. Section 5.1 covers the basic aspects regarding shape characterization and analysis. Research in shape analysis have been motivated by studies on human perception of visual form. These are briefly presented in Section 5.2. In this chapter the problem of image retrieval using shape is approached by active contours for shape segmentation (Section 5.3) and invariant moments for shape measure (Section 5.4). We discuss the traditional active contours and mention their fundamental limitations in Section 5.3.1. Based on the generalized force balance equations (Section 5.3.2) we present a method introduced by Xu and Prince [Xu and Prince, 1997] which uses the gradient vector flow (Section 5.3.3). In our experiments (Section 5.5) we compare the traditional active contour results with the ones obtained with the method proposed by Xu and Prince [Xu and Prince, 1997] using the COIL-20 database [Murase and Nayar, 1995].

Stereo matching and motion tracking applications are presented in Chapter 6. Early stereo attempts including the experiments conducted by Wheatstone and Brewster are discussed in Section 6.1. Stereo matching basic principles and problems are presented in Section 6.2. Different stereo matching algorithms from the literature are reviewed in Section 6.2.1. The stereo matching algorithms that were used in the experiments are presented in Section 6.3. We implemented a template matching algorithm (Section 6.3.1), an adaptive, multi-window algorithm by Fusiello et al. [Fusiello et al., 1997] (Section 6.3.2), and a maximum likelihood method using pixel intensities by Cox et al. [Cox et al., 1996] (Section 6.3.3). In our experiments (Section 6.4), we used international stereo data sets from Carnegie Mellon University (Castle and Tower), University of Illinois at Urbana-Champaign (Robots), and University of Stuttgart (Flat and Suburb). For the stereo pairs and the algorithms in our experiments, the maximum likelihood approach allowed us to consistently improve the accuracy of finding the correspondences in the stereo images. We also discuss about the two possible approaches of applying maximum likelihood toward improving the accuracy of matching algorithms in stereo matching. The first method recommends altering the images so that the measured noise distribution is closer to the Gaussian and then using the SSD. The second method proposed by us is to find a metric which has a distribution which is close to the real noise distribution. Motion tracking issues and experiments are presented in Section 6.5. We implemented a template matching algorithm to track pixels on a moving object in a video sequence. The idea is to trace moving facial expressions such as lips and eyes which are moving through the video sequence. In our experiments we also examine adjacent and nonadjacent frames from the video sequence.

Facial expression recognition application is presented in Chapter 7. We first discuss the importance of facial expressions in everyday interactions with others and the desire to augment the computer with the ability to interact naturally with the human, similar to the way human-human interactions take place (Section 7.1). Further, we present the emotion recognition studies (Section 7.2) with an emphasis on the studies on human facial expressions performed by Ekman and his colleagues [Ekman, 1982; Ekman, 1994]. We introduce the Facial Action Coding System and we present the six "universal categories of emotional expressions" referred to as the *basic emotions*: happiness, sadness, surprise, fear, anger, and disgust. We also present the facial expression recognition state-of-the-art (Section 7.2.2). In Section 7.3 we briefly describe a real-time face tracking system developed at University of Illinois at Urbana-Champaign and the features extracted for classification of facial expressions. The design of the classifiers is of crucial importance. We present two types of settings: dynamic and static classification. Section 7.4 describes the static setting in which Bayesian network classifiers are used for classifying frames in the video sequence to the different expressions. We focus on distribution assumptions and feature dependency structures. In particular we use Naive Bayes classifiers (Section 7.4.1) and change the distribution from Gaussian to Cauchy. Observing that the features independence assumption used by the Naive Bayes classifiers may be inappropriate we use Gaussian Tree-Augmented Naive Bayes (TAN) classifiers to learn the dependencies among different facial motion features (Section 7.4.2). In Section 7.5 we describe HMM based classifiers for facial expression recognition from presegmented video sequences (Section 7.5.1) and introduce the multi-level HMM classifier for both recognizing facial expression sequences (Section 7.5.2) and automatically segmenting the video sequence (Section 7.5.3). In our experiments (Section 7.6), we explore both person-dependent and person-independent recognition of expressions and compare the different methods using two databases. The first is a database of subjects displaying facial expressions collected by Chen [Chen, 2000]. The second is the Cohn-Kanade database [Kanade et al., 2000].

Chapter 2

MAXIMUM LIKELIHOOD FRAMEWORK

This chapter formulates a framework for a maximum likelihood approach in computer vision applications. It begins by introducing basic concepts from robust statistics including the outliers generation mechanisms. Further, we present the classical robust estimation procedure with an emphasis on Hampel's approach [Hampel et al., 1986] based on influence functions. The maximum likelihood relation with other approaches is also investigated. We draw on the ideas of robust estimation and influence functions in formulating problems in which similarity is provided by a ground truth. Our goal is to find the probability density function which maximizes the similarity probability. Furthermore, we illustrate our approach based on maximum likelihood which consists of finding the best metric to be used in an application when the ground truth is provided.

1.   Introduction

The term "robustness" does not lend itself to a clear-cut statistical definition. It seems to have been introduced by G.E.P. Box in 1953 [Box, 1953] to cover a rather vague concept described in the following way by Kendall and Buckland [Kendall and Buckland, 1981]. Their dictionary states:

> **Robustness.** Many test procedures involving probability levels depend for their exactitude on assumptions concerning the generating mechanism, e.g. that the parent variation is Normal (Gaussian). If the inferences are little affected by departure from those assumptions, e.g. if the significance points of a test vary little if the population departs quite substantially from the Normality, the test on the inferences is said to be robust. In a rather more general sense, a statistical procedure is described as robust if it is not very sensitive to departure from the assumptions on which it depends.

This quotation clearly associates robustness with applicability of the various statistical procedures. The two complementary questions that come to mind can be expressed as follows: first, how should we design a statistical procedure to be robust or, in other terms, to remain reliable in spite of possible uncertainty in the available information? Second, how wide is the field of application of a given statistical procedure or, equivalently, is it robust against some small departures from the assumptions? The word "small" can have two different interpretations, both important: either fractionally small departures for all data points, or else fractionally large departures for a small number of data points. It is the latter interpretation, leading to the notion of *outliers*, that is generally the most challenging for statistical procedures.

With the appearance of involved analytical as well as computational facilities, the field of robustness has received increased attention in the past fifty years. Mainly, progresses in non-linear mathematics and in iterative algorithms have permitted new developments. However, robustness has roots in many old studies. For instance, a mode can be looked upon as a robust estimate of location, as it also was some twenty four centuries ago. Thucydides [Thucydides, 1972] relates:

> During the same winter (428 B.C.) the Plataeans... and the Athenians, who were besieged with them, planned to leave the city and climb over the enemy's walls in the hope that they might be able to force a passage...
> They made ladders equal in height to the enemy's wall, getting the measure by counting the layers of bricks at a point where the enemy's wall on the side facing Plataea happened to have been whitewashed. Many counted the layers at the same time, and *while some were sure to make a mistake, the majority were likely to hit the true count*, especially since they counted time and again, and, besides, were at no great distance, and the part of the wall they wished to see was easily visible. In this way, the measurement of the ladders was reckoned from the thickness of the bricks.

Similar behavior can be met when fitting a line to data in the presence of outliers as is illustrated in Figure 2.1. One can see that the average effect of all points (least-squares fit) (Figure 2.1(a)) is skewed in the direction of the outliers (the points on the right). The fit recovered in Figure 2.1(b) is robust in the sense that it rejects the outliers and recovers a "better" fit to the majority of data.

2.   Statistical Distributions

The aim of this section is to provide the basic information regarding the statistical distributions that are going to be used later in this chapter. We consider here the Gaussian distribution, the exponential and the double exponential distributions, and finally the Cauchy distribution. We present their probability distributions together with the corresponding cumulative distribution functions, their characteristic functions, and where applicable the way their moments are calculated. We also show the relation between the Gaussian distribution and the Cauchy distribution.

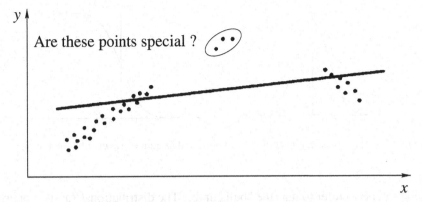

(a) Least-squares fit: average opinion of all points.

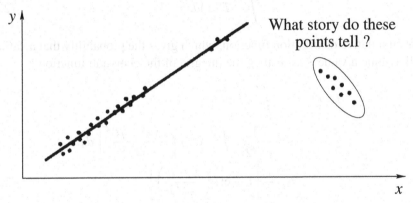

(b) Highly robust fit: clear opinion of majority of points.

Figure 2.1. Which fit do we want? When all points are used in estimation, using a least-square fit as in (a), the line fitting the data is skewed in the direction of the outliers (the points on the right). The points from above (marked as "special") suggest that a "better" fit can be recovered so that the outliers are rejected (b).

2.1 Gaussian Distribution

The Gaussian probability distribution with mean μ and standard deviation σ is a normalized Gaussian function of the form:

$$P(x) = \frac{1}{\sigma\sqrt{2\pi}} \exp\left[-\frac{(x-\mu)^2}{2\sigma^2}\right] \qquad (2.1)$$

where $P(x)dx$ gives the probability that a variate with a Gaussian distribution takes on a value in the range $[x, x + dx]$. Statisticians commonly call this distribution the normal distribution and, because of its curved flaring shape,

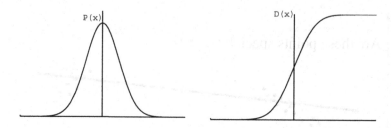

Figure 2.2. The Gaussian probability distribution and its cumulative distribution function

social scientists refer to it as the "bell curve." The distribution $P(x)$ is properly normalized for $x \in (-\infty, \infty)$ since

$$\int_{-\infty}^{\infty} P(x)dx = 1. \tag{2.2}$$

The cumulative distribution function, which gives the probability that a variate will assume a value $\leq x$, is then the integral of the Gaussian function,

$$
\begin{aligned}
D(x) &= \int_{-\infty}^{x} P(x)dx \\
&= \frac{1}{\sigma\sqrt{2\pi}} \int_{-\infty}^{x} \exp\left[-\frac{(x'-\mu)^2}{2\sigma^2}\right] dx' \\
&= \frac{1}{2}\left[1 + \mathrm{erf}\left(\frac{x-\mu}{\sigma\sqrt{2}}\right)\right]
\end{aligned}
\tag{2.3}
$$

where $\mathrm{erf}(\cdot)$ is the so-called error function.

The Gaussian distribution and its cumulative distribution function are plotted in Figure 2.2.

Gaussian distributions have many convenient properties, hence, random variates with unknown distributions are often assumed to be Gaussian, especially in physics and astronomy. Although this can be a dangerous assumption, it is often a good approximation due to a surprising result known as the central limit theorem (see Box 2.1). This theorem states that the mean of any set of variates with any distribution having a finite mean and variance approaches the Gaussian distribution. Many common attributes such as test scores, height, etc., follow roughly Gaussian distributions, with few members at the high and low ends and many in the middle.

Because they occur so frequently, there is an unfortunate tendency to invoke Gaussian distributions in situations where they may not be applicable. As Lippmann stated [Whittaker and Robinson, 1967]: "Everybody believes in the exponential law of errors: the experimenters, because they think it can be proved by mathematics; and the mathematicians, because they believe it has been established by observation."

Making the transformation

$$z \equiv \frac{x - \mu}{\sigma}, \tag{2.4}$$

so that $dz = dx/\sigma$, gives a variate with variance $\sigma^2 = 1$ and mean $\mu = 0$, transforming $P(x)dx$ into

$$P(z)dz = \frac{1}{\sqrt{2\pi}} e^{-z^2/2} dz \tag{2.5}$$

The distribution having this probability function is known as a *standard normal distribution*, and z defined in this way is known as a *z-score*.

The normal distribution function $\Phi(z)$ gives the probability that a standard normal variate assumes a value in the interval $[0, z]$,

$$\Phi(z) \equiv \frac{1}{\sqrt{2\pi}} \int_0^z e^{-x^2/2} dx = \frac{1}{2} \mathrm{erf}\left(\frac{z}{\sqrt{2}}\right) \tag{2.6}$$

where $\mathrm{erf}(\cdot)$ is the error function. Neither $\Phi(z)$ nor $\mathrm{erf}(\cdot)$ can be expressed in terms of finite additions, subtractions, multiplications, and root extractions, and so both must be either computed numerically or otherwise approximated. The value of a for which $P(x)$ falls within the interval $[-a, a]$ with a given probability P is called the P *confidence interval*.

The Gaussian distribution is also a special case of the Chi-squared distribution, since making the substitution

$$\frac{1}{2} z \equiv \frac{(x - \mu)^2}{2\sigma^2} \tag{2.16}$$

gives

$$d\left(\frac{1}{2}z\right) = \frac{(x - \mu)^2}{2\sigma^2} dx = \frac{\sqrt{z}}{\sigma} dx. \tag{2.17}$$

Now, the real line $x \in (-\infty, \infty)$ is mapped onto the half-infinite interval $z \in [0, \infty)$ by this transformation, so an extra factor of 2 must be added to $d(z/2)$, transforming $P(x)dx$ into:

$$P(z)dz = \frac{1}{\sigma\sqrt{2\pi}} e^{-z/2} \frac{\sigma}{\sqrt{z}} 2\left(\frac{1}{2} dz\right) = \frac{e^{-z/2} z^{-1/2}}{2^{1/2} \Gamma\left(\frac{1}{2}\right)} dz \tag{2.18}$$

where we used the identity $\Gamma(1/2) = \sqrt{\pi}$.

Taking into account that the probability density function of the Chi-squared distribution with r degrees of freedom is

$$P_r(z) = \frac{e^{-z/2} z^{r/2-1}}{2^{r/2} \Gamma\left(\frac{r}{2}\right)} \tag{2.19}$$

Box 2.1 (Central Limit Theorem)

*Let $x_1, x_2, \ldots, x_N$ be a set of N independent random variates and each x_i
have an arbitrary probability distribution $P(x_1, x_2, \ldots, x_N)$ with mean μ_i
and a finite variance σ_i^2. Then the normal form variate*

$$X_{norm} \equiv \frac{\sum_{i=1}^{N}(x_i - \mu_i)}{\sqrt{\sum_{i=1}^{N}\sigma_i^2}} \tag{2.7}$$

*has a limiting cumulative distribution function which approaches a normal
distribution. Under additional conditions on the distribution of the
addend, the probability density itself is also normal with mean $\mu = 0$ and
variance $\sigma^2 = 1$. If conversion to normal form is not performed, then the
variate $X \equiv \frac{1}{N}\sum_{i=1}^{N} x_i$ is normally distributed with $\mu_X = \mu_x$ and
$\sigma_X = \sigma/\sqrt{N}$.*

Consider the inverse Fourier transform of $P_X(f)$:

$$\mathcal{F}^{-1}[P_X(f)] \equiv \int_{-\infty}^{\infty} e^{2\pi i f X} P(X)dX = \int_{-\infty}^{\infty} \sum_{n=0}^{\infty} \frac{(2\pi i f X)^n}{n!} P(X)dX$$

$$= \sum_{n=0}^{\infty} \frac{(2\pi i f)^n}{n!} \int_{-\infty}^{\infty} X^n P(X)dX = \sum_{n=0}^{\infty} \frac{(2\pi i f)^n}{n!} \langle X^n \rangle \tag{2.8}$$

Now write

$$\langle X^n \rangle = \langle N^{-n}(x_1 + \cdots + x_N)^n \rangle = \int_{-\infty}^{\infty} N^{-n}(x_1 + \cdots + x_N)^n P(x_1) \cdots P(x_N)dx_1 \cdots dx_N,$$

hence, we have

$$\mathcal{F}^{-1}[P_X(f)] = \sum_{n=0}^{\infty} \frac{(2\pi i f)^n}{n!} \int_{-\infty}^{\infty} N^{-n}(x_1 + \cdots + x_N)^n P(x_1) \cdots P(x_N)dx_1 \cdots dx_N$$

$$= \sum_{n=0}^{\infty} \int_{-\infty}^{\infty} \left[\frac{2\pi i f(x_1 + \cdots + x_N)}{N}\right]^n \frac{1}{n!} P(x_1) \cdots P(x_N)dx_1 \cdots dx_N$$

$$= \int_{-\infty}^{\infty} e^{2\pi i f(x_1 + \cdots + x_N)/N} P(x_1) \cdots P(x_N)dx_1 \cdots dx_N$$

$$= \left[\int_{-\infty}^{\infty} e^{2\pi i f x/N} P(x)dx\right]^N$$

$$= \left\{\int_{-\infty}^{\infty} \left[1 + \left(\frac{2\pi i f}{N}\right)x + \frac{1}{2}\left(\frac{2\pi i f}{N}\right)^2 x^2 + \cdots\right] P(x)dx\right\}^N$$

$$= \left[\int_{-\infty}^{\infty} P(x)dx + \frac{2\pi i f}{N} \int_{-\infty}^{\infty} xP(x)dx - \frac{(2\pi f)^2}{2N^2} \int_{-\infty}^{\infty} x^2 P(x)dx + \mathcal{O}(N^{-3}) \right]^N$$

$$= \left[1 + \frac{2\pi i f}{N} \langle x \rangle - \frac{(2\pi f)^2}{2N^2} \langle x^2 \rangle + \mathcal{O}(N^{-3}) \right]^N$$

$$= \exp \left\{ N \ln \left[1 + \frac{2\pi i f}{N} \langle x \rangle - \frac{(2\pi f)^2}{2N^2} \langle x^2 \rangle + \mathcal{O}(N^{-3}) \right] \right\} \tag{2.9}$$

Now expand

$$\ln(1 + x) = x - \frac{1}{2}x^2 + \frac{1}{3}x^3 + \cdots, \tag{2.10}$$

hence,

$$\mathcal{F}^{-1}[P_X(f)] \approx \exp \left\{ N \left[\frac{2\pi i f}{N} \langle x \rangle - \frac{(2\pi f)^2}{2N^2} \langle x^2 \rangle + \frac{1}{2} \frac{(2\pi f)^2}{N^2} \langle x \rangle^2 + \mathcal{O}(N^{-3}) \right] \right\}$$

$$= \exp \left[2\pi i f \langle x \rangle - \frac{(2\pi f)^2 (\langle x^2 \rangle - \langle x \rangle^2)}{2N} + \mathcal{O}(N^{-2}) \right]$$

$$\approx \exp \left[2\pi i f \mu_x - \frac{(2\pi f)^2 \sigma_x^2}{2N} \right] \tag{2.11}$$

since $\mu_x = \langle x \rangle$, and $\sigma_x^2 = \langle x^2 \rangle - \langle x \rangle^2$.

Taking the Fourier transform,

$$P_X \equiv \int_{-\infty}^{\infty} e^{-2\pi i f x} \mathcal{F}^{-1}[P_X(f)]df = \int_{-\infty}^{\infty} e^{2\pi i f(\mu_x - x) - (2\pi f)^2 \sigma_x^2/(2N)} df \tag{2.12}$$

But, from Abramowitz and Stegun [Abramowitz and Stegun, 1972],

$$\int_{-\infty}^{\infty} e^{iaf - bf^2} df = \sqrt{\frac{\pi}{b}} e^{-a^2/(4b)} \tag{2.13}$$

Therefore, if $a \equiv 2\pi(\mu_x - x)$ and $b \equiv (2\pi\sigma_x)^2/(2N)$, then:

$$P_X = \sqrt{\frac{\pi}{\frac{(2\pi\sigma_x)^2}{2N}}} \exp \left\{ \frac{-[2\pi(\mu_x - x)]^2}{4\frac{(2\pi\sigma_x)^2}{2N}} \right\} = \frac{\sqrt{N}}{\sigma_x \sqrt{2\pi}} e^{-(x-\mu_x)^2 N/(2\sigma_x^2)} \tag{2.14}$$

But $\sigma_X = \sigma_x/\sqrt{N}$ and $\mu_X = \mu_x$, hence

$$P_X = \frac{1}{\sigma_X \sqrt{2\pi}} e^{-(\mu_X - x)^2/(2\sigma_X^2)} \tag{2.15}$$

The "fuzzy" central limit theorem says that data which are influenced by many small and unrelated random effects are approximately normally distributed.

then, Equation (2.18) is a Chi-squared distribution with $r = 1$.

The ratio of independent Gaussian-distributed variates with zero mean is distributed with a Cauchy distribution. This can be seen as follows. Let X and Y both have mean 0 and standard deviations of σ_x and σ_y, respectively, then the joint probability density function is the bivariate normal distribution (see Box 2.2) with $\rho = 0$,

$$f(x, y) = \frac{1}{2\pi\sigma_x\sigma_y} e^{-[x^2/(2\sigma_x^2) + y^2/(2\sigma_y^2)]} \tag{2.20}$$

From ratio distribution (see Box 2.3), the distribution of $U = Y/X$ is

$$
\begin{aligned}
P(u) &= \int_{-\infty}^{\infty} |x| f(x, ux)\,dx = \frac{1}{2\pi\sigma_x\sigma_y} \int_{-\infty}^{\infty} |x| e^{-[x^2/(2\sigma_x^2) + u^2 x^2/(2\sigma_y^2)]}\,dx \\
&= \frac{1}{\pi\sigma_x\sigma_y} \int_0^{\infty} x \exp\left[-x^2\left(\frac{1}{2\sigma_x^2} + \frac{u^2}{2\sigma_y^2}\right)\right]\,dx
\end{aligned}
\tag{2.29}
$$

But

$$\int_0^{\infty} x e^{-ax^2}\,dx = \left[-\frac{1}{2a}e^{-ax^2}\right]_0^{\infty} = \frac{1}{2a} \tag{2.30}$$

hence,

$$P(u) = \frac{1}{\pi\sigma_x\sigma_y} \frac{1}{2\left(\frac{1}{2\sigma_x^2} + \frac{u^2}{2\sigma_y^2}\right)} = \frac{1}{\pi} \frac{\frac{\sigma_y}{\sigma_x}}{u^2 + \left(\frac{\sigma_y}{\sigma_x}\right)^2} \tag{2.31}$$

which is a Cauchy distribution with median $\mu = 0$ and full width $a = \sigma_y/\sigma_x$.

The characteristic function (defined as the Fourier transform of the probability density function) for the Gaussian distribution is

$$\phi(t) = e^{i\mu t - \sigma^2 t^2/2} \tag{2.32}$$

and the moment-generating function is

$$
\begin{aligned}
M(t) = \langle e^{tx} \rangle &= \int_{-\infty}^{\infty} \frac{e^{tx}}{\sigma\sqrt{2\pi}} e^{-(x-\mu)^2/(2\sigma^2)}\,dx \\
&= \frac{1}{\sigma\sqrt{2\pi}} \int_{-\infty}^{\infty} \exp\left\{-\frac{1}{2\sigma^2}[x^2 - 2(\mu + \sigma^2 t)x + \mu^2]\right\}\,dx
\end{aligned}
\tag{2.33}
$$

Completing the square in the exponent,

$$\frac{1}{2\sigma^2}[x^2 - 2(\mu + \sigma^2 t)x + \mu^2] = \frac{1}{2\sigma^2}\{[x - (\mu + \sigma^2 t)]^2 + [\mu^2 - (\mu + \sigma^2 t)^2]\} \tag{2.34}$$

Box 2.2 (Bivariate Normal Distribution)

The bivariate normal distribution is given by

$$P(x_1, x_2) = \frac{1}{2\pi\sigma_1\sigma_2\sqrt{1-\rho^2}} \exp\left[-\frac{z}{2(1-\rho^2)}\right] \tag{2.21}$$

where

$$z \equiv \frac{(x_1 - \mu_1)^2}{\sigma_1^2} - \frac{2\rho(x_1 - \mu_1)(x_2 - \mu_2)}{\sigma_1\sigma_2} + \frac{(x_2 - \mu_2)^2}{\sigma_2^2} \tag{2.22}$$

and

$$\rho \equiv cor(x_1, x_2) = \frac{\sigma_{12}}{\sigma_1\sigma_2} \tag{2.23}$$

is the correlation of x_1 and x_2.
The marginal probabilities are then

$$p(x_i) = \int_{-\infty}^{\infty} P(x_i, x_j)dx_j = \frac{1}{\sigma_i\sqrt{2\pi}}e^{-(x_i-\mu_i)^2/(2\sigma_i^2)} \quad \text{with } i,j \in \{1,2\}, i \neq j \tag{2.24}$$

Box 2.3 (Ratio Distribution)

Given two distributions Y and X with joint probability density function $f(x, y)$, let $U = Y/X$ be the ratio distribution. Then the distribution function of u is

$$\begin{aligned}
D(u) &= P(U \leq u) = P(Y \leq uX|X > 0) + P(Y \geq uX|X < 0) \\
&= \int_0^{\infty} \int_0^{ux} f(x,y)dydx + \int_{-\infty}^0 \int_{ux}^0 f(x,y)dydx
\end{aligned} \tag{2.25}$$

The probability function is then

$$P(u) = D'(u) = \int_0^{\infty} xf(x,ux)dx - \int_{-\infty}^0 xf(x,ux)dx = \int_{-\infty}^{\infty} |x|f(x,ux)dx \tag{2.26}$$

For variates with a standard normal distribution, the ratio distribution is a Cauchy distribution. For a uniform distribution

$$f(x, y) = \begin{cases} 1 & \text{for } x, y \in [0, 1] \\ 0 & \text{otherwise} \end{cases} \tag{2.27}$$

the probability function is

$$P(u) = \begin{cases} 0 & \text{for } u < 0 \\ \int_0^1 xdx = \frac{1}{2} & \text{for } 0 \leq u \leq 1 \\ \int_0^{1/u} xdx = \frac{1}{2u^2} & \text{for } u > 1 \end{cases} \tag{2.28}$$

and considering $y \equiv x - (\mu + \sigma^2 t)$ and $a \equiv 1/(2\sigma^2)$, the integral becomes

$$
\begin{aligned}
M(t) &= \frac{1}{\sigma\sqrt{2\pi}} \int_{-\infty}^{\infty} \exp\left[-ay^2 + \frac{2\mu\sigma^2 t + \sigma^4 t^2}{2\sigma^2}\right] dy \\
&= \frac{1}{\sigma\sqrt{2\pi}} e^{\mu t + \sigma^2 t^2/2} \int_{-\infty}^{\infty} e^{-ay^2} dy \\
&= \frac{1}{\sigma\sqrt{2\pi}} \sqrt{\frac{\pi}{a}} e^{\mu t + \sigma^2 t^2/2} = e^{\mu t + \sigma^2 t^2/2}
\end{aligned}
\tag{2.35}
$$

hence,

$$
\begin{aligned}
M'(t) &= (\mu + \sigma^2 t) e^{\mu t + \sigma^2 t^2/2} \\
M''(t) &= \sigma^2 e^{\mu t + \sigma^2 t^2/2} + e^{\mu t + \sigma^2 t^2/2} (\mu + t\sigma^2)^2
\end{aligned}
\tag{2.36}
$$
$$
\tag{2.37}
$$

and

$$
\begin{aligned}
\mu &= M'(0) = \mu \\
\sigma^2 &= M''(0) - [M'(0)]^2 = (\sigma^2 + \mu^2) - \mu^2 = \sigma^2
\end{aligned}
\tag{2.38}
$$
$$
\tag{2.39}
$$

These can also be computed using

$$
\begin{aligned}
R(t) &= \ln[M(t)] = \mu t + \frac{1}{2}\sigma^2 t^2 \\
R'(t) &= \mu + \sigma^2 t \\
R''(t) &= \sigma^2
\end{aligned}
\tag{2.40}
$$
$$
\tag{2.41}
$$
$$
\tag{2.42}
$$

yielding as before,

$$
\begin{aligned}
\mu &= R'(0) = \mu \\
\sigma^2 &= R''(0) = \sigma^2
\end{aligned}
\tag{2.43}
$$
$$
\tag{2.44}
$$

The raw moments can also be computed directly by computing the moments about the origin $\mu'_n \equiv \langle x^n \rangle$,

$$
\mu'_n = \frac{1}{\sigma\sqrt{2\pi}} \int_{-\infty}^{\infty} x^n e^{-(x-\mu)^2/(2\sigma^2)} dx
\tag{2.45}
$$

Now let

$$
u \equiv \frac{x - \mu}{\sqrt{2}\sigma},
\tag{2.46}
$$

hence

$$
du = \frac{dx}{\sqrt{2}\sigma}
\tag{2.47}
$$

$$
x = \sigma u\sqrt{2} + \mu.
\tag{2.48}
$$

Giving the raw moments in terms of Gaussian integrals yields,

$$\mu'_n = \frac{\sqrt{2}\sigma}{\sigma\sqrt{2\pi}} \int_{-\infty}^{\infty} x^n e^{-u^2} du = \frac{1}{\sqrt{\pi}} \int_{-\infty}^{\infty} x^n e^{-u^2} du \qquad (2.49)$$

Evaluating these integrals gives

$$\begin{aligned}
\mu'_0 &= 1 & (2.50) \\
\mu'_1 &= \mu & (2.51) \\
\mu'_2 &= \mu^2 + \sigma^2 & (2.52) \\
\mu'_3 &= \mu(\mu^2 + 3\sigma^2) & (2.53) \\
\mu'_4 &= \mu^4 + 6\mu^2\sigma^2 + 3\sigma^4 & (2.54)
\end{aligned}$$

Now find the moments about the mean (the central moments) $\mu_n \equiv \langle (x-\mu)^n \rangle$,

$$\begin{aligned}
\mu_1 &= 0 & (2.55) \\
\mu_2 &= \sigma^2 & (2.56) \\
\mu_3 &= 0 & (2.57) \\
\mu_4 &= 3\sigma^4 & (2.58)
\end{aligned}$$

so the variance, skewness, and kurtosis are given by

$$\begin{aligned}
\text{var}(x) &= \sigma^2 & (2.59) \\
\gamma_1 &= \frac{\mu_3}{\sigma^3} = 0 & (2.60) \\
\gamma_2 &= \frac{\mu_4}{\sigma^4} - 3 = 0 & (2.61)
\end{aligned}$$

Cramer showed in 1936 that if X and Y are independent variates and $X + Y$ has a Gaussian distribution, then both X and Y must be Gaussian (Cramer's theorem). An easier result states that the sum of n variates each with is Gaussian distribution also has a Gaussian distribution. This follows from the result

$$P_n(x) = \mathcal{F}^{-1}\{[\phi(t)]^n\} = \frac{e^{-(x-n\mu)^2/(2n\sigma^2)}}{\sigma\sqrt{2\pi n}} \qquad (2.62)$$

where $\phi(t)$ is the characteristic function and $\mathcal{F}^{-1}[f]$ is the inverse Fourier transform.

If P(x) is a Gaussian distribution, then

$$D(x) = \frac{1}{2}\left[1 + \text{erf}\left(\frac{x-\mu}{\sigma\sqrt{2}}\right)\right] \qquad (2.63)$$

hence variates x_i with a Gaussian distribution can be generated from variates y_i having a uniform distribution in $(0, 1)$ via

$$x_i = \sigma\sqrt{2}\,\text{erf}^{-1}(2y_i - 1) + \mu \qquad (2.64)$$

However, a simpler way to obtain numbers with a Gaussian distribution is to use the Box-Muller transformation (see Box 2.4).

Box 2.4 (Box-Muller Transformation)

A transformation which transforms from a two-dimensional continuous uniform distribution to a two-dimensional bivariate normal distribution. If x_1 and x_2 are uniformly and independently distributed between 0 and 1, then z_1 and z_2 as defined below have a normal distribution with mean $\mu = 0$ and variance $\sigma^2 = 1$.

$$z_1 = \sqrt{-2 \ln x_1} \cos(2\pi x_2) \qquad (2.65)$$
$$z_2 = \sqrt{-2 \ln x_1} \sin(2\pi x_2) \qquad (2.66)$$

This can be verified by solving for x_1 and x_2,

$$x_1 = e^{-(z_1^2 + z_2^2)/2} \qquad (2.67)$$
$$x_2 = \frac{1}{2\pi} \tan^{-1}\left(\frac{z_2}{z_1}\right) \qquad (2.68)$$

Taking the Jacobian yields,

$$\frac{\partial(x_1, x_2)}{\partial(z_1, z_2)} = \begin{vmatrix} \frac{\partial x_1}{\partial z_1} & \frac{\partial x_1}{\partial z_2} \\ \frac{\partial x_2}{\partial z_1} & \frac{\partial x_2}{\partial z_2} \end{vmatrix} = -\left[\frac{1}{\sqrt{2\pi}} e^{-z_1^2/2}\right]\left[\frac{1}{\sqrt{2\pi}} e^{-z_2^2/2}\right] \qquad (2.69)$$

The differential equation having a Gaussian distribution as its solution is

$$\frac{dy}{dx} = \frac{y(\mu - x)}{\sigma^2} \qquad (2.70)$$

since

$$\frac{dy}{y} = \frac{\mu - x}{\sigma^2} dx$$
$$\ln\left(\frac{y}{y_0}\right) = -\frac{1}{2\sigma^2}(\mu - x)^2$$
$$y = y_0 e^{-(x-\mu)^2/(2\sigma^2)} \qquad (2.71)$$

This equation has been generalized to yield more complicated distributions which are named using the so-called Pearson system (see Box 2.5).

Box 2.5 (Pearson System)

A system of equation types obtained by generalizing the differential equation for the normal distribution

$$\frac{dy}{dx} = \frac{y(m-x)}{a} \qquad (2.72)$$

which has solution

$$y = Ce^{(2m-x)x/(2a)} \qquad (2.73)$$

to

$$\frac{dy}{dx} = \frac{y(m-x)}{a + bx + cx^2} \qquad (2.74)$$

which has solution

$$y = C(a + bx + cx^2)^{-1/(2c)} \exp\left[\frac{(b + 2cm)\tan^{-1}\left(\frac{b+2cx}{\sqrt{4ac-b^2}}\right)}{c\sqrt{4ac-b^2}}\right] \qquad (2.75)$$

Let c_1, c_2 be the roots of $a + bx + cx^2$. Then the possible types of curves are

0. $b = c = 0, a > 0$. E.g., normal distribution.

I. $b^2/4ac < 0, c_1 \leq x \leq c_2$. E.g., beta distribution.

II. $b^2/4ac = 0, c < 0, -c_1 \leq x \leq c_1$ where $c_1 \equiv \sqrt{-c/a}$.

III. $b^2/4ac = \infty, c = 0, c_1 \leq x < \infty$ where $c_1 \equiv -a/b$. E.g., gamma distribution. This case is intermediate to cases I and VI.

IV. $0 < b^2/4ac < 1, -\infty < x < \infty$.

V. $b^2/4ac = 1, c_1 \leq x < \infty$ where $c_1 \equiv -b/2a$. Intermediate to cases IV and VI.

VI. $b^2/4ac > 1, c_1 \leq x < \infty$ where c_1 is the larger root. E.g., beta prime distribution.

VII. $b^2/4ac = 0, c > 0, -\infty < x < \infty$. E.g., Student's t-distribution.

2.2   Exponential Distribution

Given a Poisson distribution with rate of change λ, the distribution of waiting times between successive changes (with $k = 0$) is

$$D(x) \equiv P(X \le x) = 1 - P(X > x) = 1 - \frac{(\lambda x)^0 e^{-\lambda x}}{0!} = 1 - e^{-\lambda x} \quad (2.76)$$

and

$$P(x) = D'(x) = \lambda e^{-\lambda x} \quad (2.77)$$

which is normalized since

$$\int_0^\infty P(x)dx = \lambda \int_0^\infty e^{-\lambda x}dx = -\left[e^{-\lambda x}\right]_0^\infty = 1 \quad (2.78)$$

This is the only memoryless random distribution. A variable x is memoryless with respect to t if, for all s with $t \ne 0$,

$$P(x > s + t | x > t) = P(x > s) \quad (2.79)$$

Equivalently,

$$\frac{P(x > s + t, x > t)}{P(x > t)} = P(x > s)$$

$$P(x > s + t) = P(x > s)P(x > t) \quad (2.80)$$

The exponential distribution satisfies

$$P(x > t) = e^{-\lambda t}$$

$$P(x > s + t) = e^{-\lambda(s+t)} \quad (2.81)$$

and therefore

$$P(x > s + t) = e^{-\lambda(s+t)} = P(x > s)P(x > t). \quad (2.82)$$

Define the mean waiting time between successive changes as $\theta \equiv \lambda^{-1}$. Then

$$P(x) = \begin{cases} \frac{1}{\theta}e^{-x/\theta} & x \ge 0 \\ 0 & x < 0 \end{cases} \quad (2.83)$$

The moment-generating function is

$$M(t) = \int_0^\infty e^{tx}\left(\frac{1}{\theta}\right)e^{-x/\theta}dx = \frac{1}{\theta}\int_0^\infty e^{-(1-\theta t)x/\theta}dx = \frac{1}{1 - \theta t} \quad (2.84)$$

$$M'(t) = \frac{\theta}{(1 - \theta t)^2} \quad (2.85)$$

$$M''(t) = \frac{2\theta^2}{(1 - \theta t)^3} \quad (2.86)$$

hence,

$$R(t) \equiv \ln M(t) = -\ln(1 - \theta t) \tag{2.87}$$

$$R'(t) = \frac{\theta}{1 - \theta t} \tag{2.88}$$

$$R''(t) = \frac{\theta^2}{(1 - \theta t)^2} \tag{2.89}$$

$$\mu = R'(0) = \theta \tag{2.90}$$

$$\sigma^2 = R''(0) = \theta^2 \tag{2.91}$$

The characteristic function is

$$\phi(t) = \mathcal{F}\left\{\lambda e^{-\lambda x}\left[\frac{1}{2}(1 + \mathrm{sgn}x)\right]\right\} = \frac{i\lambda}{t + i\lambda} \tag{2.92}$$

where $\mathcal{F}[f]$ is the Fourier transform.

The skewness and kurtosis are given by

$$\gamma_1 = 2 \tag{2.93}$$

$$\gamma_2 = 6 \tag{2.94}$$

The mean and variance can also be computed directly

$$\langle x \rangle \equiv \int_0^\infty x P(x) dx = \frac{1}{\theta} \int_0^\infty x e^{-x/\theta} dx \tag{2.95}$$

Use the integral

$$\int x e^{ax} dx = \frac{e^{ax}}{a^2}(ax - 1) \tag{2.96}$$

to obtain

$$\langle x \rangle = -\theta \left[e^{-x/\theta}\left(1 + \frac{x}{\theta}\right)\right]_0^\infty = \theta \tag{2.97}$$

Now, to find

$$\langle x^2 \rangle = \frac{1}{\theta} \int_0^\infty x^2 e^{-x/\theta} dx \tag{2.98}$$

use the integral

$$\int x^2 e^{ax} dx = \frac{e^{ax}}{a^3}(2 - 2ax + a^2 x^2) \tag{2.99}$$

to obtain

$$\langle x^2 \rangle = 2\theta^2 \tag{2.100}$$

giving

$$\sigma^2 \equiv \langle x^2 \rangle - \langle x \rangle^2 = \theta^2 \tag{2.101}$$

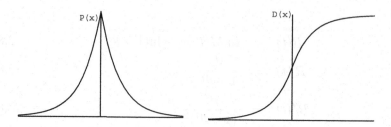

Figure 2.3. The double exponential probability distribution and its cumulative distribution function

If a generalized exponential probability function is defined by

$$P_{(\alpha,\beta)}(x) = \frac{1}{\beta} e^{-(x-\alpha)/\beta} \tag{2.102}$$

for $x \geq \alpha$, then the characteristic function is

$$\phi(t) = \frac{e^{i\alpha t}}{1 - i\beta t} \tag{2.103}$$

and the mean, variance, skewness, and kurtosis are

$$\mu = \alpha + \beta \tag{2.104}$$
$$\sigma^2 = \beta^2 \tag{2.105}$$
$$\gamma_1 = 2 \tag{2.106}$$
$$\gamma_2 = 6 \tag{2.107}$$

Consider now the distribution of differences between two independent variates with identical exponential distributions. This will yield the double exponential distribution:

$$P(x) = \frac{1}{2b} e^{-|x-\mu|/b} \tag{2.108}$$
$$D(x) = \frac{1}{2} \left[1 + \text{sgn}(x - \mu) \left(1 - e^{-|x-\mu|/b} \right) \right] \tag{2.109}$$

The double exponential distribution and its cumulative distribution function are plotted in Figure 2.3.

The moments can be computed using the characteristic function,

$$\phi(t) \equiv \int_{-\infty}^{\infty} e^{itx} P(x) dx = \frac{1}{2b} \int_{-\infty}^{\infty} e^{itx} e^{-|x-\mu|/b} dx \tag{2.110}$$

Using the Fourier transform of the exponential function

$$\mathcal{F}\left[e^{2\pi k_0 |x|} \right] = \frac{1}{\pi} \frac{k_0}{k^2 + k_0^2} \tag{2.111}$$

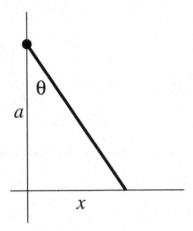

Figure 2.4. The Cauchy distribution describes the distribution of horizontal distances at which a line segment tilted at a random angle θ cuts the x-axis.

gives

$$\phi(t) = \frac{e^{i\mu t}}{1 + b^2 t^2} \qquad (2.112)$$

The moments are therefore

$$\mu_n = (-i)^n \phi(0) = (-i)^n \left[\frac{d^n \phi}{dt^n} \right]_t = 0 \qquad (2.113)$$

The mean, variance, skewness, and kurtosis are

$$\mu = \mu \qquad (2.114)$$
$$\sigma^2 = 2b^2 \qquad (2.115)$$
$$\gamma_1 = 0 \qquad (2.116)$$
$$\gamma_2 = 3 \qquad (2.117)$$

2.3 Cauchy Distribution

The Cauchy distribution, also called the Lorentzian distribution, is a continuous distribution describing resonance behavior. It also describes the distribution of horizontal distances at which a line segment tilted at a random angle cuts the x-axis. Let θ represent the angle that a line, with fixed point of rotation, makes with the vertical axis, as shown in Figure 2.4. Then

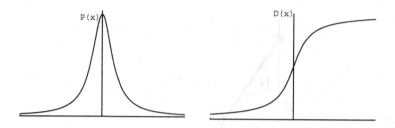

Figure 2.5. The Cauchy probability distribution and its cumulative distribution function

$$\tan\theta \;=\; \frac{x}{a} \tag{2.118}$$

$$\theta \;=\; \tan^{-1}\left(\frac{x}{a}\right) \tag{2.119}$$

$$d\theta \;=\; -\frac{1}{1+\frac{x^2}{a^2}}\frac{dx}{a} \;=\; -\frac{a\,dx}{a^2+x^2} \tag{2.120}$$

so the distribution of angle θ is given by

$$\frac{d\theta}{\pi} \;=\; -\frac{1}{\pi}\frac{a\,dx}{a^2+x^2} \tag{2.121}$$

This is normalized over all angles, since

$$\int_{-\pi/2}^{\pi/2}\frac{d\theta}{\pi} = 1 \tag{2.122}$$

and

$$-\int_{-\infty}^{\infty}\frac{1}{\pi}\frac{a\,dx}{a^2+x^2} = \frac{1}{\pi}\left[\tan^{-1}\left(\frac{x}{a}\right)\right]_{-\infty}^{\infty} = 1 \tag{2.123}$$

The general Cauchy distribution and its cumulative distribution function (see Figure 2.5) can be written as

$$P(x) \;=\; \frac{1}{\pi}\frac{a}{a^2+(x-\mu)^2} \tag{2.124}$$

$$D(x) \;=\; \frac{1}{2} + \frac{1}{\pi}\arctan\left(\frac{x-\mu}{a}\right) \tag{2.125}$$

where a is the full width and μ is the median ($\mu = 0$ in the above example).
The characteristic function is

$$\phi(t) = \frac{1}{\pi}\int_{-\infty}^{\infty}e^{itx}\frac{a}{a^2+(x-\mu)^2}dx = e^{imt-a|t|} \tag{2.126}$$

The moments μ_n of the distribution are undefined since the integrals

$$\mu_n = \int_{-\infty}^{\infty} \frac{a}{\pi} \frac{x^n}{a^2 + (x - \mu)^2} dx \tag{2.127}$$

diverge for $n \geq 1$.

If X and Y are variates with a normal distribution, then $Z \equiv X/Y$ has a Cauchy distribution with median $\mu = 0$ and full width $a = \sigma_y/\sigma_x$.

The sum of n variates each from a Cauchy distribution has itself a Cauchy distribution, as can be seen from

$$P_n(x) = \mathcal{F}^{-1}\{[\phi(t)]^n\} = \frac{1}{\pi} \frac{an}{(an)^2 + (x - n\mu)^2} \tag{2.128}$$

where $\phi(t)$ is the characteristic function and $\mathcal{F}^{-1}[f]$ is the inverse Fourier transform.

3. Robust Statistics

Statistical inferences are based in part upon the observations. An equally important base is formed by prior assumptions about the underlying situations. Even in the simplest cases, there are explicit or implicit assumptions about randomness and independence, about distributional models, perhaps prior distributions for some unknown parameters, and so on. In this context, robust statistics, in a loose, nontechnical sense, is concerned with the fact that many assumptions (such as normality, linearity, independence) are, at most, approximations to reality.

These assumptions are not supposed to be exactly true – they are mathematically convenient rationalizations of an often fuzzy knowledge or belief. As in every other branch of applied mathematics, such rationalizations or simplifications are vital, and one justifies their use by appealing to a vague continuity or stability principle: a minor error in the mathematical model should cause only a small error in the final conclusions.

Unfortunately, this does not always hold. During the past decades people have become increasingly aware that some of the common statistical procedures (in particular, those optimized for an underlying normal distribution) are excessively sensitive to seemingly minor deviations from the assumptions, and a number of alternative "robust" procedures have been proposed [Hampel et al., 1986][Rey, 1983].

The field of robust statistics [Huber, 1981] [Hampel et al., 1986] [Rousseeuw and Leroy, 1987] has developed to address the fact that the parametric models of classical statistics are often approximations of the phenomena being modeled. In particular, the field addresses how to handle *outliers*, or gross errors, which do not conform to the assumptions. While most of the work in computer vision has focused on developing optimal strategies for exact parametric models, there is a growing realization that we must be able to cope with situations for which our models were not designed.[1]

As identified by Hampel [Hampel et al., 1986] the main goals of robust statistics are:

(i) To describe the structure best fitting the bulk of data.

(ii) To identify deviating data points (outliers) or deviating substructures for further treatment, if desired.

3.1   Outliers

The intuitive definition of an outlier would be "an observation which deviates so much from other observations as to arouse suspicion that it was generated by a different mechanism" [Hawkins, 1980]. An inspection of a sample containing outliers would show up such characteristics as large gaps between "outlying" and "inlying" observations and the deviation between the outliers and the group of inliers, as measured on some suitably standardized scale.

There are two basic mechanisms which give rise to samples that appear to have outliers. It is a matter of some importance which of the mechanisms generated any particular set of observations, since this consideration certainly affects, or should affect, the subsequent analysis of the data.

Mechanism (i) The data arise from two distributions. One of these, the "basic distribution," generates "good" observations, while another, the "contaminating distribution," generates "contaminants." If the contaminating distribution has tails which are heavier than those of the basic distribution, then there will be a tendency for the contaminants to be outliers – that is, to separate visibly from the good observations, which will then constitute the inliers.

Mechanism (ii) The data come from some heavy tailed distributions such as Student's t. There is no question that any observation is in any way erroneous.

Formalizing the latter model, Green [Green, 1976] has introduced a classification of families of statistical distributions into those that are "outlier-prone" and those that are "outlier-resistant." The outlier-prone families have tails which go to zero slowly: a distribution is said to be absolutely outlier-prone if (letting $X_{n,i}$ be the ith order statistic based on a sample of size n) there exists $\varepsilon > 0, \delta > 0$, and an integer n_0 such that

$$P[X_{n,n} - X_{n,n-1} > \varepsilon] \geq \delta \qquad \text{for all } n > n_0 \qquad (2.129)$$

---

[1] As Einstein noted: "So far as mathematics is exact, it does not apply to nature; so far as it applies to nature, it is not exact."

and is relatively outlier-prone if there exist $c > 1$, $\delta > 0$ and n_0 such that

$$P[X_{n,n}/X_{n,n-1} > c] \geq \delta \qquad \text{for all } n > n_0 \qquad (2.130)$$

Clearly if either of these situations holds, then there will be a tendency for the larger order statistic to be suspiciously large relative to its predecessor, and so samples generated by outlier-prone distributions will tend to contain visual outliers.

Absolutely and relatively outlier-resistant distributions are those which are not absolutely and relatively outlier-prone, respectively.

The effect of outliers on the analysis of a set of data depends strongly on the mechanism by which the outliers are believed to be generated. If mechanism *(ii)* is assumed, then the outliers, despite appearances, are valid observations from the distribution under study. Usually, the major objective of the analysis will be to estimate a parameter - for example location - of this distribution. For doing this, a maximum likelihood estimation procedure is typically used.

4. Maximum Likelihood Estimators

Suppose that we are fitting N data points (x_i, y_i), $i = 1, \ldots, N$ to a model that has M adjustable parameters $\mathbf{a} = [a_1 \ldots a_M]$. The model predicts a functional relationship between the measured independent and dependent variables,

$$y(x) = y(x; \mathbf{a}) \qquad (2.131)$$

where the dependence on the parameters is indicated explicitly on the right-hand side.

What exactly do we want to minimize to get the fitted values for the a_j's? The first thing that comes in mind is the familiar least-squares fit,

$$\min_{\mathbf{a}} \sum_{i=1}^{N} (y_i - y(x_i; \mathbf{a}))^2 \qquad (2.132)$$

But where does this come from? What general principles is it based on? The answer to these questions takes us into the subject of maximum likelihood estimators.

Given a particular data set of x_i's and y_i's we have the intuitive feeling that some parameter sets $a_1 \ldots a_M$ are very unlikely – those for which the model function $y(x)$ looks nothing like the data – while others may be very likely – those that closely resemble the data. How can we quantify this intuitive feeling? How can we select fitted parameters that are "most likely" to be correct? In order to answer these questions we have to compute the probability that the data set could have occurred when a particular set of parameters was given. If the probability of obtaining the data set is infinitesimally small, then we can conclude that the parameters under consideration are "unlikely" to be right. Conversely, the intuition tells that the data set should not be too improbable for the correct choice of parameters. In other words, we identify the probability of the data given the parameters (which is a mathematically computable number), as the *likelihood* of the parameters given the data. Once we make this intuitive identification, however, it is only a small further step to decide to fit for the parameters $a_1 \ldots a_M$ precisely by finding those values that *maximize* the likelihood defined in the above way. This form of parameter estimation is *maximum likelihood estimation*.

In order to make a connection to (2.132), suppose that each data point y_i has a measurement error that is independently random and distributed as a normal distribution around the "true" model $y(x)$. And suppose that the standard deviations σ of these normal distributions are the same for all points. Then the probability of the data set is the product of the probabilities of each point,

$$ P \sim \prod_{i=1}^{N} \exp\left[-\frac{1}{2}\left(\frac{y_i - y(x_i; \mathbf{a})}{\sigma}\right)^2\right] \tag{2.133} $$

Maximizing (2.133) is equivalent to maximizing its logarithm, or minimizing the negative of its logarithm, namely,

$$ \sum_{i=1}^{N} \frac{(y_i - y(x_i; \mathbf{a}))^2}{2\sigma^2} \tag{2.134} $$

Since σ is constant, minimizing this equation is equivalent to minimizing (2.132).

What we see is that least-squares fitting *is* a maximum likelihood estimation of the fitted parameters *if* the measurement errors are independent and normally distributed with constant standard deviation. If the normal distribution model is a bad approximation, or outliers are important, robust estimators are employed.

In a general case, suppose we know that our measurement errors are not normally distributed. Then, in deriving a maximum likelihood formula for the estimated parameters $\mathbf{a}$ in a model $y(x; \mathbf{a})$, we would write instead of equation (2.133)

$$ P \sim \prod_{i=1}^{N} \exp[-\rho(y_i, y(x_i; \mathbf{a}))] \tag{2.135} $$

where the function ρ is the negative logarithm of the probability density. Taking the logarithm of (2.135), analogously with (2.134), we find that we want to minimize the expression

$$ \sum_{i=1}^{N} \rho(y_i, y(x_i; \mathbf{a})) \tag{2.136} $$

Very often, it is the case that the function ρ depends not independently on its two arguments, measured y_i and predicted $y(x_i)$, but only on their difference. In this case the estimate is said to be local, and we can replace (2.136) by

$$\min_{\mathbf{a}} \sum_{i=1}^{N} \rho(y_i - y(x_i; \mathbf{a})) \qquad (2.137)$$

where the function $\rho(z)$ is a function of a single variable $z \equiv y_i - y(x_i)$.

5.   Maximum Likelihood in Relation to Other Approaches

The goal of a content based retrieval system can be defined to be the minimization of the probability of retrieval error. In this way, the problem of retrieving images from a database is formulated as a classification problem. Consider a feature space $\mathcal{F}$ for the entries in the database. The retrieval system will find a map

$$g : \mathcal{F} \rightarrow \mathcal{M} = \{1, \dots, K\} \qquad (2.138)$$

from $\mathcal{F}$ to the set $\mathcal{M}$ of classes identified as useful for the retrieval operation [Vasconcelos and Lippman, 2000]. K, the cardinality of $\mathcal{M}$, can be as large as the number of items in the database (in which case each item is a class by itself) or smaller. The probability of error that should be minimized is given by $P(g(\mathbf{x}) \neq y)$. This is the probability of having a set of feature vectors $\mathbf{x}$ drawn from the class y retrieved by the system from a class $g(\mathbf{x})$ different from y. Once the problem is formulated in this way, the optimal map is given by the Bayes classifier [Devroye et al., 1996]

$$g^*(\mathbf{x}) = \max_{i} P(y = i | \mathbf{x}) \qquad (2.139)$$

It is, however, known that the posterior probabilities required by the Bayes classifier are in general difficult to compute, making the classifier of limited practical use. To cope with this difficulty, there are two important approaches proposed in the pattern recognition literature: one using discriminant classifiers and the other one using classifiers based on generative models.

Discriminant classifiers try to find the surfaces in $\mathcal{F}$ that better separate the regions associated with the different classes in the sense of Equation (2.139), classifying each point according to its position relative to those surfaces. Examples are linear discriminant classifiers, neural networks, and decision trees. The problem with these classifiers is that they must be completely retrained every time a new class is added or deleted from the database, making this approach difficult to be applied in a retrieval scenario.

Instead of dealing directly with Equation (2.139), classifiers based on generative models take the alternative provided by the Bayes rule,

$$g^*(\mathbf{x}) = \max_{i} P(\mathbf{x} | y = i) P(y = i) \qquad (2.140)$$

where $P(\mathbf{x}|y = i)$ is the likelihood function for the ith class and $P(y = i)$ is the prior probability for this class. The smallest achievable probability of error is the Bayes error [Fukunaga, 1972]

$$L^* = 1 - E_{\mathbf{x}}[\max_i P(\mathbf{x}|y = i)P(y = i)] \tag{2.141}$$

Whenever there is no prior reason to believe that one class is more likely than the others, then $P(y = i) = 1/K$, in which case we obtain the maximum likelihood (ML) classifier

$$g(\mathbf{x}) = \max_i P(\mathbf{x}|y = i) \tag{2.142}$$

Under the assumption that the query consists of a collection of N independent query features $\mathbf{x} = \{x_i, \ldots, x_N\}$ this equation can also be written as

$$g(\mathbf{x}) = \max_i \frac{1}{N} \sum_{j=1}^{N} \log P(x_j|y = i) \tag{2.143}$$

which closely resembles Equation (2.136).

If there are only two classes a and b in the classification problem then, Equation (2.141) can be written as [Young and Calvert, 1974]

$$
\begin{aligned}
L^* &= E_{\mathbf{x}}[\min(P(y = a|\mathbf{x}), P(y = b|\mathbf{x}))] \\
&= \int \min[P(\mathbf{x}|y = a)P(y = a), P(\mathbf{x}|y = b)P(y = b)] \, dx \\
&\leq \sqrt{P(y = a)P(y = b)} \int \sqrt{P(\mathbf{x}|y = a)P(\mathbf{x}|y = b)} \, dx \\
&\leq \frac{1}{2} \int \sqrt{P(\mathbf{x}|y = a)P(\mathbf{x}|y = b)} \, dx \tag{2.144}
\end{aligned}
$$

In determination of Equation (2.143) we used the following bounds $\min[p, q] \leq \sqrt{pq}$, for arbitrary $p \geq 0$ and $q \geq 0$, and $\sqrt{P(\mathbf{x}|y = a)P(\mathbf{x}|y = b)} \leq 1/2$, taking into account that $P(\mathbf{x}|y = a) = 1 - P(\mathbf{x}|y = b)$.

The relation (resembled by Equation (2.144))

$$d_B^2 = -\log \int \sqrt{P_1(\mathbf{x})P_2(\mathbf{x})} \, dx \tag{2.145}$$

represents the Bhattacharyya distance between two arbitrary distributions $\{P_i(\mathbf{x})\}_{i=1,2}$. From here we can see that the Bhattacharyya distance is an upper bound on the Bayes error probability. Note that the Bhattacharyya distance is not a metric (it does not obey the triangle inequality).

The Bhattacharyya distance was used for image retrieval in [Comaniciu et al., 1999], where it took the form

$$g(\mathbf{x}) = \min_i \int \sqrt{P(\mathbf{x}|q)P(\mathbf{x}|y = i)} \, dx \qquad (2.146)$$

where $P(\mathbf{x}|q)$ is the density of the query. The resulting classifier can thus be seen as the one which finds the lowest upper-bound of the Bayes error for the collection of two-class problems involving the query and each of the database classes.

Consider now that the distribution of features of interest is Gaussian, characterized by its mean vector μ and covariance matrix Σ

$$P(\mathbf{x}|y = i) = \frac{1}{\sqrt{(2\pi)^n |\Sigma_i|}} \exp\left(-\frac{1}{2}(\mathbf{x} - \mu_i)^T \Sigma_i^{-1}(\mathbf{x} - \mu_i)\right) \qquad (2.147)$$

the Bhattacharyya distance becomes

$$d_B^2 = \frac{1}{4}(\mu_a - \mu_b)^T (\Sigma_a + \Sigma_b)^{-1}(\mu_a - \mu_b) + \frac{1}{2} \log \frac{\left|\frac{\Sigma_a + \Sigma_b}{2}\right|}{\sqrt{|\Sigma_a||\Sigma_b|}} \qquad (2.148)$$

where $|\cdot|$ is the determinant. The first term in Equation (2.148) gives the class separability due to mean-difference, while the second term gives the class separability due to the covariance-difference.

The Mahalanobis distance is proportional to a particular case of Bhattacharyya distance when the covariances are the same $\Sigma_a = \Sigma_b = \Sigma$,

$$d_B^2 = (\mu_a - \mu_b)^T \Sigma^{-1}(\mu_a - \mu_b) \qquad (2.149)$$

A dissimilarity measure using Mahalanobis distance is unable to distinguish among distributions with the same mean but different covariance matrices.

Finally, if the covariance matrix is the identity matrix $\Sigma = I$, we obtain the Euclidean distance

$$L_2 = (\mu_a - \mu_b)^T (\mu_a - \mu_b) \qquad (2.150)$$

Other dissimilarity measures such as Fisher linear discriminant function yield useful results only for distributions that are separated by the mean-difference [Fukunaga, 1972], whereas the Kullback discriminant [Kullback, 1968] provides in various instances lower performance than the Bhattacharyya distance, as shown in [Kailath, 1967]. The Chernoff distance [Fukunaga, 1972] is in general closer to the error probability than the Bhattacharyya distance (in fact the latter is a special case of Chernoff distance), but it is difficult to evaluate.

Exposing the assumptions behind each similarity function enables a critical analysis of their usefulness and the determination of the retrieval scenarios for which they may be appropriate. While the choice between the Bayesian and the maximum likelihood criterion is a function only of the amount of prior knowledge about class probabilities, there is in general no strong justification to rely on any of the remaining measures. In this context, there is a small justification to replace the minimization of the error probability on the multi-class retrieval problem (as in maximum likelihood) by the search for the two class problem with the smallest error bound (Bhattacharyya distance). Moreover, the Mahalanobis and the Euclidean distances only make sense if the image features are Gaussian distributed for all classes.

6.   Our Maximum Likelihood Approach

In the previous sections, the standard maximum likelihood procedure was presented together with its relation with other approaches. There, the goal was to find the particular set of parameters that would maximize the probability that the data set under observation could have occurred. In our case, we consider applications that involve similarity where the ground truth is provided. The goal is to find the probability density function which maximizes the similarity probability. Furthermore, applying the maximum likelihood procedure described above, we determine the corresponding metric and use it in the experiments. By doing this we expect to obtain better retrieval/matching results.

To state the issue more concretely, consider N pairs of M-dimensional feature vectors (X_i, Y_i), $i = 1, \ldots, N$, extracted from images in a database D, which according to the ground truth G are similar: $X_i \equiv Y_i$. Further, consider that all N feature vectors X_i are concatenated in a single B-dimensional vector, x, where $B = N \times M$. The same procedure applies to the N feature vectors Y_i concatenated in a B-dimensional vector y. Applying Equation (2.135) the similarity probability can be calculated as

$$P(G) \sim \prod_{i=1}^{B} \exp[-\rho(n_i)] \qquad (2.151)$$

where $n = [n_1 \ldots n_B]$ is the "noise" vector obtained as the difference between the vectors x and y, and ρ is the negative logarithm of the probability density of the noise. We used the notation $P(G)$ to explicitly show that the similarity probability was calculated in the presence of a particular ground truth G.

The additive noise model in Equation (2.151) is the dominant model used in computer vision regarding maximum likelihood estimation. Haralick and Shapiro [Haralick and Shapiro, 1993] consider this model in defining the M-estimate: "any estimate T_k defined by a minimization problem of the form $\min_{i} \sum \rho(x_i - T_k)$ is called an M-estimate." Note that the operation "-" between the estimate and the real data implies an additive model.

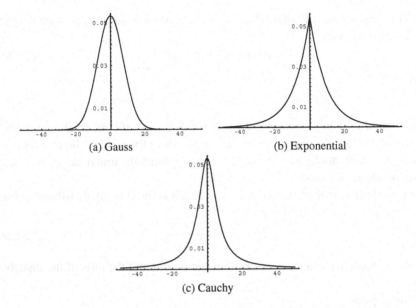

Figure 2.6. Gaussian, Exponential, and Cauchy distributions. The tails of the Gaussian and of the Exponential drop off quickly. The tails of the Cauchy distribution are more prominent.

According to Equation (2.151), we have to find the probability density function of the noise that maximizes the similarity probability: the maximum likelihood estimate for the noise distribution [Huber, 1981].

Taking the logarithm of (2.151) we find that we have to minimize the expression

$$\sum_{i=1}^{B} \rho(n_i) \tag{2.152}$$

To analyze the behavior of the estimate we take the approach described in [Hampel et al., 1986] and [Rousseeuw and Leroy, 1987] based on the influence function. The influence function characterizes the bias that a particular measurement has on the solution and is proportional to the derivative, ψ, of the estimate [Black, 1992]

$$\psi(z) \equiv \frac{d\rho(z)}{dz} \tag{2.153}$$

In the case where the noise is Gaussian distributed (Figure 2.6(a)):

$$P(n_i) \sim \exp(-n_i{}^2) \tag{2.154}$$

then,

$$\rho(z) = z^2 \qquad \text{and} \qquad \psi(z) = z \tag{2.155}$$

If the errors are distributed as a double or two-sided exponential (Figure 2.6(b)), namely,

$$P(n_i) \sim \exp(-|n_i|) \tag{2.156}$$

then,

$$\rho(z) = |z| \qquad \text{and} \qquad \psi(z) = \text{sgn}(z) \tag{2.157}$$

In this case, using Equation (2.152), we minimize the mean absolute deviation, rather than the mean square deviation. Here the tails of the distribution, although exponentially decreasing, are asymptotically much larger than any corresponding Gaussian.

A distribution with even more extensive tails is the Cauchy distribution (Figure 2.6(c)),

$$P(n_i) \sim \frac{a}{a^2 + n_i^2} \tag{2.158}$$

where the *scale* parameter a determines the height and the tails of the distribution.

This implies

$$\rho(z) = \log\left(1 + \left(\frac{z}{a}\right)^2\right) \qquad \text{and} \qquad \psi(z) = \frac{z}{a^2 + z^2} \tag{2.159}$$

For normally distributed errors, Equation (2.155) says that the more deviant the points, the greater the weight (Figure 2.7). By contrast, when tails are somewhat more prominent, as in (2.156), then (2.157) says that all deviant points get the same relative weight, with only the sign information used (Figure 2.8). Finally, when the tails are even larger, (2.159) says that ψ increases with deviation, then starts decreasing, so that very deviant points - the true outliers - are not counted at all (Figure 2.9).

Maximum likelihood gives a direct connection between the noise distributions and the comparison metrics. Considering ρ as the negative logarithm of the probability density of the noise, then the corresponding metric is given by Equation (2.152).

Consider the Minkowski-form distance L_p between two vectors x and y defined by

$$L_p(x, y) = \left(\sum_i |x_i - y_i|^p\right)^{\frac{1}{p}} \tag{2.160}$$

If the noise is Gaussian distributed, so $\rho(z) = z^2$, then Equation (2.152) is equivalent to Equation (2.160) with $p = 2$. Therefore, in this case the corresponding metric is L_2. Equivalently, if the noise is Exponential, so $\rho(z) = |z|$, then the corresponding metric is L_1 (Equation (2.160) with $p = 1$). In the case the noise is distributed as a Cauchy distribution with scale parameter a,

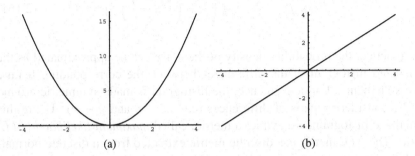

Figure 2.7. Quadratic estimator. (a) Estimate, (b) ψ-function

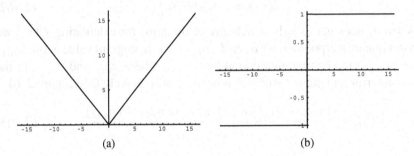

Figure 2.8. Exponential estimator. (a) Estimate, (b) ψ-function

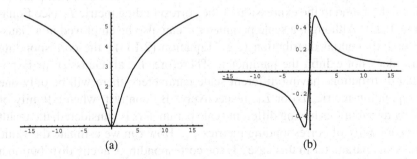

Figure 2.9. Cauchy estimator. (a) Estimate, (b) ψ-function

then the corresponding metric is no longer a Minkovski metric. However, for convenience we denote it as L_c and it is given by

$$L_c(x, y) = \sum_i \log\left(1 + \left(\frac{x_i - y_i}{a}\right)^2\right) \qquad (2.161)$$

In practice, the probability density of the noise can be approximated as the normalized histogram of the differences between the corresponding feature vectors elements. For convenience, the histogram is made symmetric around zero by considering pairs of differences (e.g., $x - y$ and $y - x$). Using this normalized histogram, we extract a metric, called *maximum likelihood (ML) metric*. The ML metric is a discrete metric extracted from a discrete normalized histogram having a finite number of bins.

The ML metric is given by Equation (2.152) where $\rho(n_i)$ is the negative logarithm of $P(n_i)$:

$$\rho(n_i) = -\log(P(n_i)). \qquad (2.162)$$

When n_i does not exactly match any of the bins, for calculating $P(n_i)$ we perform linear interpolation between $P(n_{inf})$ (the histogram value at bin n_{inf}) and $P(n_{sup})$ (the histogram value at bin n_{sup}), where n_{inf} and n_{sup} are the closest inferior and closest superior bins to n_i, respectively (see Figure 2.10)

$$P(n_i) = \frac{(n_{sup} - n_i)P(n_{inf}) + (n_i - n_{inf})P(n_{sup})}{n_{sup} - n_{inf}} \qquad (2.163)$$

6.1   Scale Parameter Estimation in a Cauchy Distribution

An interesting property of the Cauchy distribution is that the scale parameter a can be found in the expression of the corresponding metric L_c (see Equation (2.161)). Although, a scale parameter σ can also be employed in a Gaussian or Exponential distribution (e.g. Equation (2.133)), the corresponding metric does not exhibit the parameter. Therefore, for all Gaussian or Exponential distributions having different scale parameters, there will be only one corresponding metric, L_2 or L_1, respectively. By contrast, when a family of Cauchy distributions having different scale parameters is considered, the result will be a family of corresponding metrics L_c. How can we estimate the value of the scale parameter in this case? Is the corresponding Cauchy distribution a good approximation for the real noise distribution?

One solution would be to use a maximum likelihood procedure. For doing this one prior assumption is that the noise distribution is Cauchy and random samples are obtained from it. Let $x_1, \ldots, x_n$ be a random sample from a Cauchy distribution with density $a/[\pi\{a^2 + (x - \mu)^2\}]$, where μ is the location parameter and $a > 0$ is the scale parameter, both unknown. A Cauchy random

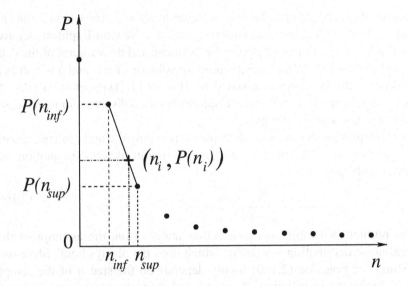

Figure 2.10. ML metric calculation procedure

sample generator can be obtained from the cumulative distribution [Haas et al., 1970] using the expression

$$F(x; \mu, a) = \frac{1}{2} + \frac{1}{\pi} \arctan\left(\frac{x - \mu}{a}\right) \tag{2.164}$$

where $-\infty < x < \infty$, $-\infty < \mu < \infty$, and $a > 0$.

Let $\hat{\mu}$ and $\hat{a}$ be the maximum likelihood estimators for μ and a. The likelihood function, $L(x_1, \ldots, x_n; \mu, a)$ is given by

$$L(x_1, \ldots, x_n; \mu, a) = \prod_{i=1}^{n} \left[\frac{a}{\pi(a^2 + (x_i - \mu)^2} \right] \tag{2.165}$$

and the logarithm of the likelihood is

$$\log L = -n \log \pi + n \log a - \sum_{i=1}^{n} \log(a^2 + (x_i - \mu)^2) \tag{2.166}$$

Hence, the maximum likelihood equations are

$$\frac{\partial \log L}{\partial \mu} = \sum_{i=1}^{n} \frac{2(x_i - \hat{\mu})}{\hat{a}^2 + (x_i - \hat{\mu})^2} = 0 \tag{2.167}$$

$$\frac{\partial \log L}{\partial a} = \frac{n}{\hat{a}} - \sum_{i=1}^{n} \frac{2\hat{a}}{\hat{a}^2 + (x_i - \hat{\mu})^2} = 0 \tag{2.168}$$

A numerical procedure must be used in order to solve (2.167) and (2.168) for $\hat{\mu}$ and $\hat{a}$. For solving these equations we used a Newton-Raphson iterative method with the starting points given by the mean and the variance of the data. We were always able to find unique positive solutions for $\hat{a}$ and $\hat{b}$ which is in accordance with the conjecture stated by Hass et al. [Haas et al., 1970]. In certain cases, however, the Newton-Raphson iteration diverged, in which cases we selected new starting points.

As noted previously, the noise distribution is symmetric and centered around zero, therefore $\mu = 0$. In this case, the maximum likelihood equation that should be solved is

$$\sum_{i=1}^{n} \frac{\hat{a}^2}{\hat{a}^2 + x_i^2} = \frac{1}{2}n \qquad (2.169)$$

The problem with this approach comes mainly from the assumption that the real noise distribution is Cauchy, which does not always hold. Moreover, a solution for Equation (2.169) highly depends on the size n of the sample extracted from the distribution. A reliable value for the parameter a can only be obtained when sufficient ground truth is available, which is not always the case.

Another way to estimate the scale parameter is by selecting that value that assures the best fit between a Cauchy model distribution and the noise distribution. A question that comes in mind is: What distance measure do we use when comparing two distributions? One solution is to use the Prokhorov distance measure [Yukich, 1989] which permits the comparison of a discrete empirical distribution with a continuous one through the association of each observation of the former with a subset of the sample space; the comparison is then performed with the help of the probability of the latter distribution over this subset.

Another solution, adopted here, is to use a Chi-square goodness-of-fit test [Watson, 1958]. The Chi-square test is frequently used in literature for comparing two binned distributions. Additionally, we can use the test not only for estimating the scale parameter but also as a goodness-of-fit indicator between the noise distribution and a model distribution (see next section). Let $\mathcal{M}$ be a binned Cauchy distribution used as a model for the noise distribution $\mathcal{R}$. The number and the location of bins for $\mathcal{M}$ are identical with the ones for $\mathcal{R}$. The Chi-square test is given by

$$\chi^2 = \sum_i \frac{(\mathcal{R}_i - \mathcal{M}_i)^2}{\mathcal{M}_i} \qquad (2.170)$$

where the sum is over all bins.

Using this simple procedure we estimate the value of the scale parameter a as that value that minimizes the χ^2.

7. Experimental Setup

In the previous section, our maximum likelihood approach was introduced for a similarity application in the presence of ground truth. An important issue is how to design a framework so that the noise distribution can be reliably constructed from the ground truth and in the same time, the performances of matching algorithms can be computed. In order to achieve the latter requirement we should also have ground truth information, so we can compare the obtained results of a matching algorithm with the ideal ones provided by the ground truth. Concretely, the setup of our experiments was the following.

We assume that representative ground truth is provided. The ground truth is split into two non-overlapping sets: the training set and the test set, as shown in Figure 2.11. Note that L_k is a notation for all possible metrics that can be used, e.g. L_1, L_2, L_c. First, for each image in the training set a feature vector is extracted. Second, the real noise distribution is computed as the normalized histogram of differences from the corresponding elements in feature vectors taken from similar images according to the ground truth. The Gaussian, Exponential, and Cauchy distributions are fitted to the real distribution. The Chi-square test is used to find the fit between each of the model distributions and the real distribution. We select the model distribution which has the best fit and its corresponding metric (L_k) is used in ranking. The ranking is done using only the test set.

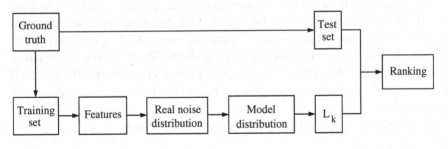

Figure 2.11. An overview of a similarity matching algorithm

It is important to note that for real applications, the parameter in the Cauchy distribution is found when fitting this distribution to the real distribution. This parameter setting would be used for the test set and any future comparisons in that application. The parameter setting can be generalized beyond the ground truth if the ground truth is representative.

For benchmarking purposes we also investigate the performance of other distance measures in matching. In all of the experiments we compare our results with the ones obtained using the Kullback relative information (K) [Kullback, 1968]. Let u and v be two discrete distributions then

$$K = \sum_i u_i \log \frac{u_i}{v_i} \tag{2.171}$$

where the sum is over all bins.

Note that the Kullback relative information is an asymmetric similarity measure between normalized probability density functions. In the applications where normalized histograms are used as feature vectors, K was computed using (2.171) where u was the feature vector corresponding to the query and v was the feature vector corresponding to a candidate match. When template matching was performed, suppose we are searching for a match for an intensity vector U from the left image. In the right image there will be many possible matching vectors and let V be one of them. Each of the intensity vectors is normalized to have the sum equal to 1 by dividing each component by the total intensity within the vector, i.e., $u_i = U_i / \sum_i U_i$. This results in two normalized vectors u and v and (2.171) can be applied for computing K.

We chose the Kullback relative information as a benchmark because it is the most frequently used similarity measure in information theory. Furthermore, Rissanen [Rissanen, 1978] showed that it serves as the foundation for other minimum description length measures such as the Akaike's information criterion [Akaike, 1973]. Regarding the relationship between the Kullback relative information and the maximum likelihood approach, Akaike [Akaike, 1973] showed that maximizing the expected log likelihood ratio in maximum likelihood estimation is equivalent to maximizing the Kullback relative information. Another interesting aspect of using the Kullback relative information as a benchmark is that it gives an example of using a logarithmically weighted function: instead of $u - v$ a weighted version of $\log u - \log v = \log(u/v)$ is computed.

In summary, our algorithm can be described as follows:

Step 1 Compute the feature vectors from the training set

Step 2 Compute the real noise distribution from the differences between corresponding elements of the feature vectors

Step 3 Compare each of the model distributions $\mathcal{M}$ to the real noise distribution $\mathcal{R}$ using the Chi-square test

$$\chi^2 = \sum_i \frac{(\mathcal{R}_i - \mathcal{M}_i)^2}{\mathcal{M}_i} \tag{2.172}$$

where the sum is over all bins.

Step 3.1 For a parameterized metric such as L_c, compute the value a of the parameter that minimizes the Chi-square test

Step 4 Select the corresponding L_k of the best fit model distribution

Step 4.1 Use the value a found from **Step 3.1** in the parameterized metrics

Step 5 Apply the L_k metric in ranking

Step 6 Compare the results with the ones obtained using the maximum likelihood (ML) metric extracted directly from the real noise distribution

8.   Concluding Remarks

In this chapter we formulated a framework for a maximum likelihood approach in computer vision applications involving similarity. The basic concepts from robust statistics were introduced and we illustrated our approach based on maximum likelihood. In the case where representative ground truth can be obtained for an application, we provided a method for selecting the appropriate metric, and proposed L_c as an alternative for both L_2 and L_1. Furthermore, we showed how to create a maximum likelihood metric (ML) based on the real noise distribution. Minimizing the ML metric is optimal with respect to maximizing the likelihood of the differences between feature vector elements when the noise distribution is representative. Therefore, the breaking points occur when there is no ground truth, or when the ground truth is not representative.

Chapter 3

COLOR BASED RETRIEVAL

In content based retrieval, color indexing is one of the most prevalent retrieval methods. The key problems in color indexing are: (1) the choice of color space, (2) color features, and (3) finding the best distance metric. In our color experiments we examine two applications from computer vision which involve distortions derived from changes in viewpoint and the process of printing and scanning. In the first experiments we use the Corel stock photo database and a color histogram method to find copies of images which were printed and subsequently scanned in. The second application deals with object based retrieval. The goal is to find all images of an object in a database where the images depicting the object were taken from different viewpoints. Both the ground truth and the algorithm come from the work by Gevers and Smeulders [Gevers and Smeulders, 1999]. Furthermore, for both applications, we implement the quadratic perceptual similarity measure proposed by Hafner et al. [Hafner et al., 1995] and the correlogram introduced by Huang et al. [Huang et al., 1997] as benchmarks.

1. Introduction

Color is an important attribute of visual information. Not only does color add beauty to objects but also gives information about objects as well. Furthermore, color information facilitates our daily life, e.g. reading a traffic light or identifying a favorite team in a sport event.

Color, in and of itself, does not exist. The color of an object is determined solely by which wavelengths of light are absorbed by the object and which ones filter back to our eyes. For instance, if we are in a forest on a sunny day, the leaves on the trees appear green. However, when we return to the same spot in the evening, the leaves now look gray. The leaves themselves are obviously unchanged, but the lighting is different, and thus our color perception is altered.

This phenomenon, along with many of its wider implications, was first noted in 1666 by 23-year-old Isaac Newton. Newton split, or refracted, a beam of sunlight by passing it through a rectangular glass prism. The colored rays of light that emerged from the other end of the prism were what Newton termed the "spectrum" of color: red, orange, yellow, green, blue, and violet (the colors of the rainbow). Later, Newton passed these colors through a second glass prism and discovered that they recombined to produce white light. Newton proved that there really are no "colors" in nature - just different wavelengths of light that were bent in different ways by the glass prism.

After Newton established the fundamentals of color in his "Optics" [Newton, 1704], color has been involved in many fields ranging from art to psychology and science. The emotional and psychological influence of color on humans was studied by Goethe in his famous book "Farbenlehre" [Goethe, 1840]. Goethe fiercely contested Newton's optics theory and its focus on physical properties. He said that colors arise in the eye and based his description of their properties on optical phenomena he himself observed. For Goethe, colors were analogous to perspective and proportions, i.e. formal categories that we process to make the observed world conform to the internal order of our brain. Light is needed to see colors because they are not part of nature but a product of our mind and eyes. Goethe's original proposal was to "marvel at color's occurrences and meanings, to admire and, if possible, to uncover color's secrets." To Goethe it was most important to understand human reaction to color, and his research marks the beginning of modern color psychology. To accomplish his goals, he created a color triangle where three primary colors red, yellow, and blue were arranged at the vertices of the triangle. The other subdivisions of the triangle were grouped into secondary and tertiary triangles, where the secondary triangle colors represented the mix of the two primary triangles to either side of it, and the tertiary triangle colors represented the mix of the primary triangle adjacent to it and the secondary triangle directly across from it. Goethe believed that his triangle was a diagram of the human mind and he linked each color with certain emotions. For example, Goethe associated blue with understanding and believed it evoked a quiet mood, while for him red evoked a festive mood and was suggestive of imagination. He chose the primaries red, yellow, and blue based on their emotional content, as well as on physical grounds, and he grouped the different subsections of the triangle by "elements" of emotion as well as by mixing level. This emotional aspect of the arrangement of the triangle reflects Goethe's concern that the emotional content of each color be taken into account by artists.

Heisenberg [Heisenberg, 1967] tried to reconcile Goethe's and and Newton's views. He suggested that the Cartesian dichotomy between an objective and subjective world - each within its own validity - would be resolved by the study of the neurological system which would ultimately be described in terms of mathematical structures.

Whoever should compare Goethe's theory of colors with Newton's preferred approach will soon become aware of two completely different attitudes to the one, single theme. These attitudes do not oppose each other, however, they complement each other - alone, neither of the systems can cover all aspects of color completely. Newton's analysis of colors is to be seen as complementary to Goethe's. Neither of the theories is wrong; each independently reproduces a valid aspect of our world, and substantiates the other.

In order to bring life to this idea of complementarity, we can compare the English scientist's and the German poet's beliefs: what for Newton is simple - pure blue, for example, being light with one wavelength ("monochromatic light") - is complicated for Goethe, since pure blue must first of all be prepared by extravagant means and is therefore artificial. In contrast, white light is simple for Goethe, since it exists completely naturally and without effort; Newton, on the other hand, sees in white light a mixture of all colors. White light is not simple for Newton; it is a combination. The essential complementarity of both color theories becomes evident when we consider the role of the subject - the human being. While Goethe, as a matter of course, views the human being as central, Newton omits him totally.

Maxwell's work in color vision is acknowledged as being the origin of quantitative color measurement (colorimetry). He developed a chart in the form of an equilateral triangle from his studies on the electromagnetic theory of light. His triangle is very similar to Goethe's, both are equilateral and both choose three primaries which are combined to produce the inner colors. Maxwell, however, believed that he could produce all the known colors within his triangle and he chose red (R), green (abbreviated to V [verde]), and blue (B) as primaries.

In painting, Munsell provided the theoretical basis in his "A Color Notation" [Munsell, 1905] on which most painters derive their notations about color ordering. His color space is based on pigment, not light. He began from two observations that he has made as painter. The first is that pure hues vary in their degree of lightness, and therefore all the pure hues (red, yellow, green, blue, violet) should not be on the same horizontal plane. The second observation is that some colors (red) are more vivid than others (green), and therefore, they should be further away from the axis. These observations pointed Munsell toward a color space whose shape is very irregular and asymmetric.

In 1931, an attempt was made to establish a world standard for measurement of color by the Commission Internationale de l'Eclairage (CIE). They generated a version of Maxwell's triangle, choosing a particular red, green, and blue from which to generate all the colors. The result became known as the CIE chromaticity chart, the updated version of which is used to measure and quantify the light produced by computer phosphor guns today.

2.   Colorimetry

All color is light. The *visible* spectrum of light, however, is only a small portion of the entire wavelength spectrum, which includes the ultraviolet portion that cannot be detected by the naked eye. The visible spectrum consists of three wavelength bands of light: red, green, and blue. The red is the longest wavelength, followed by the green, and then the blue. The various combinations of these three light wavelengths are interpreted by the human brain as a particular color.

Any color that we see represents those portions of the three bands of light that are not absorbed by the observed object and instead filter back to our eyes. An apple, therefore, appears red because all light bands except red are absorbed by the object, while the red is reflected back to us.

These three colors of light - red, green, and blue - are known as the *primary colors* (or the additive colors, or simply the primaries). They are colors that are used in video, and appear on a desktop computer screen. When combined, they produce white light; when mixed in varying intensities, they can form every other color that our eyes are capable of seeing.

To be more specific, electromagnetic radiation $F(\lambda)$ in the range of visible light ($\lambda \in \{380nm, \ldots, 780nm\}$) is perceived as color or colored light. As noticed above, it has been verified experimentally that color is perceived through three independent color receptors which have peak response at approximately red, green, and blue wavelengths, $\lambda_r = 700nm$, $\lambda_g = 546.1nm$, and $\lambda_b = 435.8nm$, respectively. By assigning each primary color receptor, $k \in \{r, g, b\}$, a response function $c_k(\lambda)$, visible light of any color $F(\lambda)$ is represented by a linear superposition of the $c_k(\lambda)$'s [Nieman, 1990], as follows: by normalizing $c_k(\lambda)$'s to reference white light $W(\lambda)$ such that

$$W(\lambda) = \overline{c_r}(\lambda) + \overline{c_g}(\lambda) + \overline{c_b}(\lambda). \tag{3.1}$$

$F(\lambda)$ produces the tristimulus responses (R, G, B) such that

$$F(\lambda) = R\,\overline{c_r}(\lambda) + G\,\overline{c_g}(\lambda) + B\,\overline{c_b}(\lambda). \tag{3.2}$$

As such, any color can be represented by a linear combination of the three primary colors (R, G, B).

3.   Color Models

There has been no consensus about which color space is most suitable for color based image retrieval. The problem is a result of the fact that there does not exist a universally accepted color space, and color perception is significantly subjective [Wyszecki and Stiles, 1982]. As a consequence, a large variety of color spaces is used in practice.

Color systems have been developed for different purposes [Smeulders et al., 2000]:

(1) display and printing process: RGB, CMY;

(2) television and video transmission efficiency: YIQ, YUV;

(3) color standardization: XYZ;

(4) color uncorrelation: $I_1 I_2 I_3$;

(5) color normalization and representation: rgb, xyz;

(6) perceptual uniformity: $U^*V^*W^*, L^*a^*b^*, L^*u^*v^*$;

(7) intuitive description: HSI, HSV.

With this large variety of color systems, the inevitable question arises which color system to use for different image retrieval applications. An important criterion is that the color system should be independent of the underlying imaging device. This is required when the images in the database are recorded by different imaging devices such as cameras and scanners. Additionally, the color system should exhibit perceptual uniformity meaning that the distances within the color space can be related to human perceptual differences. This is important when visually similar images are to be retrieved. Also, the transformation needed to compute the color system should be linear. A non-linear transformation may introduce instabilities with respect to noise, causing poor retrieval results. Moreover, to achieve robust and discriminative image retrieval, color invariance is an important criterion.

For our experiments, we chose two of the most frequently used color spaces, namely, RGB and HSV, together with the $l_1 l_2 l_3$ color model introduced by Gevers and Smeulders [Gevers and Smeulders, 1999].

3.1 RGB Color System

RGB refers to the intensity of 3 additive color primaries, red, green, and blue. The RGB space is not perceptually uniform. As such, the proximity of colors in RGB color space does not indicate color similarity. The space spanned by the R, G, and B values (see Equation 3.2) is complete in that all colors are represented as vectors in the 3D RGB space. Since it corresponds directly to the hardware, it is the easiest to be implemented and is in wide use. Typically, each primary is quantized into 256 levels and then combined to create $256 \times 256 \times 256$ possible colors.

3.2   *HSV* Color System

The *HSV* color model, introduced by Smith [Smith, 1978], approximates the perceptual properties of "hue," "saturation," and "value." Hue and saturation are taken from common speech about color, while the term value was introduced by Munsell [Munsell, 1905], although it was defined differently. The concept of value as a perceptually uniform quantity akin to brightness was created by Munsell. Roughly speaking:

(1) *hue* associates a color with some position in the color spectrum - red, green, and yellow are hue names;

(2) *saturation* describes the "vividness" of a color, pure spectral colors being "fully saturated colors" and grays being "desaturated colors";

(3) *value* corresponds to the "lightness" of a color.

A hue-saturation slice of HSV space is derived by projecting the surface of an RGB color cube onto the $R + G + B = 1$ plane: the saturation and hue of a point on the projection are its polar coordinates r and θ with respect to the center of the projected surface, while the value V of all points on the projection is simply the length of the diagonal of the color cube projected.

The transformation T_c from RGB to HSV is accomplished through the following equations [Hunt, 1989]. Let $v_c = (r, g, b)$ be the color triple of a point in normalized RGB space and let $w_c = (h, s, v)$ be the color triple of the transformed color point in HSV color space, such that $w_c = T_c(v_c)$.

For $r, g, b \in [0 \dots 1]$, T_c gives $h, s, v \in [0 \dots 1]$ as follows:

$$v = \max(r, g, b), \qquad\qquad s = \frac{v - \min(r, g, b)}{v}$$

Let

$$r' = \frac{v - r}{v - \min(r, g, b)}, \qquad g' = \frac{v - g}{v - \min(r, g, b)}, \qquad b' = \frac{v - b}{v - \min(r, g, b)}$$

then,

$$6h = \begin{cases} 5 + b' & \text{if } r = \max(r, g, b) \text{ and } g = \min(r, g, b) \\ 1 - g' & \text{if } r = \max(r, g, b) \text{ and } g \neq \min(r, g, b) \\ 1 + r' & \text{if } g = \max(r, g, b) \text{ and } b = \min(r, g, b) \\ 3 - b' & \text{if } g = \max(r, g, b) \text{ and } b \neq \min(r, g, b) \\ 3 + g' & \text{if } b = \max(r, g, b) \text{ and } r = \min(r, g, b) \\ 5 - r' & \text{otherwise} \end{cases}$$

Similarly, for $h, s, v \in [0 \dots 1]$, T_c^{-1} gives $r, g, b \in [0 \dots 1]$ as follows. Let,

$$\alpha = 6h - \text{round}(6h)$$

and,

$$\omega_1 = (1 - s)v, \quad \omega_2 = (1 - s\alpha)v, \quad \omega_3 = (1 - s(1 - \alpha))v$$

then,

$$r = \begin{cases} v & \text{if } \alpha = 0 \text{ or } \alpha = 5 \\ \omega_1 & \text{if } \alpha = 2 \text{ or } \alpha = 3 \\ \omega_2 & \text{if } \alpha = 1 \\ \omega_3 & \text{if } \alpha = 4 \end{cases} \quad g = \begin{cases} v & \text{if } \alpha = 1 \text{ or } \alpha = 2 \\ \omega_1 & \text{if } \alpha = 4 \text{ or } \alpha = 5 \\ \omega_2 & \text{if } \alpha = 3 \\ \omega_3 & \text{if } \alpha = 0 \end{cases}$$

$$b = \begin{cases} v & \text{if } \alpha = 3 \text{ or } \alpha = 4 \\ \omega_1 & \text{if } \alpha = 0 \text{ or } \alpha = 1 \\ \omega_2 & \text{if } \alpha = 5 \\ \omega_3 & \text{if } \alpha = 2 \end{cases}$$

The HSV and RGB color systems are typically used in generic content based retrieval applications.

3.3 $l_1 l_2 l_3$ Color System

Gevers and Smeulders [Gevers and Smeulders, 1999] analyzed and evaluated various color features for the purpose of image retrieval by color histogram matching under varying illumination environments. They introduced the $l_1 l_2 l_3$ color model as follows:

$$l_1(R, G, B) = \frac{(R - G)^2}{(R - G)^2 + (R - B)^2 + (G - B)^2} \tag{3.3}$$

$$l_2(R, G, B) = \frac{(R - B)^2}{(R - G)^2 + (R - B)^2 + (G - B)^2} \tag{3.4}$$

$$l_3(R, G, B) = \frac{(G - B)^2}{(R - G)^2 + (R - B)^2 + (G - B)^2} \tag{3.5}$$

where R, G, and B are the color values in the RGB color space, $0 \leq l_i \leq 1$, and $l_1 + l_2 + l_3 = 1$. They showed that the $l_1 l_2 l_3$ color model is invariant to a substantial change in viewpoint (when the viewpoint is changed, photometric changes may occur, yielding different shadows, shading, and highlighting cues for the same object), object geometry, highlights, and illumination. These invariant properties make the $l_1 l_2 l_3$ color system suitable for object recognition and retrieval applications. In their object recognition experiments, Gevers and Smeulders [Gevers and Smeulders, 1999] showed that the $l_1 l_2 l_3$ color model achieved the highest recognition rate.

4.   Color Based Retrieval

As the world enters the digital age, visual media is becoming prevalent and easily accessible. Factors such as the explosive growth of the World Wide Web, terabyte disk servers, and the digital versatile disk, reveal the growing amount of visual media which is available to society. With the availability of visual media comes the associated problem of searching for it and consequently, the focus of researchers toward providing automatic content based retrieval systems. With this new application area, color has returned to the center of interest of a growing number of scientists and artists. Aside from decorating and advertising potentials for Web-design, color information has already been used as a powerful tool in content based image and video retrieval. Different measures on the color features such as color histograms, color correlograms, prominent colors, and salient colors, have proven to be efficient in discriminating between relevant and non-relevant images. In particular, retrieval based on histograms has been widely studied in [Swain and Ballard, 1991], [Flicker et al., 1995], [Smith, 1997], [Hafner et al., 1995] and is now considered to be an effective measure for color based retrieval.

Color based retrieval may concern [Del Bimbo, 1999]:

- **Finding images containing a specified color in an assigned proportion.** This is the simplest type of color based query. The most efficient way to resolve it is to use histogram based representation of chromatic content and count the relative number of pixels that are in the histogram bin closest to the color in a query.

- **Finding images containing similar color regions as specified in a query.** A simple but generally ineffective solution to find images with color regions similar to a query, is to partition images into number of regions with fixed absolute location. Chromatic features extracted from each region are compared with those of the corresponding regions in the query. Different weights can be assigned to each region according to its relative importance [Stricker and Dimai, 1997]. However, this approach does not permit to specify arbitrary shaped regions nor their spatial relationships. To make this possible, images should be segmented into homogeneous color regions. However, size, shape, and color of regions of database images, resulting from color segmentation, in general do not fit size, shape, and color of regions specified in the query. Therefore, retrieval by color region similarity is a very complex operation.

- **Finding images containing a known object based on its color properties.** This application is similar to the previous one. Here, the object histogram is matched against parts of the database images and regions of potential interest are extracted. Histogram intersection method is suited for detecting whether an object is present in an image using its color information when objects have surfaces with fairy large homogeneous regions of color.

- **Finding image whose colors are similar to those of an example image.** When a user wants to find an image similar to a query image its interest lies on the global image chromatic content. For example, in the case of a database of paintings, this kind of query may help to find paintings of the same artist, or perceptually similar paintings, with no regard to what is represented in the picture. Image chromatic contents is usually represented through color histograms.

Queries can be expressed either through text of through visual examples. Textual specification of colors is a simple way to express queries about the presence of a color. However, it needs a commonly accepted correspondence between color names and color stimuli. Eventually, the color associated with the name selected can be visualized and the user can directly perceive the color stimuli, increasing his confidence in the color choice. Querying through visual examples is a more effective way of querying color distributions or color regions. In this approach, given a query image, the goal is to retrieve all the images whose color compositions are similar to the color composition of the query image (have colors in the same/similar proportion or location). Visual examples are also helpful for finding images containing a known object with certain color properties. Examples are expressed either by using icons [Lew and Sebe, 2000], or by extracting a sample image or a subimage from an image set [Sebe and Lew, 1999a]. In querying by example, color can be combined with other features like texture, structure, and composition.

4.1 Color Indexing

Color indexing is based on the observation that often color is used to encode functionality: grass is green, sky is blue, etc.

Color histogram is the most traditional way of describing low-level color properties of images. It can be represented as three independent color distributions, in each primary, or as two independent distributions (for color spaces which separate chromatic information from luminance) or - more frequently - as one distribution over the three primaries, obtained by discretizing image colors and counting how many pixels belong to each color.

In the last case, if we map the colors in the image $\mathcal{I}$ into a discrete color space containing n colors, then the color histogram [Swain and Ballard, 1991] [Sawhney and Hafner, 1994] $H(\mathcal{I})$ is a vector $(h_{c_1}, h_{c_2}, \cdots, h_{c_n})$, where each element h_{c_j} represents the probability of having the color c_j in the image $\mathcal{I}$.

The fundamental elements of the color histogram based approach include the selection of the color space together with the associated quantization scheme and the histogram distance metric. Color histograms are quite an efficient representation of color content; a positive aspect is that their computation is trivial. Moreover, histograms are fairly insensitive to variations originated by small camera rotations or zooming. Also they are fairly insensitive to changes in image resolution (when images have quite large homogeneous regions), and partial occlusions. However, where there are changes in lighting and large changes in view angle, histogram based representation of color may vary greatly. Moreover, histograms, by themselves, do not include spatial information so that images with very different layouts can have similar representations.

Two widely used distance metrics in color indexing are L_2 [Berman and Sapiro, 1997] and L_1 [Swain and Ballard, 1991][Gupta et al., 1997]. The L_2 distance applied to two color histograms I and M is defined as

$$L_2(I, M) = \sqrt{\sum_{i=1}^{n}(i_{c_i} - m_{c_i})^2} \tag{3.6}$$

Similarly, the L_1 distance will be

$$L_1(I, M) = \sum_{i=1}^{n}|i_{c_i} - m_{c_i}| \tag{3.7}$$

Swain and Ballard [Swain and Ballard, 1991] introduced a color matching method, known as histogram intersection. Specifically, given a pair of histograms I and M, each containing n bins, the histogram intersection measure is defined as follows:

$$H(I, M) = \frac{\sum_{i=1}^{n}\min(I_i, M_i)}{\sum_{i=1}^{n}M_i} \tag{3.8}$$

Moreover, if $\sum_{i=1}^{n}M_i = \sum_{i=1}^{n}I_i = k$, as will be the case for normalized histograms, then the histogram intersection measure is equivalent to L_1, thus

$$1 - H(I, M) = \frac{1}{2k}\sum_{i=1}^{n}|I_i - M_i| \tag{3.9}$$

For a proof consider initially the relations:

$$I_i = \begin{cases} \min(I_i, M_i) + |I_i - M_i| & \text{if } I_i > M_i \\ \min(I_i, M_i) & \text{otherwise} \end{cases} \tag{3.10}$$

and

$$M_i = \begin{cases} \min(I_i, M_i) & \text{if } I_i > M_i \\ \min(I_i, M_i) + |I_i - M_i| & \text{otherwise} \end{cases} \tag{3.11}$$

In either case

$$I_i + M_i = 2\min(I_i, M_i) + |I_i - M_i| \tag{3.12}$$

Then, using Equation (3.12)

$$k = \frac{1}{2}\sum_{i=1}^{n}(I_i + M_i) = \sum_{i=1}^{n}\min(I_i, M_i) + \frac{1}{2}\sum_{i=1}^{n}|I_i - M_i| \tag{3.13}$$

By definition,

$$1 - H(I, M) = \frac{k - \sum_{i=1}^{n}\min(I_i, M_i)}{k} \tag{3.14}$$

Replacing k in the numerator by the expression in Equation (3.13) we have

$$1 - H(I, M) = \frac{1}{2k}\sum_{i=1}^{n}|I_i - M_i| \tag{3.15}$$

and relation (3.9) is proven.

When we create a color histogram, we must quantize each component of the color model using a number of bits. We define quantization $X:Y:Z$ for color model ABC as quantizing color component A using X bits, B using Y bits, and C using Z bits. In the case of HSV, a 4:2:2 quantization refers to quantizing H using 4 bits, S using 2 bits, and V using 2 bits. When not otherwise specified RGB refers to a 3:3:2 quantization and HSV refers to a 4:2:2 quantization.

We applied the theoretical results described in Chapter 2 in two experiments. We determined the influence of the similarity noise model on finding similar images which differ due to either printer-scanner noise or change of viewpoint. We used two color image databases. The first one was the Corel Photo database and the second one consisted of 500 reference images of domestic objects, tools, art artifacts, etc.

For benchmarking purposes we compared our results with the ones obtained using Hafner's quadratic distance measure (L_q) [Hafner et al., 1995] and the color auto-correlogram (Cg) [Huang et al., 1997].

Hafner et al. [Hafner et al., 1995] introduced a sophisticated method of comparing histograms. They used a quadratic distance measure L_q which allows for similarity matching between different colors (represented by the color histograms bins)

$$L_q(x, y) = (x - y)^t A(x - y) \tag{3.16}$$

where x and y are two color histograms, $A = [a_{ij}]$ is a symmetric matrix, and the weights a_{ij} denote similarity between bins (colors) i and j. These weights can be normalized so that $0 \le a_{ij} \le 1$, with $a_{ii} = 1$, and large a_{ij} denoting similarity between bins i and j, and small a_{ij} denoting dissimilarity. In their implementation [Hafner et al., 1995], the weights a_{ij} are calculated using d_{ij}, the Euclidean distance (L_2) between colors i and j in a color space, for instance, [R(ed),G(reen),B(lue)]. Let $d_{\max} = \max\limits_{ij}(d_{ij})$ then

$$a_{ij} = 1 - \frac{d_{ij}}{d_{\max}} \tag{3.17}$$

The authors state that the quadratic distance measure more closely corresponds to human judgment of color similarity than the Euclidean distance (L_2). For simplicity, consider a histogram distribution of three colors, say red, orange, and blue, with

$$A_{\text{red, orange, blue}} = \begin{bmatrix} 1.0 & 0.9 & 0.0 \\ 0.9 & 1.0 & 0.0 \\ 0.0 & 0.0 & 1.0 \end{bmatrix} \tag{3.18}$$

where red and orange are considered highly similar. Consider a pure red image, $x = [1.0, 0.0, 0.0]^T$, and a pure orange image, $x = [0.0, 1.0, 0.0]^T$. The (squared) histogram distance given by Equation (3.16) is 0.2. This low distance reflects the perceptual similarity of the two images although their distribution populate distinct bins of the histogram so their squared Euclidean distance is 2.0.

Observing the fact that the color histograms lack information about how color is spatially distributed, Huang et al. [Huang et al., 1997], introduced a new color feature for image retrieval called color correlogram. This feature characterizes how the spatial correlation of pairs of color changes with distance in an image. A color correlogram of an image is a table indexed by color pairs, where the k-th entry for $\langle c_i, c_j \rangle$ specifies the probability of finding a pixel of color c_j at distance k from a pixel of color c_i in the image:

$$Cg_{c_i,c_j}^k(I) = P_{p_1 \in I_{c_i}}[p_2 \in I_{c_j} | \|p_1 - p_2\| = k] \tag{3.19}$$

where p_1 and p_2 are pixels in the image and $I_c = \{p | I(p) = c\}$ with $I(p)$ denoting the pixel color. Usually, because the size of color correlogram is quite large, the color auto-correlogram (simply denoted as Cg) is often used instead. This feature only captures spatial correlation between identical colors

$$Cg = Cg_{c_i,c_i}^k(I) \tag{3.20}$$

Local correlation between colors are more significant than global correlations in an image and therefore, a small subset of distances k is sufficient to capture the spatial correlation.

Since both L_q and C_g were meant to be benchmarks, they were implemented as described in the original papers. For L_q, Hafner used a 256 bin histogram in RGB color space. In computing the auto-correlograms, there were used 64 colors in RGB color space and $\{1, 3, 5, 7\}$ for spatial distances, resulting in a 256 feature vector. The comparison was made using L_1.

Clearly, the maximum likelihood approach described in Section 2.6 can also be applied to these features in the same way as it is applied to color histograms. However, in order to have a fair benchmark we consider only the implementation from the original papers.

In a typical image retrieval application the result of a query is a ranked list of images that are hopefully interesting to the user (a group of images similar to the query image). From this list only a limited number of the retrieval results are showed to the user. This is because in general a user will not want to browse through a large number of retrieval results to find the image(s) he is looking for. In this context, we consider in our experiments the best s retrieval results, where we define s as the *scope*.

The problem is formulated as follows: Let $\mathcal{Q}_1, \cdots, \mathcal{Q}_n$ be the query images and for the ith query $\mathcal{Q}_i$, and let $\mathcal{I}_1^{(i)}, \cdots, \mathcal{I}_m^{(i)}$ be the images similar with $\mathcal{Q}_i$ according to the ground truth. The retrieval method will return this set of answers with various ranks. As an evaluation measure of the performance of the retrieval method we used *precision* versus *recall* at different scopes: For a query $\mathcal{Q}_i$ and a scope $s > 0$, the recall r is defined as

$$r = \frac{|\{\mathcal{I}_j^{(i)} | rank(\mathcal{I}_j^{(i)}) \leq s\}|}{m} \tag{3.21}$$

and the precision p is defined as

$$p = \frac{|\{\mathcal{I}_j^{(i)} | rank(\mathcal{I}_j^{(i)}) \leq s\}|}{s} \tag{3.22}$$

Another interesting performance evaluation measure is the *retrieval accuracy* defined as the percentage of correct copies found within the top s matches.

5. Experiments with the Corel Database

The first experiments were done using 8,200 images from the Corel database. We used this database because it represents a widely used set of photos by both amateur and professional graphical designers. Furthermore, it is available on the Web at http://www.corel.com. In these experiments we chose two of the most frequently used color spaces, namely, RGB and HSV.

5.1 Early Experiments

Before we can measure the accuracy of particular methods, we first had to find a challenging and objective ground truth for our tests [Sebe and Lew,

1999b]. We perused the typical image alterations and categorized various kinds of noise with respect to finding image copies. Copies of images were often made with images at varying JPEG qualities, in different aspect ratio preserved scales, and in the printed media. We defined these as JPEG noise, Scaling noise, and Printer-Scanner noise.

JPEG noise was created by coding and then decoding a JPEG image using varying JPEG-quality values. Using HSV 4:2:2, JPEG quality 30, and L_1 metric, we were able to recover the exact image copy as the top rank with 100% retrieval accuracy from our large image database.

In Scale noise, we made the copy by reducing the image in size so that the image was aspect ratio preserved with maximum size 32×32. Using HSV 4:2:2 and L_1 metric, the copy was found within the top 10 ranks with 100% retrieval accuracy. We concluded that JPEG noise and Scaling noise were not sufficiently challenging to discriminate the different color indexing methods.

In Printer-Scanner noise, the idea was to measure the effectiveness of a retrieval method when trying to find a copy of an image in a magazine or newspaper. In order to create the ground truth we printed 82 images using an Epson Stylus 800 color printer at 720 dots/inch and then scanned each of them at 400 pixels/inch using an HP IIci color scanner. The noise from this copy process was the most significant in that the copy was found in the top 10 ranks using HSV 4:2:2 and L_1 metric with less than 45% accuracy. From these primary investigations in Printer-Scanner noise we concluded that this application is challenging and therefore we investigated it further.

Examples of copy pairs from the Printer-Scanner noise experiments are shown in Figure 3.1. The query image is typically very different from the target image. In the copy pair containing the child, the textures on the sleeve and on the hair are missing. Also, the cup and water jug are barely discernible. In the other copy pair, note the loss of details in the background mountainside and windows on the lower-right house wall. In conclusion, note that we purposely chose a hard ground truth in order to have a good discrimination between the retrieval methods.

5.2   Usability Issues

In creating a system for users, it is important to take into account the way in which users will interact with the system. Two important issues are: the total response time of the system and the number of results pages which the user must look at before finding the image copy. We made the following assumptions. First, in order to have an interactive experience, the total system response time should be less than 2 seconds. Furthermore, the number of results pages which are looked at by the user should reflect the usage of real professionals. Graphical artists typically flip through stock photo albums containing tens of pages, which amounts to a few hundred images for relevant material. For this

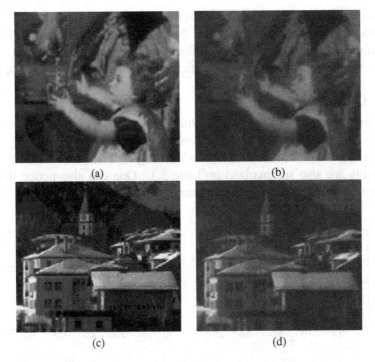

Figure 3.1. Two examples of copy pairs used in Printer-Scanner noise experiments: (a)-(c) the original image; (b)-(d) copy image. The copy image is very different from the original image.

reason we show the results regarding the top 1 to 100 ranks. We also avoid methods which require more than a few seconds of response time.

5.3 Printer-Scanner Noise Experiments

As we stated in Section 3.5.1, JPEG noise and Scaling noise were not sufficiently challenging to separate the different color indexing methods therefore, we focused on Printer-Scanner noise application. Our ground truth consists of 82 copy-pairs: the original images along with their copies obtained by printing and then scanning. The training set (see Section 2.7) was obtained by randomly choosing 50 copy-pairs from the ground truth. The test set consisted of the remaining pairs from the ground truth.

As it was noted in Section 3.3 there are various color models proposed in the literature and there has been no consensus about which one is most suitable for color based image retrieval. In our experiments with Corel database we considered the two most frequently used color models RGB and HSV. Initially, we compared the results obtained with each of these color models using the L_2 and L_1 distance measures introduced above. Further, we investigated the influence of the quantization scheme on the retrieval results. Finally, based on the previous results, we used the color model that provided the best retrieval results and investigated the influence of the similarity noise model on the retrieval results applying the theoretical framework described in Chapter 2.

5.4   Color Model

The first question we asked was: Which color model gives better retrieval accuracy? As shown in Figure 3.2, we obtained better retrieval accuracy when using the HSV color model, regardless of using L_1 or L_2 distance measures. The results are also summarized in Table 3.1. One can also notice that L_1 consistently provided better retrieval results compared to L_2.

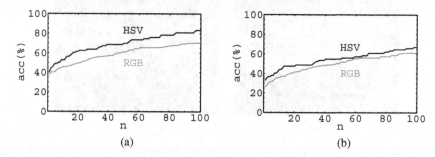

Figure 3.2.   Retrieval accuracy for the top 100 using HSV and RGB: (a) L_1; (b) L_2

Table 3.1.   Retrieval accuracy (%) for HSV and RGB using L_1 and L_2

Top		20	40	100
HSV	L_2	48.78	54.87	67.07
	L_1	62.19	68.29	84.14
RGB	L_2	40.17	48.66	61.24
	L_1	50.15	57.72	69.09

5.5   Quantization

Based upon the improvement in the retrieval accuracy it is clear that the best choice is to use the HSV color model with the L_1 metric. So, the next question is: How does the quantization scheme affect the retrieval accuracy? In Figure 3.3(a) it appears that increased resolution in H may be the cause of increased accuracy. This leads us to ask whether further H resolution will give even better results. Figure 3.3(b) shows that this is not the case.

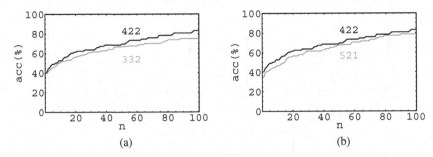

Figure 3.3. Retrieval accuracy for HSV using different quantization models (a) 4:2:2 - 3:3:2 and (b) 4:2:2 - 5:2:1

In summary, the choice of the color model and quantization can affect the accuracy by up to 15% and 7%, respectively. Our first experiments showed that the best retrieval results are obtained when using the HSV color model with a 4:2:2 quantization scheme. Consequently, we use this color model in our next experiments.

5.6   Distribution Analysis

The next question we asked was: Which distribution is a good approximation for the real color model noise? To answer this, we need to measure the noise with respect to the color model. The real noise distribution (Figure 3.4) was obtained as the normalized histogram of differences between the elements of color histograms corresponding to copy-pair images from the training set (50 image pairs).

Note that the Chi-square test was used to calculate the approximation error which measures the fit between each of the model distributions and the real distribution. The best fit Exponential had a better fit to the noise distribution than the Gaussian. Consequently, this implies that L_1 should have better retrieval results than L_2. The Cauchy distribution is the best fit overall, and the results obtained with L_c reflect this (see Figure 3.5).

If it is necessary to perform analytic computations, then the usage of one of the analytic metrics like, L_1, L_2, or L_c metrics is required. The main advantage of these metrics is the ease in implementation and analytic manipulation. However, neither corresponding distribution models the real noise distribution accurately, so we expect that we can lower the misdetection rates even further. As was shown in Section 2.6, a metric, called maximum likelihood (ML) metric can be extracted directly from the real noise distribution. We expect this metric to provide the best retrieval results.

Figure 3.5 shows the precision/recall graphs. L_c gave a significant improvement in accuracy as compared to L_2, L_1, and L_q. The Kullback relative infor-

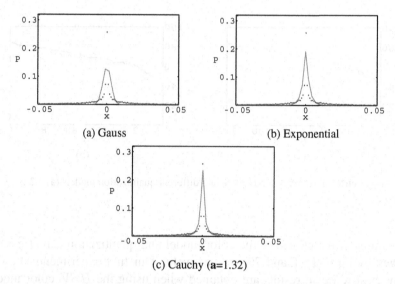

(c) Cauchy (**a**=1.32)

Figure 3.4. Noise distribution in Corel database compared with (a) the best fit Gaussian (approximation error is 0.106), (b) best fit Exponential (approximation error is 0.082) and (c) best fit Cauchy (approximation error is 0.068)

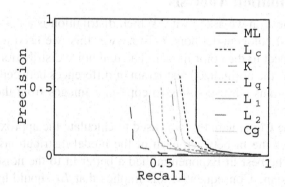

Figure 3.5. Precision/Recall in Corel database; for L_c, a=1.32

mation (K) (see Equation (2.171)), L_q, and the correlograms Cg performed better than L_2 and L_1. Overall, the ML metric gave the best accuracy.

The retrieval accuracy results are presented in Table 3.2. Note that the choice of the noise model can significantly affect the retrieval accuracy. The usage of L_q and C_g also produce improvement in retrieval accuracy compared with L_2 and L_1, since they use some extra information regarding color similarity or spatial correlation between colors. However, when the noise is modeled best, so therefore ML is used, we obtained the best retrieval results.

Table 3.2. Retrieval accuracy (%) in the Corel database

Top	20	40	100
L_2	48.78	54.87	67.07
L_1	62.19	68.29	84.14
L_q	66.34	73.66	88.29
K	68.29	75.60	86.58
L_c a=1.32	71.95	79.26	92.68
ML	75.60	82.92	96.34
Cg	71.09	79.63	88.17

6. Experiments with the Objects Database

In the next experiments we used a database [Gevers and Smeulders, 2000] consisting of 500 images of color objects such as domestic objects, tools, toys, food cans, etc. The objects were recorded in isolation (one per image) against a white cardboard background. The digitization was done in 8 bits per color. Two light sources of average day-light color were used to illuminate the objects in the scene. There was no attempt to individually control the focus of the camera or the illumination. Objects were recorded at a pace of a few shots a minute. They show a considerable amount of noise, shadows, shading, specularities, and self occlusion resulting in a good representation of views from everyday life.

As ground truth we used 48 images of 8 objects taken from different camera viewpoints (6 images for a single object). The objects were put perpendicularly in front of the camera and recordings were generated by varying the angle between the camera for $s = \{30, 45, 60, 75, 80\}$ degrees with respect to the object's surface normal. An example is shown in Figure 3.6.

For this experiment we chose to implement a method proposed in [Gevers and Smeulders, 1999] designed for indexing by color invariants. Our goal was to study the influence of the similarity noise on the retrieval results.

Using 24 images with varying viewpoint as the training set, we calculated the real noise distribution and studied the influence of different distance measures on the retrieval results. We used the $l_1 l_2 l_3$ color model introduced previously and we quantized each color component with 3 bits resulting in color histograms with 512 bins.

The Cauchy distribution was the best match for the measured noise distribution. The Exponential distribution was a better match than the Gaussian (Figure 3.7). Table 3.3 shows the precision and recall values at various scopes. The results obtained with L_c were consistently better than the ones obtained with L_2 or L_1.

Figure 3.6.   Example of images of one object taken from different camera viewpoints

Table 3.3.   Recall/Precision versus Scope; for L_c, **a=2.88**

	Precision			Recall		
Scope	5	10	25	5	10	25
L_2	0.425	0.258	0.128	0.425	0.517	0.642
L_1	0.45	0.271	0.135	0.45	0.542	0.675
L_q	0.46	0.280	0.143	0.46	0.561	0.707
K	0.466	0.279	0.138	0.466	0.558	0.692
L_c	0.525	0.296	0.146	0.525	0.592	0.733
ML	0.533	0.304	0.149	0.533	0.618	0.758
Cg	0.5	0.291	0.145	0.5	0.576	0.725

Figure 3.8 shows the precision-recall graphs. The curve corresponding to L_c is above the curves corresponding to L_1 or L_2 showing that the method using L_c is more effective. Note that the Kullback relative information performed better than L_1 or L_2.

In summary, L_c performed better than the analytic distance measures, and the ML metric performed best overall. It is interesting that the Kullback relative information performed consistently better than the well-known histogram intersection (L_1), and roughly the same as L_q. The correlogram (Cg) performed better than L_1, L_2, L_q, and K.

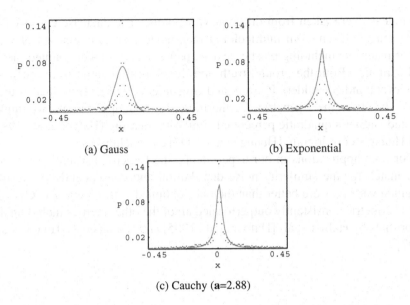

(a) Gauss   (b) Exponential

(c) Cauchy (**a=2.88**)

Figure 3.7. Noise distribution in color objects database compared with (a) the best fit Gaussian (approximation error is 0.123), (b) best fit Exponential (approximation error is 0.088) and (c) best fit Cauchy (approximation error is 0.077)

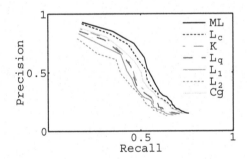

Figure 3.8. Precision/Recall for color objects database; for L_c, **a=2.88**

7. Concluding Remarks

We examined two applications from computer vision which involve distortions derived either from changes in viewpoint or from the process of printing and scanning. The first application was finding copies of images which had been printed and then scanned. For this application we used the Corel stock photo database and a color histogram method for finding the copies. The second application dealt with finding all images of an object in a database where the images were taken from different viewpoints. The database consisted of color images taken from multicolored man-made objects composed of variety of materials including plastic, textile, paper, wood, rubber, painted metal, and ceramic. Both the ground truth and the algorithm came from the work by Gevers and Smeulders [Gevers and Smeulders, 1999]. Note that in their work, they used the L_1 metric. Furthermore, for both applications, we implemented Hafner's quadratic perceptual similarity measure [Hafner et al., 1995] and Huang's correlogram [Huang et al., 1997] as benchmarks.

For both applications in our experiments, the Cauchy distribution was the best match for the similarity noise distribution and consequently the results obtained with L_c were better than the ones obtained with L_2 and L_1. Overall, the ML metric consistently outperformed all of the other metrics including the algorithms by Hafner et al. [Hafner et al., 1995] and Huang et al. [Huang et al., 1997].

Chapter 4

ROBUST TEXTURE ANALYSIS

Textures are one of the basic features in visual searching and computer vision. In the research literature, most of the attention has been focussed on the texture features with minimal consideration of the noise models. In this chapter we investigate the problem of texture classification from a maximum likelihood perspective. We take into account the texture models (e.g., Gabor and wavelet models and texture distribution models such as gray-level differences, Laws' models, covariance models, and local binary patterns), the noise distribution, and the inter-dependence of the texture features. We use the Brodatz's texture database [Brodatz, 1966] in two experiments. Firstly, we use a subset of nine textures from the database in a texture classification experiment. The goal is to classify correctly random samples extracted from the original textures. In these experiments we use the texture distribution models for extracting features as in the work by Ojala et al. [Ojala et al., 1996]. Secondly, we consider a texture retrieval application where we extract random samples from all the 112 original Brodatz's textures and the goal is to retrieve samples extracted from the same original texture as the query sample. As texture models we use the wavelet model as in the work by Smith and Chang [Smith and Chang, 1994] and the Gabor texture model as in the work by Ma and Manjunath [Ma and Manjunath, 1996].

1. Introduction

Texture is an intuitive concept. Every child knows that leopards have spots but tigers have stripes, that curly hair looks different from straight hair, etc. In all these examples there are variations of intensity and color which form certain repeated patterns called *visual texture*. The patterns can be the result of physical surface properties such as roughness or oriented strands which often have a tactile quality, or they could be the result of reflectance differences such as the color on a surface. Even though the concept of texture is intuitive (we recognize texture when we see it), a precise definition of texture has proven difficult to formulate. This difficulty is demonstrated by the number of different texture definitions attempted in the literature [Bovik et al., 1990][Richards and Polit, 1974][Haralick, 1979][Chaudhuri et al., 1993][Tamura et al., 1978].

Despite the lack of a universally accepted definition of texture, all researchers agree on two points:

(1) within a texture there is significant variation in intensity levels between nearby pixels; that is, at the limit of resolution, there is non-homogeneity

(2) texture is a homogeneous property at some spatial scale larger than the resolution of the image.

It is implicit in these properties of texture that an image has a given resolution. A single physical scene may contain different textures at varying scales. For example, at a large scale the dominant pattern in a floral cloth may be a pattern of flowers against a white background, yet at a finer scale the dominant pattern may be the weave of the cloth. The process of photographing a scene, and digitally recording it, creates an image in which the pixel resolution implicitly defines a finest scale. It is conventional in the texture analysis literature to investigate texture at the pixel resolution scale; that is, the texture which has significant variation at the pixel level of resolution, but which is homogeneous at a level of resolution about an order of magnitude coarser.

Some researchers finesse the problem of formally defining texture by describing it in terms of the human visual system: textures do not have uniform intensity, but are nonetheless perceived as homogeneous regions by a human observer. Other researchers are completely driven in defining texture by the application in which the definition is used. Some examples are given here:

- "An image texture may be defined as a local arrangement of image irradiances projected from a surface patch of perceptually homogeneous irradiances." [Bovik et al., 1990]

- "Texture is defined for our purposes as an attribute of a field having no components that appear enumerable. The phase relations between the components are thus not apparent enumerable. The phase relations between the components are thus not apparent. Nor should the field contain an obvious gradient. The intent of this definition is to direct attention of the observer to the global properties of the display, i.e., its overall "coarseness," "bumpiness," or "fineness." Physically, nonenumerable (aperiodic) patterns are generated by stochastic as opposed to deterministic processes. Perceptually, however, the set of all patterns without obvious enumerable components will include many deterministic (and even periodic) textures." [Richards and Polit, 1974]

- "An image texture is described by the number and types of its (tonal) primitives and the spatial organization or layout of its (tonal) primitives ... A fundamental characteristic of texture: it cannot be analyzed without a frame of reference of tonal primitive being stated or implied. For any smooth gray tone surface, there exists a scale such that when the surface is examined, it has no texture. Then as resolution increases, it takes on a fine texture and then a coarse texture." [Haralick, 1979]

- "Texture regions give different interpretations at different distances and at different degrees of visual attention. At a standard distance with normal attention, it gives the notion of macroregularity that is characteristic of the particular texture." [Chaudhuri et al., 1993]

A definition of texture based on human perception is suitable for psychometric studies and for discussion on the nature of texture. However, such a definition poses problems when used as the theoretical basis for a texture analysis algorithm. Consider the three images in Figure 4.1. All three images are constructed by the same method, differing in only one parameter. Figures 4.1(a) and (b) contain perceptually different textures, whereas Figures 4.1(b) and (c) are perceptually similar. Any definition of texture, intended as the theoretical foundation for an algorithm and based on human perception, has to address the problem that a family of textures, as generated by a parameterized method, can vary smoothly between perceptually distinct and perceptually similar pairs of textures.

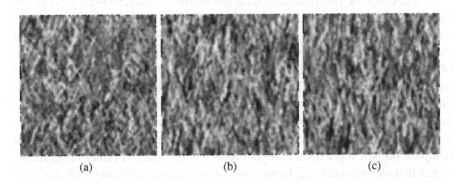

(a)   (b)   (c)

Figure 4.1. Visibility of texture distinctions; Each of the images is composed of lines of the same length having their intensity drawn from the same distribution and their orientations drawn from different distributions. The lines in (a) are drawn from the uniform distribution, with a maximum deviation from the vertical of 45°. The orientation of lines in (b) is at most 30° from the vertical and in (c) at most 28° from the vertical.

2.   Human Perception of Texture

Julesz has studied texture perception extensively in the context of texture discrimination [Julesz et al., 1973][Julesz, 1975]. The question he posed was: "When is a texture pair discriminable, given that the textures have the same brightness, contrast, and color?" His approach was to embed one texture in the other. If the embedded patch of texture visually stood out from the surrounding texture, then the two textures were considered to be dissimilar. In order to analyze if two textures are discriminable, he compared their first and second order statistics.

First order statistics measure the likelihood of observing a gray value at a randomly chosen location in the image. These statistics can be computed from the histogram of pixel intensities in the image. These depend only on individual pixel values and not on the interaction or co-occurrence of neighboring pixel values. The average intensity in an image is an example of a first order statistic. Second order statistics are defined as the likelihood of observing a pair of gray values occurring at the endpoints of a dipole of random length placed in the image at a random location and orientation. These are properties of pairs of pixel values.

Julesz found that textures with similar first order statistics, but different second order statistics were easily discriminated. However, he could not find any textures with the same first and second order statistics that could be discriminated. This led him to the conjecture that "iso-second-order textures are indistinguishable." [Julesz et al., 1973]

Later Caelli et al. [Caelli et al., 1978] did produce iso-second-order textures that could be discriminated with pre-attentive human visual perception. Further work by Julesz [Julesz, 1981a][Julesz, 1981b] revealed that his original conjecture was wrong. Instead, he found that the human visual perception mechanism did not necessarily use third order statistics for the discrimination of these iso-second-order textures, but rather use the second order statistics of features he called *textons*. These textons are described as being the fundamentals of texture. Three classes of textons were found: *color*, *elongated blobs*, and the *terminators* (end points) of these elongated blobs. The original conjecture was revised to state that "the pre-attentive human visual system cannot compute statistical parameters higher than second order." Furthermore, Julesz stated that the pre-attentive human visual system actually uses only the first order statistics of these textons.

Since these pre-attentive studies into the human visual perception, psychophysical research has focused on developing physiologically plausible models of texture discrimination. These models involved determining which measurements of textural variations humans are most sensitive to. Textons were not found to be the plausible textural discriminating measures as envisaged by Julesz [Bergen and Adelson, 1988][Voorhees and Poggio, 1988]. Beck et al. [Beck et al., 1987] argued that the perception of texture segmentation in certain types of patterns is primarily a function of spatial frequency analysis and not the result of a higher level symbolic grouping process. Psychophysical research suggested that the brain performs a multi-channel, frequency, and orientation analysis of the visual image formed on the retina [Campbell and Robson, 1968][De Valois et al., 1982]. Campbell and Robson [Campbell and Robson, 1968] conducted psychophysical experiments using various grating patterns. They suggested that the visual system decomposes the image into filtered images of various frequencies and orientations. De Valois et al. [De Valois et al., 1982] have studied the brain of the macaque monkey which is assumed to be close to the human brain in its visual processing. They recorded the response of the simple cells in the visual cortex of the monkey to sinusoidal gratings of various frequencies and orientations and concluded that these cells are tuned to narrow ranges of frequency and orientation. These studies have motivated vision researchers to apply multi-channel filtering approaches to texture analysis. Tamura et al. [Tamura et al., 1978] and Laws [Laws, 1980] identified the following properties as playing an important role in describing texture: uniformity, density, coarseness, roughness, regularity, linearity, directionality, direction, frequency, and phase. Some of these perceived qualities are not independent. For example, frequency is not independent of density, and the property of direction only applies to directional textures. The fact that the perception of texture has so many different dimensions is an important reason why there is no single method of texture representation which is adequate for a variety of textures.

3. Texture Features

Interest in visual texture was triggered by the phenomenon of texture discrimination which occurs when a shape is defined purely by its texture, with no associated change in color or brightness: color alone cannot distinguish between tigers and cheetahs! This phenomenon gives clear justification for texture features to be used in content based retrieval together with color and shape. Several systems have been developed to search through image databases using combination of texture, color, and shape attributes (QBIC [Flicker et al., 1995], Photobook [Pentland et al., 1996], Chabot [Ogle and Stonebracker, 1995], VisualSEEk [Smith and Chang, 1996], etc.). Although, in these systems texture features are used in combination with color and shape features, texture alone can also be used for content based retrieval.

In practice, there are two different approaches in which texture is used as the main feature for content based retrieval. In the first approach, texture features are extracted from the images and then are used for finding similar images in the database [Ma and Manjunath, 1998] [Gorkani and Picard, 1994] [Smith and Chang, 1994]. Texture queries can be formulated in a similar manner to color queries, by selecting examples of desired textures from a palette, or by supplying an example query image. The system then retrieves images with texture measures most similar in value to the query. The systems using this approach may use already segmented textures as in the applications with Brodatz database [Picard et al., 1993], or they first have a segmentation stage after which the extracted features in different regions are used as queries [Ma and Manjunath, 1998]. The segmentation algorithm used in this case may be crucial for the content based retrieval. In the second approach, texture is used for annotating the image [Picard and Minka, 1995]. Vision based annotation assists the user in attaching descriptions to large sets of images and video. If a user labels a piece of an image as "water," a texture model can be used to propagate this label to other visually similar regions.

The method of texture analysis chosen for feature extraction is critical to the success of texture classification. However, the metric used in comparing the feature vectors is also clearly critical. Many methods have been proposed to extract texture features either directly from the image statistics, e.g. co-occurrence matrix [Haralick et al., 1973], or from the spatial frequency domain [Van Gool et al., 1985]. Ohanian and Dubes [Ohanian and Dubes, 1992] studied the performance of four types of features: Markov Random Fields parameters, Gabor multi-channel features, fractal based features, and co-occurrence features. Comparative studies to evaluate the performance of some texture measures were made in [Reed and Du Buf, 1993][Ojala et al., 1996]. Recently there has been a strong push to develop multiscale approaches to the texture problem. Smith and Chang [Smith and Chang, 1994] used the statistics (mean and variance) extracted from the wavelet subbands as the texture representation. To explore the middle-band characteristics, tree-structured wavelet transform was used by Chang and Kuo [Chang and Kuo, 1993]. Ma and Manjunath [Ma and Manjunath, 1995] evaluated the texture image annotation by various wavelet transform representations, including orthogonal and bi-orthogonal wavelet transforms, tree-structured wavelet transform, and the Gabor wavelet transform (GWT). They found out that the Gabor transform was the best among the tested candidates, which matched the human vision study results [Beck et al., 1987].

Most of these previous studies have focussed on the features, but not on the metric, nor on modeling the noise distribution. Here, we study the effect of the similarity noise, the metric, and their interrelationship within the maximum likelihood paradigm, using texture distribution models, Gabor, and wavelet features.

3.1   Texture Distribution Models

Texture distribution methods use probability density function (PDF) models which are sensitive to high order interactions. Typically, these methods use a histogram model in which the partitioning of the intensity space is sensitive to high order interactions between pixels. This sensitivity is made feasible by quantizing the intensity values to a small number of levels, which considerably reduces the size of the space. The largest number of levels used is four, but two levels, or thresholding, is more common. These methods can be categorized into the following classes: gray-level differences, Laws' texture measures, center-symmetric covariance measures, and local binary patterns. We briefly describe them and give references to the original papers.

3.1.1 Gray-level differences

The class of gray-level differences were used by Unser [Unser, 1986]. These methods capture the distribution of local contrast in different directions. Since they rely on the differences, they provide reduced dependence on intensity. In our implementation, we used four measures based on the gray-level difference method. By accumulating the differences of the adjacent gray levels in the horizontal and vertical directions, we create histograms DIFFX and DIFFY. When we accumulate the absolute differences in both horizontal and vertical directions, we arrive at DIFF2, and in DIFF4, we accumulate the absolute differences in all four principal directions, which also gives rotational invariance.

3.1.2 Laws' texture energy measures

Beyond gray-level differences, we examine larger convolution masks which measure the energy of local patterns. From Laws' work [Laws, 1980] on texture energy measures, we used four Laws' 3×3 operators (see Figure 4.2): two perform edge detection in vertical (L3E3) and horizontal directions (E3L3) and the other ones are line detectors in these two orthogonal directions (L3S3 and S3L3).

-1	0	1	-1	-2	-1	-1	2	-1	-1	-2	-1
-2	0	2	0	0	0	-2	4	-2	2	4	2
-1	0	1	1	2	1	-1	2	-1	-1	-2	-1
L3E3			E3L3			L3S3			S3L3		

Figure 4.2. Four 3×3 Laws' masks used in the experiments

3.1.3 Center-symmetric covariance measures

We also consider statistical concepts of symmetry and covariance. Harwood et al. [Harwood et al., 1995] introduced measures for gray-level symmetry (positive) and anti-symmetry (negative) by computing local auto-covariances or auto-correlations of center-symmetric pixel values of suitably sized neighborhoods. We implemented a local center-symmetric auto-correlation measure based on neighborhood rank-order (SRAC) and a related covariance measure (SCOV).

SCOV is a measure of the pattern correlation as well as the local pattern contrast.

$$\text{SCOV} = \frac{1}{4}\sum_{i=1}^{4}(g_i - \mu)(g'_i - \mu) \tag{4.1}$$

where g_i refers to the gray level of pixel i (see Figure 4.3) and μ denotes the local mean.

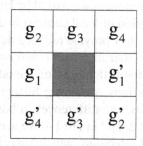

Figure 4.3.   A 3×3 neighborhood with 4 center-symmetric pairs of pixels

SRAC is a gray-scale invariant measure which ignores the local means and variances but preserves local linear and ranked ordering.

$$\text{SRAC} \;=\; 1 - \frac{12\left\{\sum_{i=1}^{4}(r_i - r'_i)^2 + T_x\right\}}{m^3 - m} \tag{4.2}$$

$$T_x \;=\; \frac{1}{12}\sum_{i=1}^{l}(t_i^3 - t_i) \tag{4.3}$$

where m is n^2 (considering a $n \times n$ neighborhood), each t_i is the number of ties at rank r_i, r_i refers to the rank of the gray level pixel i, and l defines the number of different ranks. The values of SRAC are bounded between -1 and 1.

Since SCOV it is not normalized with respect to local gray scale variation, it provides more texture information than SRAC. However, there is a tradeoff here: since the unnormalized SCOV is more sensitive to local sample variation, it is not so invariant as SRAC which is very robust in the presence of local gray scale variability or noise.

3.1.4   Local binary patterns and trigrams

Another way of analyzing local patterns is to binarize the local pattern information and measure the distribution of these patterns in the texture. Ojala et al. [Ojala et al., 1996] proposed a texture unit represented by eight elements, each of which has two possible values $\{0, 1\}$ obtained from a neighborhood of 3×3 pixels. These textures units are called local binary patterns (LBP) and their occurrence of distribution over a region forms the texture spectrum. The LBP is computed by thresholding each of the noncenter pixels by the value of the center pixel, resulting in 256 binary patterns. The LBP method is gray-scale invariant and can be easily combined with a simple contrast measure by computing for each neighborhood the difference of the average gray-level of those pixels which after thresholding have the value 1, and those which have the value 0, respectively. The algorithm is detailed below:

For each 3×3 neighborhood, consider P_i the intensities of the component pixels with P_0 the intensity of the center pixel. Then,

1 Threshold pixels P_i by the value of the center pixel: $P_i' = \begin{cases} 0 & \text{if } P_i < P_0 \\ 1 & \text{otherwise} \end{cases}$

2 Count the number n of resulting non-zero pixels: $n = \sum\limits_{i=1}^{8} P_i'$

3 Calculate the local binary pattern: $\text{LBP} = \sum\limits_{i=1}^{8} P_i' 2^{i-1}$

4 Calculate the local contrast:

$$C = \begin{cases} 0 & \text{if } n = 0 \text{ or } n = 8 \\ \frac{1}{n} \sum\limits_{i=1}^{8} P_i' P_i - \frac{1}{8-n} \sum\limits_{i=1}^{8} (1 - P_i') P_i & \text{otherwise} \end{cases}$$

A numerical example is given in Figure 4.4.

Another texture unit called **trigram** was introduced by Huijsmans et al. [Huijsmans et al., 1996]. This texture unit is represented by 9 elements each of which has two possible values $\{0, 1\}$ obtained from a neighborhood of 3×3 pixels. The value 0 or 1 associated with each element is calculated by applying a threshold in gradient space. If the pixel value is greater than the threshold then, the assigned value of the corresponding trigram element is 1, otherwise 0. This results in 512 trigrams which are accumulated in a histogram. Note that for the trigrams it is important to select the threshold properly.

3.1.5   Complementary feature pairs

In many cases a single texture measure cannot provide sufficient information about the spatial and frequency oriented structure of the local texture. Better

Example			Thresholded			Weights		
6	5	2	1	0	0	1	0	0
7	6	1	1		0	8		0
9	3	7	1	0	1	32	0	128

LBP=1+8+32+128=169   C=(6+7+9+7)/4-(5+2+1+3)/4=4.5

Figure 4.4.   Computation of Local Binary Pattern (LBP) and contrast measure (C).

discrimination of textures can be obtained considering joint occurrences of two or more features. Therefore, we consider pairs of features which provide complementary information.

The center-symmetric covariance measures provide robust information about the local texture, but little about the exact local spatial pattern. This suggests that as complementary features we should consider measures that provide spatial patterns such as LBP, trigrams, or any difference measure. We consider two different features combined with LBP. LBP/C is based on the contrast measure already introduced and the other pair is LBP/SCOV. Laws' masks perform edge and line detections in horizontal and vertical directions. Since these patterns can be in arbitrary directions, the joint use of edge and line detectors in the orthogonal directions should be considered. Similarly, the joint use of histograms of differences between neighboring pixels computed in the horizontal and vertical directions should provide useful information for texture discrimination. The pair L3E3/E3L3 corresponds to edge detection, L3S3/S3L3 to line detection, DIFFX/DIFFY to absolute gray-level in the horizontal and vertical direction, respectively, and DIFFY/SCOV combines absolute gray-scale differences in the vertical direction with the center-symmetric covariance measure.

3.2   Gabor and Wavelet Models

The Fourier transform is an analysis of the global frequency content in the signal. Many applications require the analysis to be localized in the spatial domain. This is usually handled by introducing spatial dependency into the Fourier analysis. The classical way of doing this is through what is called the window Fourier transform. Considering a one dimensional signal $f(x)$, the window Fourier transform is defined as:

$$F_w(u, \psi) = \int_{-\infty}^{\infty} f(x)w(x - \psi)e^{-j2\pi ux}dx \qquad (4.4)$$

When the window function $w(x)$ is Gaussian, the transform becomes a Gabor transform. The limits of the resolution in the time and frequency domain of the window Fourier transform are determined by the *time-bandwidth product* or the *Heisenberg uncertainty inequality* given by $\Delta t \Delta u \geq \frac{1}{4\pi}$. Once a window is chosen for the window Fourier transform, the time-frequency resolution is fixed over the entire time-frequency plane. To overcome the resolution limitation of the window Fourier transform, one lets the Δt and Δu vary in the time-frequency domain. Intuitively, the time resolution must increase as the central frequency of the analyzing filter is increased. That is, the relative bandwidth is kept constant in a logarithmic scale. This is accomplished by using a window whose width changes as the frequency changes. Recall that when a function $f(t)$ is scaled in time by a, which is expressed as $f(at)$, the function is contracted if $a > 1$ and it is expanded when $a < 1$. Using this fact, the Wavelet transform can be written as:

$$W_{f,a}(u, \psi) = \frac{1}{\sqrt{a}} \int_{-\infty}^{\infty} f(t)h\left(\frac{t - \psi}{a}\right) dt \qquad (4.5)$$

Setting in Equation (4.5),

$$h(t) = w(t)e^{-j2\pi ut} \qquad (4.6)$$

we obtain the wavelet model for texture analysis. Usually the scaling factor will be based on the frequency of the filter.

Daugman [Daugman, 1980] proposed the use of Gabor filters in the modeling of receptive fields of simple cells in the visual cortex of some mammals. The proposal to use the Gabor filters in texture analysis was made by Turner [Turner, 1986] and Clark and Bovik [Clark and Bovik, 1987]. Gabor filters produce spatial-frequency decompositions that achieve the theoretical lower bound of the uncertainty principle [Daugman, 1985]. They attain maximum joint resolution in space and spatial-frequency bounded by the relations $\Delta x \Delta u \geq \frac{1}{4\pi}$ and $\Delta y \Delta v \geq \frac{1}{4\pi}$, where $[\Delta x, \Delta y]$ gives the resolution in space and $[\Delta u, \Delta v]$ gives the resolution in spatial-frequency.

A two-dimensional Gabor function consists of a sinusoidal plane wave of a certain *frequency* and *orientation* modulated by a Gaussian envelope. It is given by:

$$g(x, y) = \exp\left(-\frac{1}{2}\left(\frac{x^2}{\sigma_x^2} + \frac{y^2}{\sigma_y^2}\right)\right)\cos(2\pi u_0(x\cos\theta + y\sin\theta)) \qquad (4.7)$$

where u_0 and θ are the frequency and phase of the sinusoidal wave, respectively. The values σ_x and σ_y are the sizes of the Gaussian envelope in the x and y directions, respectively. The Gabor function at an arbitrary orientation θ_0 can be obtained from (4.7) by a rigid rotation of the xy plane by θ_0.

The Gabor filter is a frequency and orientation selective filter. This can be seen from the Fourier domain analysis of the function. When the phase θ is 0, the Fourier transform of the resulting even-symmetric Gabor function $g(x, y)$ is given by:

$$
\begin{aligned}
G(u, v) \;=\; A\left(\exp\left(-\frac{1}{2}\left(\frac{(u-u_0)^2}{\sigma_u^2} + \frac{v^2}{\sigma_v^2}\right)\right) + \right. \\
\left. \exp\left(-\frac{1}{2}\left(\frac{(u+u_0)^2}{\sigma_u^2} + \frac{v^2}{\sigma_v^2}\right)\right)\right)
\end{aligned}
\tag{4.8}
$$

where $\sigma_u = 1/(2\pi\sigma_x)$, $\sigma_v = 1/(2\pi\sigma_y)$, and $A = 2\pi\sigma_x\sigma_y$. This function is real-valued and has two lobes in the spatial frequency domain, one centered around u_0, and another centered around $-u_0$. For a Gabor filter of a particular orientation, the lobes in the frequency domain are also appropriately rotated. An example of a 1D Gabor function in spatial and frequency domains is given in Figure 4.5.

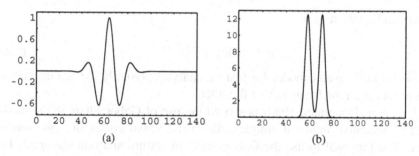

Figure 4.5.   1D Gabor function in (a) spatial domain and (b) frequency domain

The Gabor filter masks can be considered as orientation and scale tunable edge and line detectors. The statistics of these microfeatures in a given region can be used to characterize the underlying texture information. A class of such self similar functions referred to as Gabor wavelets is discussed in [Ma and Manjunath, 1996]. This self-similar filter dictionary can be obtained by appropriate dilations and rotations of $g(x, y)$ through the generating function,

$$
g_{mn}(x, y) = a^{-m} g(x', y'), \quad m = 0, 1, \cdots, S-1
\tag{4.9}
$$

$$
x' = a^{-m}(x\cos\theta + y\sin\theta), \quad y' = a^{-m}(-x\sin\theta + y\cos\theta)
$$

where $\theta = n\pi/K$, K the number of orientations, S the number of scales in the multiresolution decomposition, and $a = (U_h/U_l)^{-1/(S-1)}$ with U_l and U_h the lower and the upper center frequencies of interest, respectively.

Another approach which uses the trade-off between space and spatial-frequency resolution without using Gabor functions is using a wavelet filter bank. The wavelet filter bank produces octave bandwidth segmentation in spatial-frequency. It allows simultaneously for high spatial resolutions at high spatial-frequencies and high spatial-frequency resolution at low spatial-frequencies. Furthermore, the wavelet tiling is supported by evidence that visual spatial-frequency receptors are spaced at octave distances [Daugman, 1989]. A quadrature mirror filter (QMF) bank was used for texture classification by Kundu and Chen [Kundu and Chen, 1992]. A two band QMF bank utilizes orthogonal analysis filters to decompose data into low-pass and high-pass frequency bands. Applying the filters recursively to the lower frequency bands produces wavelet decomposition as illustrated in Figure 4.6.

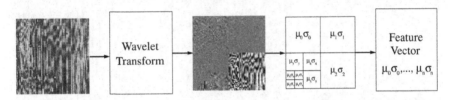

Figure 4.6. Texture classifier for Brodatz textures samples using QMF-wavelets based features

4. Texture Classification Experiments

In our first experiments, nine classes of textures - herringbone, wool, calf, sand, waves, wood, raffia, pigskin, and plastic - taken from Brodatz's album [Brodatz, 1966] were used (Figure 4.7). The texture images were normalized to have the same gray-level mean and standard deviation in order to avoid gray-level bias which is unrelated to the image texture. The test samples were obtained by randomly subsampling the original texture images. 1000 subsamples each consisted of rectangular blocks of 32×32 or 16×16 pixels in size were extracted from every texture class, resulting in a classification of 9000 random samples in total. Regarding implementation, we used the same number of bins for the texture classification methods as in the survey by Ojala [Ojala et al., 1996]. In the case of Trigrams, 512 bins were used.

As feature vectors we used the texture distribution features introduced in Section 4.3.1. In order to obtain better texture discrimination we also considered joint occurrences of two features, as described in Section 4.3.1.

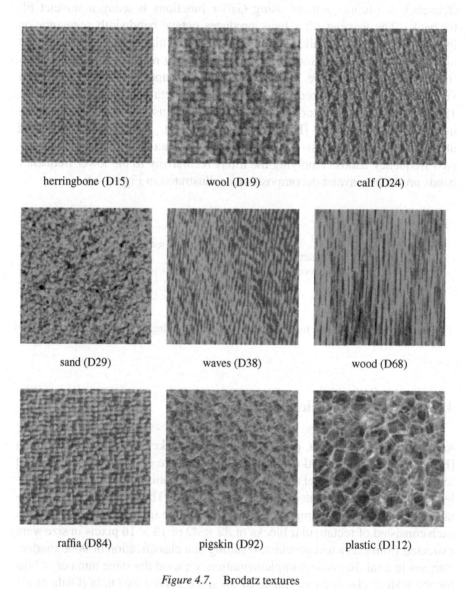

Figure 4.7. Brodatz textures

class labels. The sample was assigned the label of the model that was found to be more similar, using a certain similarity measure.

Consider that s and m are the sample and the model distributions, n is the number of bins, and s_i, m_i are respective sample and model probabilities at bin i. In this context, the L_1 metric will have the expression:

$$L_1(s,m) = \sum_{i=1}^{n} |m_i - s_i| \qquad (4.10)$$

The other metrics, such as L_2 and L_c, can be defined similarly. As benchmark we use the Kullback discriminant (see Equation (2.171)). In this case, the Kullback discriminant measures likelihoods that samples are from an alternative texture class, based on exact probabilities of feature values of pre-classified texture prototypes:

$$K(s,m) = \sum_{i=1}^{n} s_i \log \frac{s_i}{m_i} \qquad (4.11)$$

The model distribution for each class was obtained by scanning the original gray-scale 256×256 texture image with the local texture operator. The number of bins used in quantization of feature space is important. Histograms with small number of bins will not provide enough discriminative information about the distributions. Furthermore, if histograms have too many bins and the average number of entries per bin is small, then the histograms become sparse and unstable.

4.2 Distribution Analysis

From the maximum likelihood paradigm, the first critical step is to determine the real noise distribution. Considering m the feature vector corresponding to a texture class M and x_i the feature vector corresponding to the sample block i extracted from M then the real noise distribution is seen as the normalized histogram of differences between the elements of the two vectors x_i and m.

The next step is to determine the distortion between the real noise distribution and the distributions associated with the L_1, L_2, and L_c distance measures, namely, the Exponential, the Gaussian, and the Cauchy distributions. We present the quantitative results in Table 4.1. For all the features considered, L_1 has a lower modeling error than L_2 and therefore, L_1 is a more appropriate distance measure than L_2 regarding modeling the noise distribution. The Cauchy distribution is the best match for the noise distribution so, consequently, the results obtained with L_c will outperform the results obtained with L_1 and L_2.

Furthermore, we visually display in Figure 4.8 the similarity noise distribution for LBP matched by the best fit Exponential, best fit Gaussian, and the best

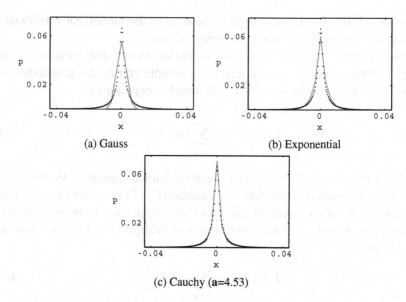

(a) Gauss   (b) Exponential

(c) Cauchy (**a**=4.53)

Figure 4.8.   Noise distribution for LBP compared with the best fit Gaussian (a) (approximation error is 0.065), best fit Exponential (b)(approximation error is 0.052), and best fit Cauchy (c) (approximation error is 0.05)

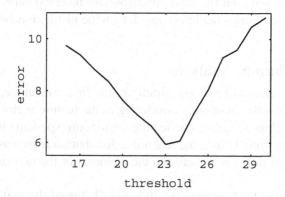

Figure 4.9.   Trigrams error rate (%) for different threshold values using L_1 and 32 × 32 samples

fit Cauchy, respectively. We can further conclude that the noise distribution is not Gaussian as assumed with regard to the L_2 measure.

For the feature pairs, we show the numerical modeling errors in Table 4.2. The results are consistent with the single feature tests.

Table 4.1.   The approximation error for the corresponding noise distribution using single features

	LBP	Trig	DIFFX	DIFFY	DIFF2	DIFF4
L_2	0.065	0.06	0.041	0.042	0.068	0.09
L_1	0.052	0.051	0.029	0.032	0.05	0.078
L_c	0.05	0.047	0.025	0.027	0.048	0.073
	L3E3	E3L3	L3S3	S3L3	SCOV	SRAC
L_2	0.03	0.035	0.039	0.042	0.03	0.037
L_1	0.023	0.026	0.029	0.027	0.021	0.031
L_c	0.019	0.017	0.024	0.021	0.018	0.029

Table 4.2.   The approximation error for the corresponding noise distribution using pairs of features

	LBP/C	LBP/SCOV	DIFFX/DIFFY	DIFFY/SCOV	L3E3/E3L3	L3S3/S3L3
L_2	0.05	0.064	0.041	0.037	0.031	0.039
L_1	0.045	0.044	0.026	0.019	0.015	0.028
L_c	0.041	0.039	0.025	0.017	0.012	0.022

4.3   Misdetection Rates

The next step is to determine the misdetection rates from Brodatz's test database. We compute the misdetection rate as the percentage of misclassified texture blocks.

Since the Trigrams require a threshold, this parameter affects the performance of the method. For the tests, we used the optimal threshold which provided the best accuracy. In Figure 4.9 is presented the trigrams misdetection error as a function of the threshold when L_1 was used and the sample size was 32×32. The optimal value for the threshold in this case is 23.

In Figure 4.10, we display the misdetection rates for various distance measures versus the sample size for each of the texture distribution features. Note that L_c consistently yields lower misdetection rates, which agrees with the maximum likelihood paradigm. Note that ML consistently has lower misdetection rates for all sample sizes. As expected, the misdetection rate is getting smaller when the sample size increases.

In order to have an overall measure of the performance of a particular feature we calculated the average error rate when the sample size varied from 16×16 to 48×48 pixels (Table 4.3). LBP has the lowest average misdetection rate followed by DIFF4, DIFF2, and Trigrams.

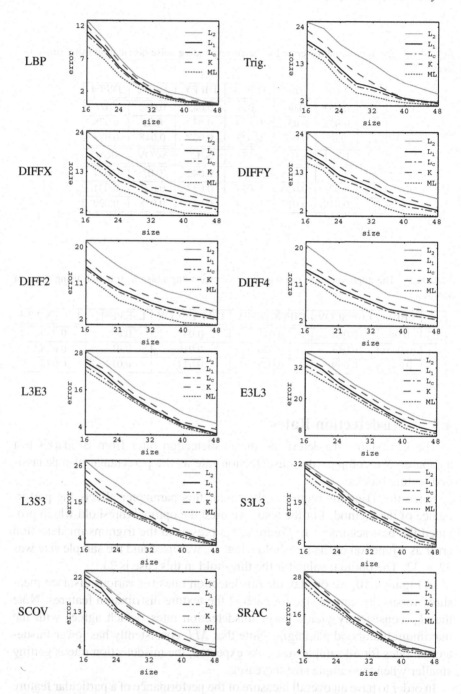

Figure 4.10. Error rates (%) for single features as function of sample size using L_1, L_2, L_c, the Kullback discriminant (K), and ML.

Regarding the feature pairs, the misdetection rates are shown in Figure 4.11. These results are consistent with the single feature tests. Moreover, the use of joint occurrences of features produces a much lower misdetection rate comparing with the case when only one feature is considered.

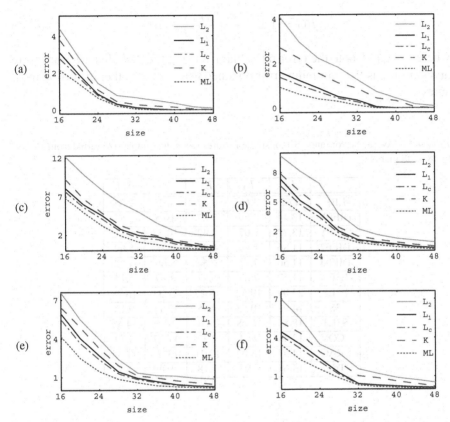

Figure 4.11. Error rates (%) for pairs of features as function of sample size using L_1, L_2, L_c, the Kullback discriminant (K), and ML: (a) LBP/C, (b) LBP/SCOV, (c) DIFFX/DIFFY, (d) DIFFY/SCOV, (e) L3E3/E3L3, (f) L3S3/S3L3.

The average error rate for pairs of features when the sample size varied from 16×16 to 48×48 pixels is presented in Table 4.4. LBP/C and LBP/SCOV have the lowest average misdetection rates.

When looking at the results one can ask if there really is a significant gain in accuracy when using ML comparing with the other metrics. This question is even more legitimate when pairs of features are considered. Consider for example the case where LBP/C pair is used in classification (Figure 4.11(a)). When the sample size is greater than 32 the misdetection rates for all metrics are getting very close to zero, so the absolute improvement is very small. However, if one would compute the improvement relative to the ML result, the gain will be significant. In this context, in order to give a quantitative value for the improvement in accuracy introduced by the ML distortion measure we define the *relative gain* as being:

$$RG = \left(1 - \frac{err_{ML}}{err_{MIN}}\right) \times 100 \qquad (4.12)$$

where err_{ML} denote the error rate obtained using the ML distortion measure and err_{MIN} is the minimum error obtained using all the other distortion measures.

Table 4.3.   Average error rates (%) for single features when the sample size varied from 16×16 to 48×48 pixels

	L_2	L_1	L_c	K	ML
LBP	4.62	3.68	3.47	4.1	2.84
DIFFX	13.44	8.89	7.87	10.5	5.84
DIFFY	13.22	8.07	7.42	10.53	6.11
DIFF2	11.86	7.46	6.86	8.78	5.09
DIFF4	11.56	7.15	6.54	8.66	4.72
L3E3	11.67	7.63	6.57	8.89	5.14
E3L3	23.09	19.57	18.27	21.33	16.98
L3S3	14.98	10.53	9.85	12.11	9.17
S3L3	18.85	16.68	15.4	17.5	14.48
SCOV	12.48	9.64	9.25	11.77	8.79
SRAC	14.97	13.02	12.21	13.82	11.35
Trig	13.64	7.93	7.18	9.4	5.7

Table 4.4.   Average error rates (%) for pairs of features when the sample size varied from 16×16 to 48×48 pixels

	L_2	L_1	L_c	K	ML
LBP/C	1.24	0.7	0.63	0.93	0.49
LBP/SCOV	1.53	0.51	0.43	0.79	0.26
DIFFX/DIFFY	5.61	2.97	2.68	3.41	2.11
DIFFY/SCOV	3.94	2.4	2.17	2.81	1.72
L3E3/E3L3	2.74	1.84	1.67	2.24	1.16
L3S3/S3L3	2.61	1.42	1.29	1.95	0.98

Tables 4.5 and 4.6 summarize the results for single and feature pairs across the L_2, L_1, L_c, K, and ML distortion measures when 32×32 samples were

considered. Note that using the maximum likelihood approach one can lower the misdetection rate by significant percentages.

Table 4.5. Error rates (%) for single features considering 32×32 samples. The last column represent the *relative gain* (RG) in % obtained using the ML distortion measure in comparison with the best of the other measures (L_c)

	L_2	L_1	L_c	K	ML	RG
LBP	2.42	1.98	1.86	3.05	1.51	18.81
DIFFX	12.71	7.14	6.1	8.37	4.04	33.77
DIFFY	12.40	8.47	7.2	10.05	4.67	35.13
DIFF2	10.73	6.03	5.34	7.56	4.91	8.05
DIFF4	10.87	6.57	5.9	7.12	3.62	38.64
L3E3	13.73	9.95	9.35	10.62	8.75	6.41
E3L3	22.12	18.47	17.35	19.33	15.24	12.16
L3S3	13.93	9.65	9.06	10.66	8.48	6.4
S3L3	17.77	15.49	14.54	15.64	13.12	9.76
SCOV	11.26	8.71	7.9	10.38	7.29	7.72
SRAC	13.38	11.18	10.5	11.85	9.83	6.38
Trig	13.02	5.94	5.05	7.30	3.27	35.24

Table 4.6. Error rates for pairs of features considering 32×32 samples. The last column represent the *relative gain* (RG) in % obtained using the ML distortion measure in comparison with the best of the other measures (L_c)

	L_2	L_1	L_c	K	ML	RG
LBP/C	0.66	0.12	0.09	0.28	0.04	55.55
LBP/SCOV	1.27	0.35	0.27	0.88	0.12	55.55
DIFFX/DIFFY	4.91	1.91	1.62	2.32	1.05	35.18
DIFFY/SCOV	2.24	1.12	1.02	1.48	0.83	18.62
L3E3/E3L3	1.33	0.92	0.83	1.12	0.58	30.12
L3S3/S3L3	1.56	0.42	0.38	1.03	0.31	18.42

Overall, for the single features LBP had the least error rate and for the feature pairs LBP/C and LBP/SCOV provide the best results. The *relative gain* obtained by using the ML distortion measure has significant values. Moreover, for pairs of features the relative gain is in general greater than in the case of single features.

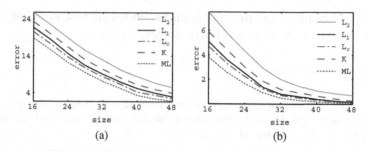

Figure 4.12. Average error rates (%) over all features for single feature (a) and for pairs of features (b) using: L_1, L_2, L_c, the Kullback discriminant (K), and ML

4.3.1   Summary

Most of the pattern recognition literature uses the Kullback discriminant or the sum of squared differences (L_2). By linking the distributions with the metrics, we can directly show why a particular metric would outperform another metric. Specifically, the metric which will have the least misdetection rate should be the metric whose distribution best matches the real noise distribution from the test set.

Given that the modeling of the real noise distribution is linked with the misdetection rate, the next logical question is, What is the misdetection rate when we directly model the real noise distribution? It is also validated that the lowest misdetection rate occurs when we use an approximate, quantized model for the real noise distribution. The corresponding distortion measure clearly outperforms the rest of the distortion measures as shown in Figures 4.10 and 4.11.

Regarding completeness we have given the absolute error rates. We have also provided one of the possible measures of improvement denoted as *relative gain*. This measure reflects the significance of the ML distortion measure in comparison with the best of the other measures. It should be noted that the real significance of a change in error rate can only be made with regard to a particular application - whether the acceptable error rate is 1 in a hundred or a thousand.

In the summary Figure 4.12 we show the average comparative results over all features for L_1, L_2, L_c, K, and ML for single and complementary feature pairs. Note that ML consistently provided lower misdetection rate comparing with all the other measures.

5.   Texture Retrieval Experiments

What distinguishes image search for database related applications from traditional pattern classification methods is the fact that there is a human in the loop (the user), and in general there is a need to retrieve more than just the best match. In typical applications, a number of top matches with rank ordered similarities to the query pattern will be retrieved. Comparison in the feature space should preserve visual similarities between patterns. In this context, the next experiments dealt with a texture database retrieval application.

The textures used in these experiments are the 112 Brodatz textures. We extract random samples from the textures and store them in a texture database. The goal here is to retrieve as many as possible similar samples in top n retrieved samples. The similar samples, by definition, are the ones previously extracted from the same original texture as the query sample. The database was formed by randomly subsampling 20 samples of 128×128 pixels in size from the 112 original textures, resulting in a number of 2240 texture samples.

5.1 Texture Features

As noted before, there has recently been a strong push to develop multiscale approaches to the texture problem. These methods were found to be the best choices for texture retrieval applications. Moreover, they match the human vision study results. In our study we consider the Gabor and wavelet models introduced in Section 4.3.2.

As shown before, the wavelet transformation involves filtering and subsampling. A compact representation needs to be derived in the transform domain for classification and retrieval. The mean and the variance of the energy distribution of the transform coefficients for each subband at each decomposition level are used to construct the feature vector (Figure 4.6). Let the image subband be $W_n(x, y)$, with n denoting the specific subband. The resulting feature vector is $f = \{\mu_n, \sigma_n\}$ with,

$$\mu_n = \int |W_n(x, y)| dx \, dy \tag{4.13}$$

$$\sigma_n = \sqrt{\int \int (|W_n(x, y)| - \mu_n)^2 dx \, dy} \tag{4.14}$$

Consider two image patterns i and j and let $f^{(i)}$ and $f^{(j)}$ represent the corresponding feature vectors. The distance between the two patterns in the features space is:

$$d(f^{(i)}, f^{(j)}) = \sum_n \left(\left| \frac{\mu_n^{(i)} - \mu_n^{(j)}}{\alpha(\mu_n)} \right|_{L_k} + \left| \frac{\sigma_n^{(i)} - \sigma_n^{(j)}}{\alpha(\sigma_n)} \right|_{L_k} \right) \tag{4.15}$$

where $\alpha(\mu_n)$ and $\alpha(\sigma_n)$ are the standard deviations of the respective features over the entire database and L_k is a notation for all possible metrics that can be used, e.g. L_1, L_2, L_c.

Note that in the case of Gabor wavelet transform (GWT) there are two indexes m and n, with m indicating a certain scale and n a certain orientation.

5.2   Experiments Setup

First the ground truth was known since the samples were extracted from the original textures. The ground truth was split into two non-overlapping sets: the training set and the test set. In our experiments the training set consisted of 1000 samples from the ground truth. Second, for each sample in the training set a feature vector was extracted using the scheme in Figure 4.6. Note that in these experiments, the feature vector was composed from two features: the mean and the variance. For each of them the real noise distribution was estimated as the normalized histogram of the absolute difference of corresponding elements from the feature vectors in the training set. The Gaussian, Exponential, and Cauchy distributions were fitted to each real noise distributions using the Chi-square test. We selected the model distribution which had the best fit and its corresponding metric (L_k) was used in ranking. The ranking was done using only the test set. It is important to note that for real applications, the parameter in the Cauchy distribution was found by fitting this distribution to the real distribution from the training set. This parameter setting was used for the test set and any further comparisons in the application.

Note that there were two ML metrics calculated, one from the mean distribution and the other one from the variance distribution. It is also interesting to note that metric values were already normalized through the histogram so the normalization factors (the standard deviations) in this case were not necessary.

Recall that our database was composed by randomly extracting 20 subsamples from the 112 original textures. When doing retrieval, in the ideal case all the top 19 retrievals should be from the same original texture as the query sample. The performance was measured in term of the average retrieval rate defined as the percentage of retrieving the 19 correct patterns when top n matches were considered.

5.3   Similarity Noise for QMF-Wavelet Transform

A QMF wavelet filter bank was used for texture classification by Kundu and Chen [Kundu and Chen, 1992]. The authors identified several properties of the QMF filter bank as being relevant to texture analysis: orthogonality and completeness of basic functions, filter outputs that are spatially localized, and the reduction of complexity afforded by decimation of filter outputs. In our implementation we used five levels of decomposition of the wavelet transform. We extracted the mean and the variance of each subband in a 32 (16 subbands $\times$ 2) dimensional feature vector.

As noted before, we had to compute two similarity noise distributions corresponding to mean and variance features. The similarity noise distributions are displayed in Figure 4.13 and 4.14. The similarity noise distribution was obtained as the normalized histogram of differences between the corresponding feature elements from the training set.

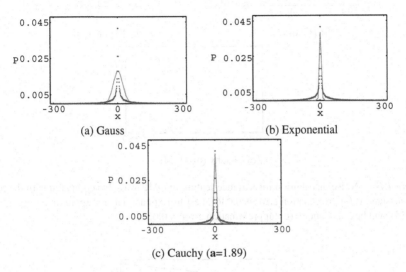

(a) Gauss   (b) Exponential

(c) Cauchy (a=1.89)

Figure 4.13. Noise distribution for mean feature in QMF-wavelets compared with the best fit Gaussian (a) (approximation error is 0.279), best fit Exponential (b) (approximation error is 0.207), and best fit Cauchy (c) (approximation error is 0.174)

For both features, the Exponential had a better fit to the noise distribution than the Gaussian. Consequently, this implies that L_1 should have a better retrieval rate than L_2. The Cauchy distribution was the best fit overall and the results obtained with L_c reflect this. Figure 4.15 presents the average retrieval rate for the correct patterns when top n matches are considered. This results are also contained in Table 4.7. Note that using ML we obtained the best average retrieval.

Table 4.7. Comparison of retrieval performances using QMF-wavelets for different metrics

Top	5	10	25	50
L_2	62.43	68.86	78.83	85.14
L_1	72.36	76.34	81.41	89.62
L_c	76.32	79.15	83.67	90.18
ML	80.06	83.58	88.66	94.24

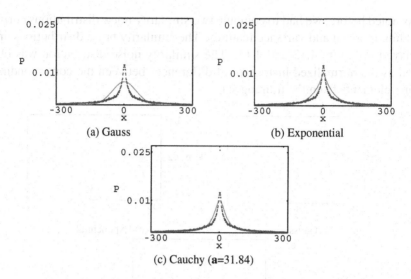

(a) Gauss   (b) Exponential

(c) Cauchy (**a**=31.84)

Figure 4.14. Noise distribution for variance feature in QMF-wavelets compared with the best fit Gaussian (a) (approximation error is 0.036), best fit Exponential (b) (approximation error is 0.0255), and best fit Cauchy (c) (approximation error is 0.023)

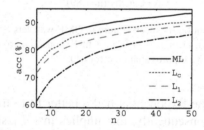

Figure 4.15. Average retrieval rate using QMF-wavelets

5.4   Similarity Noise for Gabor Wavelet Transform

A Gabor wavelet transform (GWT) enables us to obtain image representations which are locally normalized in intensity and decomposed in spatial frequency and orientation. It thus provides a mechanism for obtaining (1) invariance under intensity transformations, (2) selectivity in scale by providing a pyramid representation, and (3) it permits investigation of the local oriented features. In this paper, for the non-orthogonal Gabor wavelet transform we used 4 scales (S=4) and 6 orientations/scale ($K = 6$).

The mean and the variance of the energy distribution of the transform coefficients for each subband at each decomposition level were used to construct a 48 ($6 \times 4 \times 2$) dimensional feature vector. We calculated the similarity noise distribution for both features and fitted them with the model distributions. As seen from Table 4.8, the Cauchy distribution was the best match for the measured noise distribution. The Exponential was a better match than the Gaussian.

Table 4.8. The approximation error for the noise distribution using GWT

Feature	Gauss	Exponential	Cauchy
Mean	0.186	0.128	0.114
Variance	0.049	0.035	0.027

Figure 4.16 presents the average retrieval rate when different metrics were used. Note that L_c had better retrieval rate than L_1 and L_2. ML provided the best results.

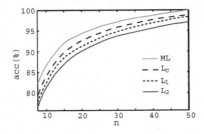

Figure 4.16. Average retrieval rate using GWT

In summary, L_c performed better than the analytic distance measures, and the ML metric performed best overall. Note that the results obtained with GWT were superior to the ones obtained using QMF-wavelet transform.

6. Concluding Remarks

This research is differentiated from the previous works in texture analysis in that we had investigated the role of the underlying noise distribution and corresponding metric in the paradigm of maximum likelihood. Our experiments on both the noise distribution and the retrieval rates from using a particular distortion measure provided strong evidence of the maximum likelihood theory.

We considered two kind of applications involving texture and we used the well-known Brodatz's textures. First, we investigated the influence of the noise distribution in a typical texture classification application using a nearest neighbor classifier. The classification of a sample was based on comparing the sample distribution of feature values to several pre-defined model distributions of feature values with known true-class labels. The second application was a typical database retrieval application. The textures in the database were obtained by randomly subsampling the original textures. The goal was to retrieve as many samples as possible among the top n retrieved samples, which were extracted from the same texture as the query texture.

In both experiments, we have found that the noise distribution is modeled better by the Cauchy distribution than the Exponential or Gaussian distributions. Consequently, among the analytic distortion measures, L_c consistently had a better misdetection/retrieval rate than L_1 or L_2.

Given that the modeling of the real noise distribution is linked with the retrieval rate, the next logical question was, What is the misdetection/retrieval rate when we directly model the real noise distribution? It was also validated that the best misdetection/retrieval rate occurs when we used an approximate, quantized model for the real noise distribution. The corresponding distortion measure (ML) clearly outperformed the rest of the distortion measures.

Chapter 5

SHAPE BASED RETRIEVAL

Together with color and texture, shape is one of the basic features in computer vision. Shape analysis methods play an important role in systems for object recognition, matching, registration, and analysis. Research in shape analysis has been motivated, in part, by studies of human visual form perception systems. Several theories of visual form are briefly mentioned here. A proper definition of shape similarity calls for the distinctions between shape similarity in images (similarity between actual geometrical shapes appearing in the images) and shape similarity between the objects depicted by the images, i.e. similarity modulo a number of geometrical transformations corresponding to changes in view angle, optical parameters, and scale. In our shape-based retrieval experiments we concentrate on active contour methods for shape segmentation and invariant moments for shape measures. We implemented two algorithms from the research literature and we applied them on a standard object database.

1. Introduction

Shape is a concept which is widely understood yet difficult to define formally. For human beings perception of shape is a high-level concept whereas mathematical definitions tend to describe shape with low-level attributes. Therefore, there exists no uniform theory of shape. However, the word shape can be defined in some specific frameworks. For object recognition purposes Marshall [Marshall, 1989] defined shape as a function of position and direction of a simply connected curve within a two-dimensional field. Clearly, this definition is not general, nor even sufficient for general pattern recognition.

In pattern recognition, the definition suggested by Marshall [Marshall, 1989] is suitable for two dimensional image objects whose boundaries or pixels inside the boundaries can be identified. It must be pointed out that this kind of definition requires that there are some objects in the image and, in order to code or describe the shape, the objects must be identified by segmentation. Therefore, either manual or automatic segmentation is usually performed before shape description.

How can we separate the objects from the background? Difficulties come from discretization, occlusions, poor contrast, viewing conditions, noise, complicated objects, complicated background etc. In the cases where the segmentation is less difficult and possible to overcome, the object shape is a characteristic which can contribute enormously in further analysis. If segmentation is not an option, a global search in the form of template matching is a possibility [Jain et al., 1996]. Here, the template represents the desired object to be found. However, performing template matching over a dense structure of scales and rotations of an image is not an interactive solution regarding searches in large image databases.

We are interested in using shape descriptors in content-based retrieval. Our problem is as follows: assume that we have a large number of images in the database. Given a query image, we would like to obtain a list of images from the database which are most similar (here we consider the shape aspect) to the query image. For solving this problem, we need two things - first, a measure which represents the shape information of the image, and second a similarity measure to compute the similarity between corresponding features of two images.

We addressed the problem of choosing a similarity metric in Chapter 2. There we showed that in the case where representative ground truth is available, there is a way to select the appropriate metric, and we proposed L_c as an alternative for both L_2 and L_1. Furthermore, we showed how to create a maximum likelihood metric (ML) based on the real noise distribution.

In this chapter, the problem of image retrieval using shape was approached by active contours for segmentation and invariant moments for shape measure. Active contours were first introduced by Kass et al. [Kass et al., 1988], and were termed snakes by the nature of their movement. Active contours are a sophisticated approach to contour extraction and image interpretation. They are based on the idea of minimizing energy of a continuous spline contour subject to constraints on both its autonomous shape and external forces derived from a superposed image that pull the active contour toward image features such as lines and edges.

Moments describe a shape in terms of its area, position, orientation, and other parameters. The set of invariant moments [Hu, 1962] makes a useful feature vector for the recognition of objects which must be detected regardless of position, size, or orientation. Matching of the invariant moments feature vectors is computationally inexpensive and is a promising candidate for interactive applications.

2.   Human Perception of Visual Form

The goal of this section is to emphasize the role and the importance of research in interdisciplinary fields like visual perception, cognition, psychology, and physiology towards the development of new shape analysis techniques.

From the broad field of cognitive science, the areas of visual cognition and perception are of particular interest for the study of shape description. If the structure of the human shape analysis system were known, it would be possible to develop analog artificial systems. For this reason the study of shape analysis methods is often motivated by and utilizes the results of research in the area of human visual perception. An exhaustive survey of human visual perception research is beyond the scope of this chapter. Some introductory and more advanced books and articles dealing with visual perception and cognition include [Zusne, 1970; Cornsweet, 1970; Granrath, 1981; Lowe, 1985; Posner, 1989; Loncaric, 1998]. In this section, a brief overview of visual perception research related to shape description is presented.

The Gestalt school of psychology [Zusne, 1970] has played a revolutionary role with its novel approach to visual form. The Gestalt theory is a noncomputational theory of visual form, and thus a disadvantage for practical engineering applications. However, according to Zusne "it is still the only theory to deal with form in a comprehensive fashion" ([Zusne, 1970], p. 108). There have been many books on Gestalt laws presenting various lists of principles. These lists range from six to more than one hundred. Here, we provide a list of laws for visual forms as proposed by Zusne [Zusne, 1970]:

- Visual form is the most important property of a configuration.

- Visual form is either dynamic or the outcome of dynamic processes which underlie them.

- All visual forms possess at least two aspects, a figured portion called figure and a background called ground.

- Visual forms may possess one or several centers of gravity about which the form is organized.

- Visual forms are transposable (with respect to translation, size, orientation, and color) without loss of identity.

- Visual forms resist change. They tend to maintain their structure against disturbing forces.

- Visual forms will always be as good (regular, symmetric, simple, uniform, exhibiting the minimum amount of stress) as the conditions (pattern stimulus) allow.

- Forms may fuse to produce new ones.

- A change in one part of form affects other parts of the form (law of compensation).

- Visual forms tend to appear and disappear as wholes.

- Visual forms leave an aftereffect that make them easier to remember (law of reproduction).

- Space is anisotropic, it has different properties in different directions.

Another approach to the theory of visual form is found in Hebb's work. Hebb presented a neuropsychological theory of behavior in his book "The Organization of Behavior" [Hebb, 1949]. In his theory, Hebb emphasized the role of neural structures in the mechanism of visual perception. His work influenced a number of researchers in the field of artificial neural networks. As opposed to the Gestalt school, Hebb argues that form is not perceived as a whole but consists of parts. The organization and mutual spatial relation of parts must be learned for successful recognition. This learning aspect of perception is the central point in Hebb's theory.

Gibson [Gibson, 1950] developed another comprehensive theory of visual perception. The first principle of his theory is that space is not a geometric or abstract entity, but a real visual one characterized by the forms that are in it. Gibson's theory is centered around perceiving real three-dimensional objects, not their two-dimensional projections. The second principle is that a real world stimulus exists behind any simple or complex visual perception. This stimulus is in the form of a gradient which is a property of the surface. Examples of physical gradients are the change in size of texture elements (depth dimension), degree of convergence of parallel edges (perspective), hue and saturation of colors, and shading. Gibson points out that the Gestalt school has been occupied with the study of two-dimensional projections of the three-dimensional world and that its dynamism is no more than the ambiguity of the interpretation of projected images. In his classification there are ten different kinds of form:

- Solid form. (Seeing an object means seeing a solid form.)

- Surface form. (Slanted forms and forms with edges.)

- Outline form. (A drawing of edges of a solid form.)

- Pictorial form. (Representations which are drawn, photographs, paintings, etc.)

- Plan form. (A drawing of edges of a surface projected on a flat surface.)

- Perspective form. (A perspective drawing of a form.)

- Nonsense form. (Drawings which do not represent a real object.)

- Plane geometric form. (An abstract geometric form not derived from or attempting to make a solid form visible.)

- Solid geometric form. (An abstract part of a three-dimensional space bounded with imaginary surfaces.)

- Projected form. (A plane geometric form which is a projection of a form.)

These forms are grouped into three classes as follows:

- Real objects: solid and surface forms.

- Representations of real objects: outline, pictorial, plan, perspective, and nonsense forms.

- Abstract (non-real) objects: Plane geometric forms, solid geometric forms, and projected forms.

The first class is the "real" class consisting of objects from the real world. The second class are representations of real objects. The third class are abstractions that can be represented using symbols but do not correspond to real objects (because they have no corresponding stimulus in the real world).

Marr et al. [Marr, 1976; Marr and Poggio, 1979; Marr, 1982] made significant contributions to the study of the human visual perception system. In Marr's paradigm [Marr, 1982], the focus of research is shifted from applications to topics corresponding to modules of the human visual system. An illustration of this point is the so-called *shape from x* research which represents an important part of the total research in computer vision [Aloimonos, 1988]. Papers dealing with *shape from x* techniques include: shape from shading [Zhang et al., 1999], shape from contour [Horaud and Brady, 1988], shape from texture [Malik and Rosenholtz, 1997], shape from stereo [Hoff and Ahuja, 1989], and shape from fractal geometry [Chen et al., 1990].

In [Marr, 1976] Marr developed a primal sketch paradigm for early processing of visual information. In his method, a set of masks is used to measure discontinuities in first and second derivatives of the original image. This information is then processed by subsequent procedures to create a primal sketch of the scene. The primal sketch contains locations of edges in the image and is used by subsequent stages of the shape analysis procedure. Marr and Hildreth [Marr and Hildreth, 1980] further developed the concept of the primal sketch and proposed a new edge detection filter based on the zero crossings of the Laplacian of the two-dimensional Gaussian distribution function. In this approach, zeros of Laplacian indicate the inflection point in the edge to detect edge positions.

Koenderink [Koenderink, 1984] and Koenderink and van Doorn [Koenderink and Van Doorn, 1986] have studied the psychological aspects of visual perception and proposed several interesting paradigms. Conventional approaches to shape are often static in the sense that they treat all shape details equally as global shape features [Koenderink and Van Doorn, 1986]. A dynamic shape model was developed where visual perception is performed on several scales of resolution. Such notions of order and relatedness are present in visual psychology and are absent in conventional geometrical theories of shape. It has been argued in [Koenderink and Van Doorn, 1986] that there exist manuals of art theory (such as [Gombrich, 1960]) which have not been given the attention they deserve and which contain practical knowledge accumulated over centuries. In art as well as in perception, a shape is viewed as a hierarchical structure. A procedure for morphogenesis based on multiple levels of resolution has been developed [Koenderink and Van Doorn, 1986]. Any shape can be embedded in a "morphogenetic sequence" based on the solution of the partial differential equation that describes the evolution of the shape through multiple resolutions.

Many authors agree on the significance of high curvature points for visual perception. Attneave [Attneave, 1954] performed psychological experiments to investigate the significance of corners for perception. In the famous Attneave's cat experiment a drawing of a cat was used to locate points of high curvature which were then connected to create a simplified drawing of the cat. After a brief presentation the cat could be reliably recognized in the drawing. It has been suggested that such points have high information content. Attneave's work has initiated further research on the topic of curve partitioning [Wuescher and Boyer, 1991; Fischler and Wolf, 1994; Katzir et al., 1994]. To approximate curves by straight lines, high curvature points are the best place to break the lines, thereby the resulting image retains the maximal amount of information necessary for successful shape recognition. For the purpose of shape description, corners are used as points of high curvature and the shape can be approximated by a polygon. Davis [Davis, 1977] combined the use of high curvature points and line segment approximations for polygonal shape approximations. Stokely and Wu [Stokely and Wu, 1992] investigated methods for measurement of the curvature of 3-D surfaces that evolve in many applications (e.g. tomographic medical images).

Hoffman and Richards [Hoffman and Richards, 1984] argue that when the visual system decomposes objects it does so at points of high negative curvature. This agrees with the principle of transversality [Guillemin and Pollack, 1974] found in nature. This principle contends that when two arbitrarily shaped convex objects interpenetrate each other, the meeting point is a boundary point of concave discontinuity of their tangent planes.

Leyton [Leyton, 1987] demonstrated the Symmetry-Curvature theorem which claims that any curve section that has only one curvature extremum has one and only one symmetric axis which terminates at the extremum itself. This is an important result because it establishes the connection between two important notions in visual perception. In [Leyton, 1989], Leyton developed a theory which claims that all shapes are basically circles which changed form as a result of various deformations caused by external forces like pushing, pulling, stretching, etc. Two problems were considered: the first was the inference of the shape history from a single shape, and the second was the inference of shape evolution between two shapes. The concept of symmetry-curvature was used to explain the process that deformed the object. Symmetric axes show the directions along which a deformation process most likely took place. In [Leyton, 1987], Leyton proposed a theory of nested structures of control which, he argues, governs the functioning of the human perceptual system. It is a hierarchical system where at each level of control all levels bellow any given level are also included in information processing.

Pentland [Pentland, 1984; Pentland, 1986] investigated methods for representation of natural forms by means of fractal geometry. He argued that fractal functions are appropriate for natural shape representation because many physical processes produce fractal surface shapes. This is due to the fact that natural forms repeat whenever possible and non-animal objects have a limited number of possible forms [Stevens, 1974]. Most existing schemes for shape representation were developed for engineering purposes and not necessarily to study perception. Fractal representations produce objects which correspond much better to the human model of visual perception and cognition.

Lowe [Lowe, 1987] proposed a computer vision system that can recognize three-dimensional objects from unknown viewpoints and single two-dimensional images. The procedure is non-typical and uses three mechanisms of perceptual grouping to determine three-dimensional knowledge about the object as opposed to a standard bottom-up approach. The disadvantage of bottom-up approaches is that they require an extensive amount of information to perform recognition of an object. Instead, the human visual system is able to perform recognition even with very sparse data or partially occluded objects. The conditions that must be satisfied by perceptual grouping operations are the following.

- The viewpoint invariance condition. This means that observed primitive features must remain stable over a range of viewpoints.

- The detection condition. There must be enough information available to avoid accidental mis-interpretations.

The grouping operations used by Lowe are the following. Grouping on the basis of proximity of line end points was used as one viewpoint invariant operation. The second operation was grouping on the basis of parallelism, which is also viewpoint independent. The third operation was grouping based on collinearity. The preprocessing operation consisted of edge detection using Marr's zero crossings in the image convolved with a Laplacian of Gaussian filter. In the next step a line segmentation was performed. Grouping operations on line-segmented data were performed to determine possible locations of objects.

3.   Active Contours

Active contours challenge the widely held view of bottom-up vision processes. The principal disadvantage with the bottom-up approach is its serial nature; errors generated at a low-level are passed on through the system without the possibility of correction. The principal advantage of active contours is that the image data, the initial estimate, the desired contour properties, and the knowledge-based constraints are integrated into a single extraction process.

Snakes [Kass et al., 1988], or active contours, are curves defined within an image domain which can move under the influence of internal forces coming from within the curve itself and external forces computed from the image data. The internal and external forces are defined so that the snake will conform to the boundary of an object or other desired features within an image. Snakes are widely used in many applications, including edge detection [Kass et al., 1988], shape modeling [Terzopoulos and Fleischer, 1988; McInerney and Terzopoulos, 1995], segmentation [Leymarie and Levine, 1993; Durikovic et al., 1995], and motion tracking [Leymarie and Levine, 1993; Terzopoulos and Szeliski, 1992].

In the literature, del Bimbo et al. [Del Bimbo and Pala, 1997] deformed active contours over a shape in an image and measured the similarity between the two based on the degree of overlap and on how much energy the active contour had to spend in the deformation. Jain et al. [Jain et al., 1996] used a matching scheme with deformable templates. The approach taken here is different in that we use a Gradient Vector Flow (GVF) based method [Xu and Prince, 1997] to improve the automatic fit of the snakes to the object contours.

Active contours are defined as energy-minimizing splines under the influence of internal and external forces. The internal forces of the active contour serve as a smoothness constraint designed to hold the active contour together (elasticity forces) and to keep it from bending too much (bending forces). The external forces guide the active contour towards image features such as high intensity gradients. The optimal contour position is computed such that the total energy is minimized. The contour can hence be viewed as a reasonable balance between geometrical smoothness properties and local correspondence with the intensity function of the reference image.

Let the active contour be given by a parametric representation $\mathbf{x}(s) = [x(s), y(s)]$, with s the normalized arc length of the contour. The expression for the total energy can then be decomposed as follows:

$$E_{total} = \int_0^1 E(\mathbf{x}(s))ds = \int_0^1 [E_{int}(\mathbf{x}(s)) + E_{ext}(\mathbf{x}(s)) + E_{con}(\mathbf{x}(s))]\,ds \quad (5.1)$$

where E_{int} represents the internal forces (or energy) which encourage smooth curves, E_{ext} represents the local correspondence with the image function, and E_{con} represents a constraint force that can be included to attract the contour to specific points in the image plane. In the following discussions the E_{con} will be ignored. E_{ext} is typically defined such that locations with high image gradients or short distances to image gradients are assigned low energy values.

Internal Energy

E_{int} is the internal energy term which controls the natural behavior of the active contour. It is designed to minimize the curvature of the active contour and to make the active contour behave in an elastic manner. According to Kass et al. [Kass et al., 1988], the internal energy is defined as

$$E_{int}(\mathbf{x}(s)) = \alpha(s)\left|\frac{d\mathbf{x}(s)}{ds}\right|^2 + \beta(s)\left|\frac{d^2\mathbf{x}(s)}{ds^2}\right|^2 \quad (5.2)$$

The first order continuity term, weighted by $\alpha(s)$, makes the contour behave elastically, while the second order curvature term, weighted by $\beta(s)$, makes it resistant to bending. Setting $\beta(s) = 0$ at a point s allows the active contour to become second order discontinuous at that point and to develop a corner. Setting $\alpha(s) = 0$ at a point s allows the active contour to become discontinuous. Active contours can interpolate gaps in edges phenomena known as subjective contours due to the use of the internal energy. It should be noted that $\alpha(s)$ and $\beta(s)$ are defined to be functions of the curve parameter s, and hence segments of the active contour may have different natural behavior. Minimizing the energy of the derivatives gives a smooth function.

External Energy

E_{ext} is the image energy term derived from the image data over which the active contour lies and is constructed to attract the active contour to desired feature points in the image, such as edges and lines. Given a gray-level image $I(x, y)$, viewed as a function of continuous position variables (x, y), typical external energies designed to lead an active contour toward step edges are [Kass et al., 1988]:

$$E_{ext}^{(1)}(x, y) = -|\nabla I(x, y)|^2 \tag{5.3}$$

$$E_{ext}^{(2)}(x, y) = -|\nabla(G_\sigma(x, y) * I(x, y))|^2 \tag{5.4}$$

where $G_\sigma(x, y)$ is a two-dimensional Gaussian function with standard deviation σ and ∇ is the gradient operator. If the image is a line drawing (black on white), then appropriate external energies include [Cohen, 1991]:

$$E_{ext}^{(3)}(x, y) = I(x, y) \tag{5.5}$$

$$E_{ext}^{(4)}(x, y) = G_\sigma(x, y) * I(x, y) \tag{5.6}$$

It is easy to see from these definitions that larger σ will cause the boundaries to become blurry. Such large σ are often necessary, however, in order to increase the capture range of the active contour.

A snake that minimizes E_{total} (see Eq 5.1) must satisfy the Euler equation:

$$\alpha \mathbf{x}''(s) - \beta \mathbf{x}''''(s) - \nabla E_{ext} = 0 \tag{5.7}$$

This can be viewed as a force balance equation:

$$F_{int} + F_{ext}^{(p)} = 0 \tag{5.8}$$

where $F_{int} = \alpha \mathbf{x}''(s) - \beta \mathbf{x}''''(s)$ and $F_{ext}^{(p)} = -\nabla E_{ext}$. The internal force F_{int} discourages stretching and bending while the external potential force $F_{ext}^{(p)}$ pulls the snake towards the desired image edge.

To find a solution to Eq. (5.7), the snake is made dynamic by treating $\mathbf{x}$ as function of time t as well as s i.e., $\mathbf{x}(s, t)$. The partial derivative of $\mathbf{x}$ with respect to t is then set equal to the left hand side of Eq. (5.7) as follows:

$$\mathbf{x}_t(s, t) = \alpha \mathbf{x}''(s, t) - \beta \mathbf{x}''''(s, t) - \nabla E_{ext} \tag{5.9}$$

When the solution $\mathbf{x}(s, t)$ stabilizes, the term $\mathbf{x}_t(s, t)$ vanishes and we achieve a solution of Eq. (5.7). A numerical solution to Eq. (5.9) can be found by discretizing the equation and solving the discrete system iteratively (cf. [Kass et al., 1988]). Note that most snake implementations use either a parameter which multiplies $\mathbf{x}_t$ in order to control the temporal step-size, or a parameter to multiply ∇E_{ext} which permits separate control of the external force strength.

3.1   Behavior of Traditional Active Contours

An example of the behavior of a traditional snake is shown in Figure 5.1. Figure 5.1(a) shows a 64×64-pixel linedrawing of a U-shaped object (shown in gray) having a boundary concavity at the top. It also shows a sequence of

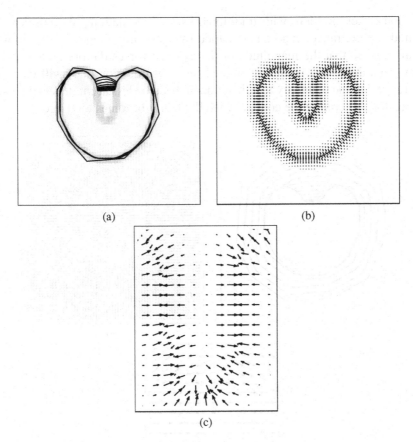

Figure 5.1. (a) The convergence of an active contour using (b) traditional potential forces. (c) Close-up within the boundary concavity.

curves (in black) depicting the iterative progression of a traditional snake ($\alpha = 0.6, \beta = 0.0$) initialized outside the object but within the capture range of the potential force field. The potential force field $F_{ext}^{(p)} = -\nabla E_{ext}^{(4)}$ where $\sigma = 1.0$ pixel is shown in Figure 5.1(b). Note that the final solution in Figure 5.1(a) solves the Euler equations of the snake formulation, but remains split across the concave region.

The reason for the poor convergence of this snake is revealed in Figure 5.1(c) where a close-up of the external force field within the boundary concavity is shown. Although the external forces correctly point toward the object boundary, within the boundary concavity the forces point horizontally in opposite directions. Therefore, the active contour is pulled apart toward each of the "fingers" of the U-shape, but not made to progress downward into the concavity. There is no choice of α and β that will correct this problem.

Another key problem with traditional snake formulations, the problem of limited capture range, can be understood by examining Figure 5.1(b). In this figure, we see that the magnitude of the external forces die out quite rapidly away from the object boundary. Increasing σ in Equation (5.6) will increase this range, but the boundary localization will become less accurate and distinct, ultimately obliterating the concavity itself when σ becomes too large.

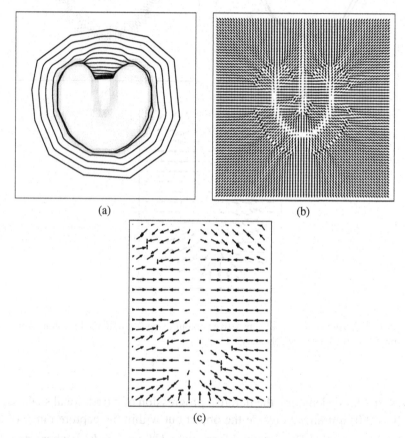

(a)   (b)

(c)

Figure 5.2. (a) The convergence of an active contour using (b) distance potential forces. (c) Close-up within the boundary concavity.

Cohen and Cohen [Cohen and Cohen, 1993] proposed an external force model that significantly increases the capture range of a traditional snake. These external forces are the negative gradient of a potential function that is computed using a Euclidean (or chamfer) distance map. We refer to these forces as *distance potential forces* to distinguish them from the *traditional potential forces* defined above. Figure 5.2 shows the performance of a snake using distance potential forces. Figure 5.2(a) shows both the U-shaped object (in gray) and a sequence of contours (in black) depicting the progression of the snake from its initialization far from the object to its final configuration. The distance potential forces shown in Figure 5.2(b) have vectors with large magnitudes far away from the object, explaining why the capture range is large for this external force model.

As shown in Figure 5.2(a), this snake also fails to converge to the boundary concavity. This can be explained by inspecting the magnified portion of the distance potential forces shown in Figure 5.2(c). We see that, like traditional potential forces, these forces also point horizontally in opposite directions, which pulls the snake apart but not downward into the boundary concavity. We note that Cohen and Cohen's modification to the basic distance potential forces, which applies a nonlinear transformation to the distance map [Cohen and Cohen, 1993], does not change the direction of the forces, only their magnitudes. Therefore, the problem of convergence to boundary concavities is not solved by distance potential forces.

In summary, several fundamental problems exist with active contours. Furthermore, solutions to these problems may create problems in other components of the active contour model.

- **Initialization** - The final extracted contour is highly dependent on the position and shape of the initial contour due to the presence of many local minima in the energy function. The initial contour must be placed near the required feature otherwise the contour can become obstructed by unwanted features like JPEG compression artifacts, closeness of a nearby object, and different other noises.

- **Non-convex shapes** - How do we extract non-convex shapes without compensating the importance of the internal forces, or without a corruption of the image data? For example pressure forces [Cohen, 1991] (addition to the external force) can push an active contour into boundary concavities, but cannot be too strong or otherwise weak edges will be ignored. Pressure forces must also be initialized to push out or push in, a condition that mandates careful initialization.

The original method of Kass et al. [Kass et al., 1988] suffered from three main problems: dependence on the initial contour, numerical instability, and lack of guaranteed convergence to the global energy minimum. Amini et al. [Amini et al., 1988] improved the numerical instability by minimizing the energy functional using dynamic programming, which allows inclusion of hard constraints into the energy functional. However, memory requirements are large, being $O(nm^2)$, and the method is slow, being $O(nm^3)$ where n is the number of contour points and m is the neighborhood size to which a contour point is allowed to move in a single iteration. Seeing the difficulties with both

previous methods Williams and Shah [Williams and Shah, 1992] developed
the *greedy algorithm* which combines speed, flexibility, and simplicity. The
greedy algorithm is faster $O(nm)$ than the dynamic programming and is more
stable and flexible for including constraints than the variational approach of
Kass et al. [Kass et al., 1988]. During each iteration, a neighborhood of each
point is examined and a point in the neighborhood with the smallest energy
value provides the new location of the point. Iterations continue till the number of points in the active contour that moved to a new location in one iteration
is below a specified threshold.

3.2   Generalized Force Balance Equations

The snake solutions shown in Figures 5.1(a) and 5.2(a) both satisfy the Euler equation (5.7) for their respective energy model. Accordingly, the poor
final configurations can be attributed to convergence to a local minimum of
the objective function (5.1). Several researchers have sought solutions to this
problem by formulating snakes directly from a force balance equation in which
the standard external force $F_{ext}^{(p)}$ is replaced by a more general external force
$F_{ext}^{(g)}$ as follows

$$F_{int} + F_{ext}^{(g)} = 0 \tag{5.10}$$

The choice of $F_{ext}^{(g)}$ can have a profound impact on both the implementation
and the behavior of a snake. Broadly speaking, the external forces $F_{ext}^{(g)}$ can
be divided into two classes: static and dynamic. Static forces are those that
are computed from the image data, and do not change as the snake progresses.
Standard snake potential forces are static external forces. Dynamic forces are
those that change as the snake deforms.

Several types of dynamic external forces have been invented to try to improve upon the standard snake potential forces. For example, the forces used
in multiresolution snakes [Leroy et al., 1996] and the pressure forces used in
balloons [Cohen, 1991] are dynamic external forces. The use of multiresolution schemes and pressure forces, however, adds complexity to a snake's implementation and unpredictability to its performance. For example, pressure
forces must be initialized to either push out or push in, and may overwhelm
weak boundaries if they act too strongly [Tek and Kimia, 1995]. Conversely,
they may not move into boundary concavities if they are pushing in the wrong
direction or act too weakly.

Here, we discuss the type of static external force proposed by Xu and
Prince [Xu and Prince, 1997]. This force does not change with time or depend on the position of the snake itself. The underlying mathematical premise
for this force comes from the Helmholtz theorem (cf. [Morse and Feshbach,
1953]), which states that the most general static vector field can be decomposed

into two components: an irrotational (curl-free) component and a solenoidal (divergence-free) component. Irrotational fields are sometimes called conservative fields; they can be represented as the gradient of a scalar potential function. An external potential force generated from the variational formulation of a traditional snake must enter the force balance equation (5.7) as a static irrotational field, since it is the gradient of a potential function. Therefore, a more general static field $F_{ext}^{(g)}$ can be obtained by allowing the possibility that it comprises both an irrotational component and a solenoidal component. In the following section, a more natural approach in which the external force field is designed to have the desired properties of both a large capture range and the presence of forces that point into boundary concavities is presented. The resulting formulation produces external force fields that can be expected to have both irrotational and solenoidal components.

3.3 Gradient Vector Flow

Since the greedy algorithm easily accommodates new changes, there are three things we would like to add to it: the ability to inflate the contour as well as deflate it, the ability to deform to concavities, and to increase the capture range of the external forces. These three additions reduce the sensitivity to initialization of the active contour and allow deformation inside concavities. This can be done by replacing the existing external force with the gradient vector flow (GVF) [Xu and Prince, 1997]. The GVF is an external force computed as a diffusion of the gradient vectors of an image, without blurring the edges. The idea of the diffusion equation is taken from physics. An example of the effect of the GVF external force can be seen in Figure 5.3. Figures 5.3(b) and (c) show the differences between the deformation with the gradient magnitude (the greedy algorithm) and the deformation with the gradient vector flow in the presence of a concavity.

The overall approach taken by Xu and Prince [Xu and Prince, 1997] is to use the force balance condition (5.8) as a starting point for designing a snake. The *gradient vector flow* (GVF) field is defined as new static external force field $F_{ext}^{(g)} = \mathbf{v}(x, y)$. To obtain the corresponding dynamic snake equation, we replace the potential force $-\nabla E_{ext}$ in (5.9) with $\mathbf{v}(x, y)$, yielding

$$\mathbf{x}_t(s, t) = \alpha \mathbf{x}''(s, t) - \beta \mathbf{x}''''(s, t) + \mathbf{v} \tag{5.11}$$

The parametric curve solving the above dynamic equation is called a *GVF snake*. It is solved numerically by discretization and iteration, in identical fashion to the traditional snake.

Although the final configuration of a GVF snake will satisfy the force-balance equation (5.8), this equation does not, in general, represent the Euler equations of the energy minimization problem in (5.1). This is because $\mathbf{v}(x, y)$

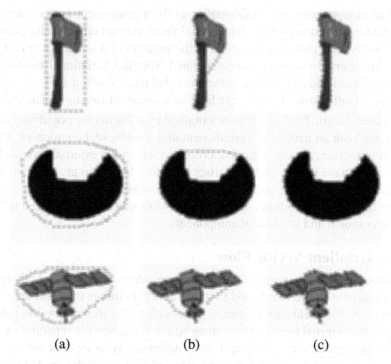

Figure 5.3. Initialization across the shape: (a) initial position, (b) deformation with the gradient magnitude, (c) deformation with the GVF.

will not, in general, be an irrotational field. The loss of this optimality property, however, is well-compensated by the significantly improved performance of the GVF snake.

Consider an edge map $f(x, y)$ derived from the image $I(x, y)$ having the property that it is larger near the image edges. We can use any gray-level or binary edge map defined in the image processing literature (cf. [Jain, 1989]); for example, we could use

$$f(x, y) = -E_{ext}^{(i)}(x, y) \quad i = 1, 2, 3, \text{ or } 4 \qquad (5.12)$$

Three general properties of edge maps are important in the present context. First, the gradient of an edge map ∇f has vectors pointing toward the edges, which are normal to the edges at the edges. Second, these vectors generally have large magnitudes only in the immediate vicinity of the edges. Third, in homogeneous regions, where $I(x, y)$ is nearly constant, ∇f is nearly zero.

Now consider how these properties affect the behavior of a traditional snake when the gradient of an edge map is used as an external force. Because of the first property, a snake initialized close to the edge will converge to a stable configuration near the edge. This is a highly desirable property. Because of the second property, however, the capture range will be very small, in general. Because of the third property, homogeneous regions will have no external forces whatsoever. These last two properties are undesirable. The approach is to keep the highly desirable property of the gradients near the edges, but to extend the gradient map farther away from the edges and into homogeneous regions using a computational diffusion process. As an important benefit, the inherent competition of the diffusion process will also create vectors that point into boundary concavities.

Consider the gradient vector flow field to be the vector field $\mathbf{v}(x, y) = (u(x, y), v(x, y))$ that minimizes the energy functional

$$\mathcal{E} = \int \int \mu(u_x^2 + u_y^2 + v_x^2 + v_y^2) + |\nabla f|^2 |\mathbf{v} - \nabla f|^2 dx dy \qquad (5.13)$$

This variational formulation follows a standard principle, that of making the result smooth when there is no data. In particular, we see that when $|\nabla f|$ is small, the energy is dominated by sum of the squares of the partial derivatives of the vector field, yielding a slowly-varying field. On the other hand, when $|\nabla f|$ is large, the second term dominates the integrand, and is minimized by setting $\mathbf{v} = \nabla f$. This produces the desired effect of keeping $\mathbf{v}$ nearly equal to the gradient of the edge map when it is large, but forcing the field to be slowly-varying in homogeneous regions. The parameter μ is a regularization parameter governing the tradeoff between the first term and the second term in the integrand. This parameter should be set according to the amount of noise present in the image (more noise, increase μ).

Note that the smoothing term – the first term within the integrand of (5.13) – is the same term used by Horn and Schunck in their classical formulation of optical flow [Horn and Schunck, 1981]. Gupta and Prince [Gupta and Prince, 1996] also showed that this term corresponds to an equal penalty on the divergence and curl of the vector field. Therefore, the vector field resulting from this minimization can be expected to be neither entirely irrotational nor entirely solenoidal.

Using the calculus of variations, it can be shown that the GVF field can be found by solving the following Euler equations

$$\mu \nabla^2 u - (u - f_x)(f_x^2 + f_y^2) = 0 \qquad (5.14)$$

$$\mu \nabla^2 v - (v - f_y)(f_x^2 + f_y^2) = 0 \qquad (5.15)$$

where ∇^2 is the Laplacian operator. These equations provide further intuition behind the GVF formulation. Note that in a homogeneous region (where $I(x, y)$ is constant), the second term in each equation is zero because the gradient of $f(x, y)$ is zero. Therefore, within such a region, u and v are each determined by Laplace's equation, and the resulting GVF field is interpolated from the region's boundary, reflecting a kind of competition among the boundary vectors. This explains why GVF yields vectors that point into boundary concavities.

Equations (5.14) and (5.15) can be solved by treating u and v as functions of time and solving

$$u_t(x, y, t) = \mu \nabla^2 u(x, y, t) - (u(x, y, t) - f_x(x, y))(f_x^2(x, y) + f_y^2(x, y)) \quad (5.16)$$
$$v_t(x, y, t) = \mu \nabla^2 v(x, y, t) - (v(x, y, t) - f_y(x, y))(f_x^2(x, y) + f_y^2(x, y)) \quad (5.17)$$

The steady-state solution of these linear parabolic equations is the desired solution of the Euler equations (5.14) and (5.15). Note that these equations are decoupled, and therefore can be solved as separate scalar partial differential equations in u and v. The equations in (5.16) and (5.17) are known as generalized diffusion equations. They have appeared here from the description of desirable properties of snake external force fields as represented in the energy functional of (5.13).

For convenience, we rewrite the equations as follows

$$u_t(x, y, t) = \mu \nabla^2 u(x, y, t) - b(x, y)u(x, y, t) + c^1(x, y) \quad (5.18)$$
$$v_t(x, y, t) = \mu \nabla^2 v(x, y, t) - b(x, y)v(x, y, t) + c^2(x, y) \quad (5.19)$$

where

$$b(x, y) = f_x^2(x, y) + f_y^2(x, y)$$
$$c^1(x, y) = b(x, y)f_x(x, y)$$
$$c^2(x, y) = b(x, y)f_y(x, y)$$

Any digital image gradient operator can be used to calculate f_x and f_y. In the examples shown in this chapter, we used simple central differences. The coefficients $b(x, y)$, $c^1(x, y)$, and $c^2(x, y)$, can then be computed and fixed for the entire iterative process.

To set up the iterative solution, let the indices i, j, and n correspond to x, y, and t, respectively. Then the required partial derivatives can be approximated as

$$u_t = u_{i,j}^{n+1} - u_{i,j}^n$$
$$v_t = v_{i,j}^{n+1} - v_{i,j}^n$$
$$\nabla^2 u = u_{i+1,j} + u_{i,j+1} + u_{i-1,j} + u_{i,j-1} - 4u_{i,j}$$
$$\nabla^2 u = v_{i+1,j} + v_{i,j+1} + v_{i-1,j} + v_{i,j-1} - 4v_{i,j}$$

Substituting these approximations into (5.18) and (5.19) gives the iterative solution to GVF:

$$u_{i,j}^{n+1} = (1 - b_{i,j})u_{i,j}^n + (u_{i+1,j}^n + u_{i,j+1}^n + u_{i-1,j}^n + u_{i,j-1}^n - 4u_{i,j}^n) + c_{i,j}^1 \quad (5.20)$$
$$v_{i,j}^{n+1} = (1 - b_{i,j})v_{i,j}^n + (v_{i+1,j}^n + v_{i,j+1}^n + v_{i-1,j}^n + v_{i,j-1}^n - 4v_{i,j}^n) + c_{i,j}^1 \quad (5.21)$$

The intuition behind the diffusion equations is that in homogeneous regions, the first and third terms are zeros since the gradient is zero, and within those regions, u and v are each determined by Laplace's equation. This results in a type of "filling-in" of information taken from the boundaries of the region. In regions of high gradient v is kept nearly equal to the gradient.

Creating GVF field yields streamlines to a strong edge. In the presence of these streamlines, blobs and thin lines in the way to strong edges do not form any impediments to the movement of the active contour. It can be considered as an advantage if the blobs are in front of the shape, nevertheless it can be considered as a disadvantage if the active contour enters the shape's silhouette.

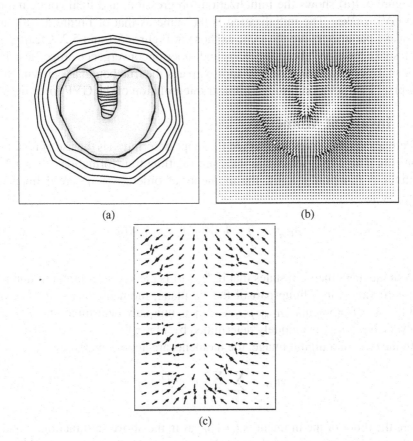

(a)   (b)

(c)

Figure 5.4.   (a) The convergence of an active contour using (b) GVF external forces. (c) Close-up within the boundary concavity.

In Figure 5.4 we computed the GVF field for the same U-shaped object used in Figures 5.1 and 5.2. Comparing the GVF field, shown in Figure 5.4(b), to the traditional potential force field of Figure 5.1(b), reveals several key differences.

First, like the distance potential force field (Figure 5.2(b)), the GVF field has a much larger capture range than traditional potential forces. A second observation, which can be seen in the closeup of Figure 5.4(c), is that the GVF vectors within the boundary concavity at the top of the U-shape have a downward component. This stands in stark contrast to both the traditional potential forces of Figure 5.1(c) and the distance potential forces of Figure 5.2(c). Finally, it can be seen from Figure 5.4(b) that the GVF field behaves in an analogous fashion when viewed from the inside of the object. In particular, the GVF vectors are pointing upward into the "fingers" of the U shape, which represent concavities from this perspective.

Figure 5.4(a) shows the initialization, progression, and final configuration of a GVF snake. The initialization is the same as that of Figure 5.2(a), and the snake parameters are the same as those in Figures 5.1 and 5.2. Clearly, the GVF snake has a broad capture range and superior convergence properties. The final snake configuration closely approximates the true boundary, arriving at a sub-pixel interpolation through bilinear interpolation of the GVF force field.

4.   Invariant Moments

Perhaps the most popular method for shape description is the use of invariant moments [Hu, 1962] which are invariant to affine transformations. For a 2-D continuous function $f(x, y)$, the moments of order $(p + q)$ are defined for $p, q \in \mathcal{N}$ as

$$m_{pq} = \int_{-\infty}^{\infty} \int_{-\infty}^{\infty} x^p y^q f(x, y) dx dy \qquad (5.22)$$

A uniqueness theorem states that if $f(x, y)$ is piecewise continuous and has non-zero values in a finite part of the xy plane, moments of all orders exist and the set of moments $\{m_{pq}, p, q \in \mathcal{N}\}$ is uniquely determined by $f(x, y)$. Conversely, $\{m_{pq}\}$ is uniquely determined by $f(x, y)$.

In the case of a digital image, the moments are approximated by

$$m_{pq} = \sum_x \sum_y x^p y^q f(x, y) \qquad (5.23)$$

where the order of the moment is $(p + q)$ as in the above formulation, x and y are the pixel coordinates relative to some arbitrary standard origin, and $f(x, y)$ represents the pixel brightness.

To have moments that are invariant to translation, scale, and rotation, first the central moments μ are calculated

$$\mu_{pq} = \sum_x \sum_y (x - \overline{x})^p (y - \overline{y})^q f(x, y) \qquad (5.24)$$

where $\bar{x} = \frac{m_{10}}{m_{00}}$ and $\bar{x} = \frac{m_{01}}{m_{00}}$.

Further, the normalized central moments η_{pq} are calculated as

$$\eta_{pq} = \frac{\mu_{pq}}{\mu_{00}^{\lambda}} \quad (5.25)$$

where $\lambda = \frac{(p+q)}{2} + 1$, and $p + q \geq 2$.

From these normalized parameters a set of invariant moments $\{\phi\}$ found by Hu [Hu, 1962], may then be calculated. The seven equations of the invariant moments contain terms up to order 3:

$$\begin{aligned}
\phi_1 &= \eta_{20} + \eta_{02} \\
\phi_2 &= (\eta_{20} - \eta_{02})^2 + 4\eta_{11}^2 \\
\phi_3 &= (\eta_{30} - 3\eta_{12})^2 + (3\eta_{21} - \eta_{03})^2 \\
\phi_4 &= (\eta_{30} - \eta_{12})^2 + (\eta_{21} - \eta_{03})^2 \\
\phi_5 &= (\eta_{30} - 3\eta_{12})(\eta_{30} + \eta_{12})\left((\eta_{30} + \eta_{12})^2 - 3(\eta_{21} + \eta_{03})^2\right) + \\
&\quad (3\eta_{21} - \eta_{03})(\eta_{21} + \eta_{03})\left(3(\eta_{30} + \eta_{12})^2 - (\eta_{21} + \eta_{03})^2\right) \\
\phi_6 &= (\eta_{20} - \eta_{02})\left((\eta_{30} + \eta_{12})^2 - (\eta_{21} + \eta_{03})^2\right) + \\
&\quad 4\eta_{11}(\eta_{30} + \eta_{12})(\eta_{21} + \eta_{03}) \\
\phi_7 &= (3\eta_{21} - \eta_{30})(\eta_{30} + \eta_{12})\left((\eta_{30} + \eta_{12})^2 - 3(\eta_{21} + \eta_{03})^2\right) + \\
&\quad (3\eta_{12} - \eta_{03})(\eta_{21} + \eta_{03})\left(3(\eta_{30} + \eta_{12})^2 - (\eta_{21} + \eta_{03})^2\right)
\end{aligned}$$

Global (region) properties provide a firm common base for similarity measure between shapes silhouettes where gross structural features can be characterized by these moments. Since we do not deal with occlusion, the invariance to position, size, and orientation, and the low dimensionality of the feature vector represent good reasons for using the invariant moments in matching shapes. The logarithm of the invariant moments is taken to reduce the dynamic range.

5. Experiments

In our experiments we used a database of 1,440 images of 20 common house hold objects from the COIL-20 database [Murase and Nayar, 1995]. Each object was placed on a turntable and photographed every $5°$ for a total of 72 views per object. Examples are shown in Figure 5.5.

In creating the ground truth we had to take into account the fact that the images of one object may look very different when an important rotation is considered. Therefore, for a particular instance (image) of an object we consider as similar the images taken for the same object when it was rotated within $\pm r \times 5°$. In this context, we consider two images to be r-similar if the rotation angle of the object depicted in the images is smaller than $r \times 5°$. In our experiments we used $r = 3$ so that one particular image is considered to be similar

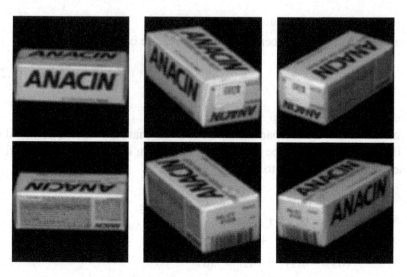

Figure 5.5.   Example of images of one object rotated with 60°

with 6 other images of the same object rotated within ±15°. We prepared our training set by selecting 18 equally spaced views for each object and using the remaining views for testing.

The first question we asked was, "Which distribution is a good approximation for the similarity noise distribution?" To answer this we needed to measure the similarity noise caused by the object rotation and depending on the feature extraction algorithm (greedy or GVF). The real noise distribution was obtained as the normalized histogram of differences between the elements of feature vectors corresponding to similar images from the training set.

Figure 5.6 presents the real noise distribution obtained for the greedy algorithm. The best fit Exponential had a better fit to the noise distribution than the Gaussian. Consequently, this implies that L_1 should provide better retrieval results than L_2. The Cauchy distribution is the best fit overall, and the results obtained with L_c should reflect this. However, when the maximum likelihood metric (ML) extracted directly from the similarity noise distribution is used we expect to obtain the best retrieval results.

In the case of GVF algorithm the approximation errors for matching the similarity noise distribution with a model distribution are given in Table 5.1. Note that the Gaussian is the worst approximation. Moreover, the difference between the Gaussian fit and fit obtained with the other two distributions is larger than in the previous case and therefore the results obtained with L_2 will be much worse. Again the best fit by far is provided by the Cauchy distribution.

The results are presented in Figure 5.7 and Table 5.2. In the precision-recall graphs the curves corresponding to L_c is above the curves corresponding to

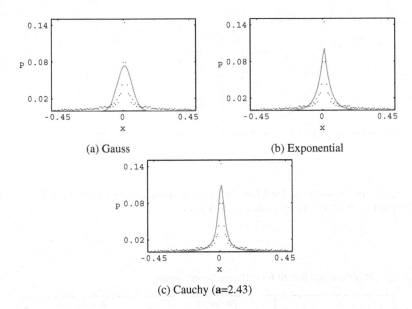

(a) Gauss   (b) Exponential

(c) Cauchy (a=2.43)

Figure 5.6. Similarity noise distribution for the greedy algorithm compared with (a) the best fit Gaussian (approximation error is 0.156), (b) the best fit Exponential (approximation error is 0.102), and (c) the best fit Cauchy (approximation error is 0.073)

Table 5.1. The approximation error for matching the similarity noise distribution with one of the model distributions in the case of GVF algorithm (for Cauchy a=3.27)

Gauss	Exponential	Cauchy
0.0486	0.0286	0.0146

L_1 and L_2 showing that the method using L_c is more effective. Note that the choice of the noise model significantly affects the retrieval results. The Cauchy distribution was the best match for the measured similarity noise distribution and the results in Table 5.2 show that the Cauchy model is more appropriate for the similarity noise than the Gaussian and Exponential models. However, the best results are obtained when the metric extracted directly from the noise distribution is used. One can also note that the results obtained with the GVF method are significantly better than the ones obtained with the greedy method.

In summary, L_c performed better than the analytic distance measures, and the ML metric performed best overall.

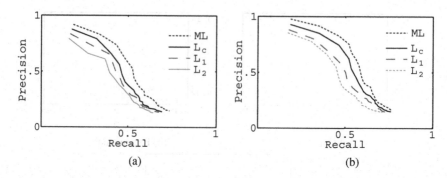

Figure 5.7. Precision/Recall for COIL-20 database using (a) the greedy algorithm (for L_c **a=2.43**) and (b) the GVF algorithm (for L_c **a=3.27**)

Table 5.2. Precision and Recall for different Scope values

		Precision			Recall		
Scope		6	10	25	5	10	25
greedy	L_2	0.425	0.258	0.128	0.425	0.517	0.642
	L_1	0.45	0.271	0.135	0.45	0.542	0.675
	L_c **a=2.43**	0.466	0.279	0.138	0.466	0.558	0.692
	ML	0.525	0.296	0.146	0.525	0.592	0.733
GVF	L_2	0.46	0.280	0.143	0.46	0.561	0.707
	L_1	0.5	0.291	0.145	0.5	0.576	0.725
	L_c (a=3.27)	0.533	0.304	0.149	0.533	0.618	0.758
	ML	0.566	0.324	0.167	0.566	0.635	0.777

6.   Conclusions

We showed that the GVF based snakes give better retrieval results than the traditional snakes. In particular, the GVF snakes have the advantage over traditional snakes in that it is not necessary to know apriori whether the snake must be expanded or contracted to fit the object contour. Furthermore, the GVF snakes have the ability to fit into concavities of the object, which traditional snakes cannot do. Both of these factors resulted in significant improvement in the retrieval results.

We also considered the choice of the similarity metric in a shape based retrieval application. From our experiments, L_2 is typically not justified because the similarity noise distribution is not Gaussian. We showed that better accuracy was obtained when the Cauchy metric was substituted for the L_2 and L_1.

Chapter 6

ROBUST STEREO MATCHING AND MOTION TRACKING

Despite the wealth of information contained in a photograph, the depth of a scene point along the corresponding projection ray is not directly accessible in a single image. With at least two pictures, depth can be measured through triangulation. This is of course one of the reasons that most animals have at least two eyes and/or move their head when looking for friend or foe, as well as the motivation for equipping an autonomous robot with a stereo and motion analysis system.

In the human visual system, two of the fundamental methods of obtaining information about the world are stereo matching and motion tracking. Stereo matching refers to finding correspondences between a pair of binocular images of a scene. When the correspondences to all of the pixels in the image pair are found, a three dimensional model of the world can be mathematically derived. Stereo matching is typically performed at a single instant in time. However, the world changes and evolves over time which is where motion tracking becomes important. Motion tracking describes how the world changes over time. Instead of matching pixels between images at a single instant in time, we trace the movement of a pixel over a sequence of images taken at different instants in time. In this chapter we explore several promising stereo matching methods from the research literature which include pixel and template based algorithms. For the motion tracking, we examine the topic of tracking facial expressions through a video sequence.

1. Introduction

It is a well known fact that for the visual perception of depth in humans stereoscopic vision has an important contribution. Evidence of this must have been known to the Greek geometer Euclid, who around the year 280 BC demonstrated that the right and left eyes see a slightly different version of the same scene. Leonardo da Vinci studied and sketched human anatomy quite extensively in the 1500's, but his drawings of the eye, while showing the optic nerve stretching into the brain, did not reveal the true anatomical arrangement of binocular vision. However, his artistic observations on the problem of representing space were far ahead of his time. Leonardo wrote that the art of painting can never reproduce space because painting lacks the quality he called "relievo," the relief of objects in space [Layer, 1979]. Yet, however easy it is to link the perception of depth to stereoscopic vision, it still took more than two millenniums for scientists to be in a position to guess at the complex mechanism by which objects are perceived as 3D structures in space.

Though some experiments in stereo viewing were conducted earlier (most notably pairs of "stereo" drawings made by the sixteenth century Florentine painter Jacopo Chimenti [Slama (ed.), 1980]), the advent of photography really made widespread 3D viewing possible. Chimenti made a drawing of a man from two slightly different viewpoints (and on a slightly different scale). The small differences give the impression of 3D depth effects, when one fuses the pair binocularly. However, von Helmholtz [Helmholtz, d ed] said: "... it seems to me very unlikely that Chimenti intended them [the drawings] for a stereoscopic experiment ... It seems more probable to me that the artist was not satisfied with the first figure and did it over again ..."

One of the fundamental milestones in the science of stereo vision was laid in 1838 by Sir Charles Wheatstone when addressing the Royal Society in London [Ferwerda, 1987]. Wheatstone came across a peculiar effect: when two hand-drawn images of an object depicted from two different perspectives were viewed by means of a special apparatus, the result was a full 3D experience. The key factor behind this perception relied on isolating the two images so that each eye would only see one drawing. In order to ensure this, Wheatstone built a complex viewing device that made use of mirrors. The small experiment proved that the perception of depth was a psychological effect that took place entirely in the human brain.

No other scientists before him were so close to a theory of stereo vision. Naturally, it was not until Niepce discovered a means of retaining the physically transformed lattice of silver-halide crystals exposed to light, that stereo images were really feasible to be produced. A major contribution in this respect came from Daguerre, who published in 1839 the foundations of the photographic process: the Daguerreotype. The first stereoscope, was built in 1849 by Brewster. His stereoscope resembled greatly the binocular lens, whereby a stereo pair of images would be placed on a support frame just in front of the optics. Stereography soon became a very popular form of art and entertainment, particularly after the 1851 World Fair in London. Legend says that Queen Victoria was so attracted by the stereoscopes on display that she initiated an enthusiasm for stereo photography that lasts to these days.

1.1 Stereoscopic Vision

In retrospect, it is difficult to understand why the basic cause for stereoscopic vision and the revelation that 3D drawings could be created and viewed stereoscopically were not discovered until Wheatstone's magnificent breakthrough in 1838. Since 3D drawings can be easily made and viewed without instruments or optical devices of any kind, there is no technical reason why these discoveries could not have occurred 2000 years ago. Wheatstone's demonstration of his 3D drawings required his mirror stereoscope, which was called by Sir John Herschel, "one of the most curious and beautiful for its simplicity in the entire range of experimental optics." [Layer, 1979]

Since Wheatstone, the overwhelming conclusion of more than one hundred years of perception research is that retinal image disparities, alone, determine the quality and nature of the stereoscopic experience. Of course the cues of accommodation and convergence play an important role in assisting the eyes to "lock on" objects at various distances, but do not seem to affect seriously our psychic reconstruction of space.

Another aspect of this issue lies in a perceptual phenomenon that is unique to 3D, the separation of accommodation and convergence planes. In natural viewing, these planes always coincide; that is, we automatically converge our eyes for the same distance that we focus. This is also true in viewing a hologram. However, a stereoscopic image cannot be viewed without a separation of these two functions - a fact that is quite important in 3D projection systems, especially large theaters.

Stereoscopic vision has been called a primary factor in spatial orientation. It exists in babies at the earliest ages that can be measured, and thereby seems to be an innate quality of vision. Most other depth cues of vision are considered secondary in the sense that they are learned cues, derived from our previous experiences with objects.

Also, stereoscopic vision is considered a perception of relative depth rather than absolute distance. The eyes do not work like a camera rangefinder for the purpose of determining a specific distance. It is nearly impossible to gauge the distance from one point of light in a totally dark room, although it is quite easy to tell which of two adjacent lights is closer. Our stereoscopic acuity for small differences in depth comparisons is quite high - as little as ten seconds of arc. And, since stereoscopic acuity is measured by parallax angle - a numerical constant regardless of object distance - the minimum distances between objects with a perceived change of relief vary dramatically.

Note that just as monoscopic illusions can be ambiguous, so can perceptual conflicts be created between monocular and binocular depth cues. Ittelson and other psychologists [Ittelson, 1960] have studied the dynamics of cue conflicts in order to evaluate their relative importance, the underlying factors, the effect of learning, and the influence of cross-sensory conflicts, such as between vision and hearing. The classic subject for a stereo cue conflict is the human face. If the right-eye view of a face is displayed only to the left eye and the left-eye view to the right eye, the physical shape of the face should appear inverted, with the result that it will look like the inside of a mask, but it does not. Monocular depth cues in the picture conflict with the stereo disparity cues, as well as with our previous knowledge of a human face, and suppress the inversion. On the other hand, abstract subjects invert easily. There are little or no monocular cues to counter the stereo cues. A general rule should be remembered: the more familiar a subject is, the more its monocular depth cues will suppress any contradictory stereo depth cues in the final spatial perception.

An agreed upon theory of stereoscopic vision has yet to be found. Artists are familiar with the wealth of known visual illusions, such as used so ingeniously by the artist M.C. Escher, but almost no visual illusions centering on the stereoscopic experience have been discovered. Julesz [Julesz, 1971][Julesz, 1995] introduced the random dot stereograms (RDS) technique. Briefly, in an RDS, each of two pictures presents a random pattern of dots or other elements with no apparent meaning. Only when fused into one image does the impression of a recognizable object in 3D emerge. The use of Julesz stereograms in perception experiments, described as "incredible" by Harvard psychologists, indicates the brain's ability to extract depth cues from the integration of disparate images and establishes that this process enhances our ability to recognize objects that are otherwise obscure or even invisible. In this, the RDS effect provides a powerful metaphor concerning our ability to gain insights from the integration of competing perspectives.

Based on this power of stereoscopic vision to aid the accuracy of recognition and the clarity of perception, Julesz refers to stereo 3D effects as "breaking camouflage." By analogy, this is the process at work when aerial reconnaissance experts take two photographs of the ground while flying overhead and then fuse these images with the help of a stereoscope to locate hidden enemy weapons. It is also the process at work when a hunter sees a white rabbit standing in the snow. In these ways, stereoscopic vision confers considerable survival value. This beneficial effect may help to explain the deep sense of satisfaction that often accompanies the stereo 3D experience.

2.   Stereo Matching

The projection of light rays onto the retina presents our visual system with an image of the world that is inherently two-dimensional, and yet we are able to interact with the three-dimensional world, even in situations new to us, or with unknown objects. That we accomplish this task easily implies that one of the functions of the human visual system is to reconstruct a 3D representation of the world from its 2D projection onto our eyes. The quest to depict reality as seen by our naked eyes has been pursued by countless individuals throughout the history of human kind. Beginning with the early cave painters, people have attempted to capture the reality. Photography - or in more general, imaging - is a natural extension of this will.

The problem with conventional images is that they have an inherent limitation: they do not retain the psychological perception of depth. Objects depicted in images are flat. It is the observer who - via accumulated knowledge of shapes and forms - perceives their true volume. It could be argued that photographs are accepted amongst us simply because we are used to them; we have learned to deal with their inherent limitation. However, a means to retain depth alongside shape, color, and other features is clearly a significant increase in information content. An image that captures shapes and volumes equally, enables navigation through space and thus a higher degree of realism. Furthermore, since these types of images stand in 3D space, measurements unavailable before can readily be made for them. Depths of interiors, separation distance between objects and backgrounds, height of terrain seen from satellite imagery, are all examples of its applications.

Stereo imaging offers an intuitive way to reconstruct the lost depth information. It relies on one fundamental finding: if two shots of a given static (e.g., without egomotion) scene are captured from two different viewpoints, then the resulting images will differ slightly due to the effect of perspective projection. The correspondences of the stereo pair can be used effectively to reconstruct the three-dimensions of the scene depicted, via a procedure known as *stereo matching*.

Stereo matching stated simply is the process of finding a pair of corresponding image elements produced by a unique object in a stereo arrangement. These elements can be decomposed into sets of corresponding points. The distance that one of the points has shifted with respect to the second one - relative to its local coordinate system - is termed *disparity*, and is the fundamental measure required to reconstruct a scene.

The minimum system requirements for stereo vision are a pair of cameras positioned with overlapping fields of view (Figure 6.1). These cameras could be arranged in any number of ways, but to simplify the forthcoming discussion we will restrict our attention to a simple case: both cameras on a horizontal plane with optical and vertical axes parallel, and known baseline (distance between them). A constraint that is often applied to stereo systems is the *epipolar constraint*. The main idea is that given a pixel in the left image, one does not need to search through the entire right image looking for a correspondent. Instead, attention may be limited to a straight line, the so-called *epipolar line*. Why is it a line instead of some 2D region? The object represented by a pixel in the left image must lie on a ray that extends in the world from the left focal point through that pixel on the left image plane. The epipolar line is the image on the right image plane of that ray in the world; the projection of a straight line is still a straight line. An introduction to epipolar analysis can be found in [Boufama and Mohr, 1995], and a very detailed description in [Faugeras, 1993]. When the optical axes are parallel, as we have assumed here, we enjoy the further property that epipolar lines are guaranteed to be horizontal, and therefore all correspondents will lie on the same-numbered scanline in the other image.

At first finding correspondences in a stereo pair seems to be a simple task, but there are several sources of errors that makes it very difficult to locate the correct pairs. There are systematic errors that appear due to the way the stereo system is constructed. Changes in intensity of the same 3D point in the stereo pair may appear due to the different viewing position. Moreover, some points in the left image simply have no match in the right image, because projection takes place from two different viewpoints (Figure 6.1). This is known as the *occlusion* problem. Another source of errors is related to the symmetries present in the stereo pair. When two or more parts of an image pair are similar in appearance, as can happen when a repetitive pattern like a checkerboard or a brick wall is present, a part of the pattern in one image might seem to match several parts in the other. When this happens, when there are multiple potential correspondents for a given pixel, an *ambiguous* match is said to exist.

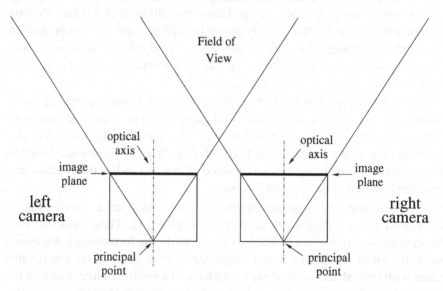

Figure 6.1. Stereo arrangement with a pair of cameras positioned with overlapping fields of view. Some points in the left image simply have no match in the right image, because projection takes place from two different viewpoints.

Consider the case in which the position of the principal point in the left camera is located at distance b from the principal point in the right camera. Assume that the image plane is at distance f in front of each camera lens and that both cameras are oriented identically, with their optical axes parallel and their image planes aligned (Figure 6.2). Let $O(x, y, z)$ be a 3D point and let $L(x_L, y_L)$ and $R(x_R, y_R)$ be its perspective projections on the left and right images, respectively. Note that in this situation $y_L = y_R$, so that the y disparity is zero. From Figure 6.2 by means of similar triangles we can derive the relations:

$$\frac{x_L}{f} = \frac{x}{z} \tag{6.1}$$

$$-\frac{x_R}{f} = \frac{b - x}{z} \tag{6.2}$$

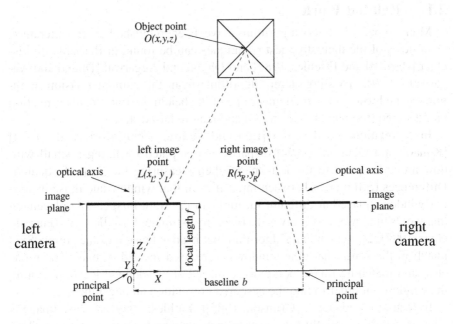

Figure 6.2. Top view of a stereo arrangement

The solution for (x, y, z), given the (x_L, y_L) and (x_R, y_R), can be obtained from the difference $x_L - x_R$, which is referred to as *disparity*. Now

$$x_L - x_R = \frac{f \cdot b}{z}. \tag{6.3}$$

Hence,

$$z = \frac{f \cdot b}{x_L - x_R}. \tag{6.4}$$

Once the depth z is determined, the (x, y) coordinates are easily determined from the perspective projection equations.

$$\left(\begin{array}{c} x \\ y \end{array} \right) = \frac{z}{f} \left(\begin{array}{c} x_L \\ y_L \end{array} \right) \tag{6.5}$$

Generally the *baseline* distance b between the two cameras' optical axes and the *focal length* f are known parameters of the geometry. The *disparity* however, is unknown and needs to be estimated in order to recover the depth information. Current stereo matching algorithms estimate disparity by making use of a metric function that is minimized.

2.1   Related Work

Many types of stereo algorithms have been published in the literature. Overviews of the then-strongest techniques can be found in Barnard and Fischler [Barnard and Fischler, 1982] and Dhond and Aggarwal [Dhond and Aggarwal, 1989]. Existing stereo algorithms from the computer vision literature can be loosely classified under one of the headings: traditional correlation based stereo (template based stereo) and feature based stereo.

In correlation based stereo [Luo and Maitre, 1990][Mori et al., 1973] [Kanade and Okutomi, 1994] disparity is computed by fixing a small window around a pixel in the left image, then measuring the Sum-of-Squared-Differences (SSD) error between intensities in that window and those in similar windows placed at different locations in the right image. The placement that yields the lowest error gives the disparity estimate. Fusiello et al. [Fusiello et al., 1997] implemented an algorithm that is an extension of the simple SSD match in the sense that nine windows were used instead of one. The reference and matching image points were placed at pre-defined locations within the windows in order to find the best area-correlation amongst them.

In feature based stereo [Grimson, 1985][Matthies, 1989], a dense image is converted into a spatially sparse set of features which are then matched. This results into a sparse disparity map which must be interpolated to yield disparities at every pixel. Semantic features (with known physical properties and/or spatial geometry) or intensity anomaly features (isolated anomalous intensity patterns not necessarily having any physical significance) are the basic units that are matched. Semantic features of the generic types include occlusion edges, vertices of linear structures, and prominent surface markings; domain specific semantic features may include such features as the corner or peak of a building, or a road surface marking. Intensity anomaly features include zero crossings or salient points [Loupias et al., 2000]. Methods used for feature matching often include symbolic classification techniques, as well as correlation.

Obviously, feature matching alone cannot provide a depth map of the desired density, and so it must be augmented by a model based interpretation step (e.g., we recognize the edges of a building and assume that the intermediate space is occupied by planar walls and roofs), or by template matching. When used in conjunction with template matching, the feature matches are generally considered to be more reliable than the template matching alone, and can constrain the search for correlation matches.

Jones and Malik [Jones and Malik, 1992] applied 2D oriented derivative-of-Gaussian filters to a stereo pair and used the magnitude of the filter responses at each pixel as matching features. The original signal may also be transformed to Fourier space, and some part of the transformed signal is used to compute the disparity [Sanger, 1988]. Often the phase of the transformed signal is used [Jenkin and Jepson, 1994], [Maimone, 1996].

A post-processing refinement technique of the template based stereo algorithm is the Kanade/Okutomi variable-window method [Kanade and Okutomi, 1994]. This method addresses the occlusion and foreshortening problems by dynamically adjusting the size of the matching windows according to constraints on the local variations of both intensity and disparity. The difficulty of a locally adaptive window lies in a difficulty in evaluating and using disparity variances. While the intensity variation is directly measurable from the image, evaluation of the disparity variation is not easy, since the disparity is what we intend to calculate as the end product of stereo. To resolve the dilemma, the authors employ a statistical model of the disparity distribution within the window: the difference of disparity at a point in the window from that of the center point has a zero-mean Gaussian distribution with variance proportional to the distance between these points. This modeling enables the computation of the uncertainty of the disparity estimate by taking into account both intensity and disparity variances. As a result, their method searches for a window that produces the estimate of disparity with the least uncertainty for each pixel of an image: the method controls not only the size but also the shape (rectangle) of the window. Finally, this adaptive-window method is embedded in an iterative stereo matching algorithm: starting with an initial estimate of the disparity map, the algorithm iteratively updates the disparity estimate for each point by choosing the size and shape of a window until it converges. In this way the authors attempt to avoid the boundary problems that arise when the correlation window encompasses two objects at different depths.

The use of multiple cameras for stereo was described by Kanade et al. [Kanade et al., 1992]. Their approach, known as multibaseline stereo, advocates using a simple Sum-of-Absolute-Differences (SAD) stereo matching algorithm over several image pairs. By incorporating multiple views of the world using known camera calibration, many of the shortcomings of the direct yet simple SAD method are eliminated: e.g., specular highlights are ignored, noisy disparity maps become smoother, and some occluded surfaces become visible.

An interesting approach using a maximum likelihood cost function optimization was proposed by Cox et al. [Cox et al., 1996]. This function assumes that corresponding features in the left and right images are normally distributed about a common true value. However, the authors [Cox et al., 1996] noticed that the normal distribution assumption used to compare corresponding intensity values is violated for some of their test sets. They altered the stereo pair so that the noise distribution would be closer to a Gaussian.

Recent research by [Bhat and Nayar, 1998] concluded that the SSD is sensitive to outliers and therefore robust M-estimators should be used regarding stereo matching. However, the authors [Bhat and Nayar, 1998] did not consider metrics based on similarity distributions. They considered ordinal metrics, where an ordinal metric is based on relative ordering of intensity values in windows - rank permutations.

Most of the efforts mentioned above were concentrated on finding a better algorithm or feature that can provide a more accurate and dense disparity map. Some of them use a simple SSD or SAD metric in matching correspondences or make assumptions about the corresponding features in the left and right stereo images. Our goal is to use the maximum likelihood framework introduced in Chapter 2 and to find a better model for the noise distribution in a stereo pair. We implemented a template based matching algorithm, the multi-window algorithm by Fusiello et al. [Fusiello et al., 1997], and the maximum likelihood method by Cox et al. [Cox et al., 1996]. Note that for the last two algorithms in order to have a good benchmark we used the original source codes provided by the authors and only the line of code where the metric was involved was modified.

3.   Stereo Matching Algorithms

Several algorithms have been proposed to estimate the disparity map of a stereo arrangement. They all agree to a large extent in their form: some sort of metric function SSD (L_2) or SAD (L_1) is minimized to yield the best match for a given reference point. The choice of the metric function is the subject of our investigations. We implemented the algorithms mentioned before and investigated the influence of the metric function on the matching accuracy.

3.1   Template Based Algorithm

A template based algorithm makes minimal assumptions (e.g., constant depth inside the template) about the underlying geometry of the stereo pair and uses a simple translational model to estimate the disparity. An implementation of this technique gives good disparity estimates for points located at constant depths, but it is less robust with receding features - i.e. image facets that recede in depth - that can become severely distorted due to perspective projection.

Considering the stereo arrangement illustrated in Figure 6.2, pixels of a left and right image of a stereo pair are matched using a simple pair of equations of the form

$$\text{SSD}(x, y, d) = \sum_{w_x, w_y \in W} \left(R(x + w_x, y + w_y) - L(x + w_x + d, y + w_y)\right)^2 \quad (6.6)$$

$$disparity\ (x, y) = \min_{m \leq d \leq M} \text{SSD}(x, y, d) \quad (6.7)$$

or

$$\text{SAD}(x, y, d) = \sum_{w_x, w_y \in W} |R(x + w_x, y + w_y) - L(x + w_x + d, y + w_y)| \quad (6.8)$$

$$disparity\ (x, y) = \min_{m \leq d \leq M} \text{SAD}(x, y, d) \quad (6.9)$$

These equations are employed to estimate the disparity by placing a window W of a predefined size (w_x, w_y), centered around a reference point in the right image. A second window of identical size (see Figure 6.3) would be placed in the left image and moved around its x axis (the epipolar constraint is assumed). Generally the matching window would be moved from a minimum disparity m to a maximum disparity M which in turn determines the disparity search range. The position at which the minimum error occurs for each candidate point, is chosen as the best disparity estimate for a given reference point. Sub-pixel precision can be obtained by fitting a curve through the chosen values, yielding more accurate disparity estimates [Fusiello et al., 2000].

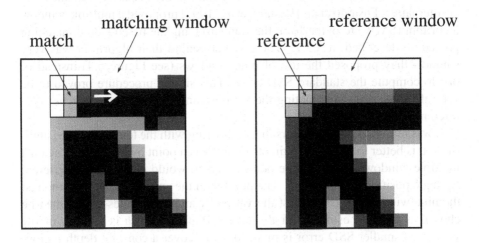

Figure 6.3. Example of a template matching procedure

An important problem that has to be considered is the occlusion. Some points in the left image simply have no match in the right image, because projection takes place from two different viewpoints (see Figure 6.1). The algorithm will still try to match these occluded points, and will even produce an incorrect disparity estimation for them. The situation can be detected in a post-processing stage whereby two disparity maps - d_{RtoL} (right to left), and d_{LtoR} (left to right) - are checked for consistency, using equation (6.10). For example, if the disparity of a point x in the right image is d, then the match of x is located at $x + d$ in the right image, and vice versa.

$$d_{RtoL}(x) = d_{LtoR}(x + d_{RtoL}(x)) \qquad (6.10)$$

Points that satisfy this expression are retained while the others are signaled as occluded pixels and disparity is assigned heuristically. Following [Little and Gillet, 1990], we assumed that occluded areas, occurring between two planes at different depth, take the disparity of the deeper plane.

3.2   Multiple Windows Algorithm

As observed by Kanade and Okutomi [Kanade and Okutomi, 1994], when the correlation window covers a region with non-constant disparity, template based matching is likely to fail, and the error in the depth estimates grows with the window size. Reducing the latter, on the other hand, makes the estimated disparities more sensitive to noise.

To overcome such difficulties, Kanade and Okutomi [Kanade and Okutomi, 1994] proposed a statistically adaptive technique which selects at each pixel the window size that minimizes the uncertainty in the disparity estimates. As an alternative, Fusiello et al. [Fusiello et al., 1997] proposed a multiple window algorithm (SMW) to outperform the standard template based stereo matching procedure described in 6.3.1. The concept behind their algorithm was very simple - they proposed the use of nine windows (see Figure 6.4) instead of one to compute the standard SSD error. This simple procedure proved to be very effective at disambiguating the various candidate disparity matches of a reference point.

It was reasoned by the authors that comparing with the template based algorithm it is better to obtain an estimate of any given point by matching it against multiple windows, in which the point to match would be located at different strategic positions within them. The point with the smallest disparity amongst the nine windows, and amongst the various search candidates would then be chosen as the best estimate for the given point. The idea is that a window yielding a smaller SSD error is more likely to cover a constant depth region; in this way, the disparity profile itself drives the selection of the appropriate window. Consider the case of a piecewise-constant surface: points within a window close to surface discontinuities come from two different planes, there-

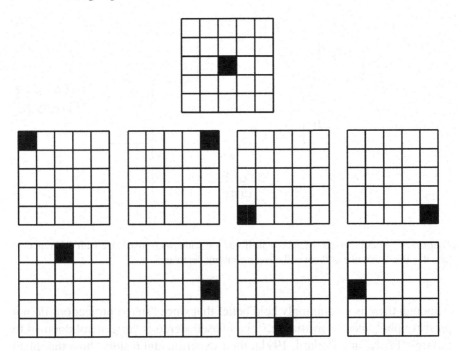

Figure 6.4. The nine asymmetric correlation windows in Fusiello's algorithm. The black pixel in the array denotes the position where the reference image-point is located in each matching window. The template based algorithm would use only the top window where the matching pixel is at center.

fore a single "average" disparity cannot be assigned to the whole window without making a gross error. The multiple window approach can be regarded as a robust technique able to fit a constant disparity model to data consisting of piecewise-constant surface, that is, capable of "drawing the line" between two different populations (see Figure 6.5).

While this is nothing else than a more involved form of the conventional template matching strategy, it was shown in their paper that computation of the disparity estimate was more accurate compared with the adaptive algorithm proposed by Kanade and Okutomi [Kanade and Okutomi, 1994].

A left-right consistency test (see equation 6.10) was also employed for detecting the occluded points.

3.3 Cox' Maximum Likelihood Algorithm

A different approach was proposed by Cox et al. [Cox et al., 1996]. Their interesting idea was to perform matching on the individual pixel intensity, instead of using an adaptive window as in the area based correlation methods.

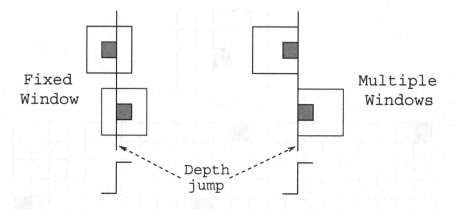

Figure 6.5. Multiple windows approach. If one use windows of fixed size with different centers, it is likely that one of them will cover a constant depth area.

Although there is a commonly held belief that since "stereo projections do not preserve photometric invariance," pixel based stereo is "in general doomed to failure" [Frisby and Pollard, 1991], their experimental results show that pixel based stereo can be considered as a practical alternative.

   Their algorithm assumed that any two corresponding features (pixels) in the left and right images are normally distributed about their true value. This leads to a local matching cost that is the weighted SSD error between the features. The global cost function that is eventually minimized is the sum of the local costs of matching pixels plus the sum of occlusion costs for unmatched pixels. The global optimization is efficiently performed in 1D along each epipolar line.

   Initially, the local cost of matching two points z_{i_1} and z_{i_2} is calculated. The condition that measurement z_{i_1} from camera 1, and measurement z_{i_2} from camera 2 originate from the same location, X, in space, i.e. that z_{i_1} and z_{i_2} correspond to each other, is denoted by Z_{i_1,i_2}. The likelihood that the measurement pair Z_{i_1,i_2} originated from the same point X is denoted by $\Lambda(Z_{i_1,i_2}|X)$ and is given by

$$\Lambda(Z_{i_1,i_2}|X) = \left(\frac{1 - P_D}{\phi}\right)^{\delta_{i_1,i_2}} [P_D\,p(z_{i_1}|X) \times P_D\,p(z_{i_2}|X)]^{1-\delta_{i_1,i_2}} \quad (6.11)$$

where δ_{i_1,i_2} is an indicator variable that is unity if a measurement is not assigned a corresponding point, i.e. is occluded, and zero otherwise, ϕ is the field of view of the camera, and the term $p(z|X)$ is a probability density distribution that represents the likelihood of measurement z assuming it originated from a point X in the scene. The parameter P_D represents the probability of detecting a measurement originating from X at sensor s and is a function of the number of occlusions, noise, etc. Conversely, $(1 - P_D)$ may be viewed as the probability of occlusion.

As mentioned before, the authors assume that the measurement vectors z_{i_s}, $s = \{1, 2\}$, are normally distributed about their ideal value z, so

$$p(z_{i_s}|X) = |(2\pi)^d S_s|^{-\frac{1}{2}} \exp\left\{-\frac{1}{2}(z - z_{i_s})' S_s^{-1}(z - z_{i_s})\right\} \qquad (6.12)$$

where d is the dimension of the measurement vectors z_{i_s} and S_s is the co-variance matrix associated with the error $(z - z_{i_s})$. Since the true value z is unknown, it is approximated by maximum likelihood estimate $\hat{z}$ obtained from the measurement pair Z_{i_1, i_2} and given by

$$z \approx \hat{z} = \frac{S_{i_1}^{-1} z_{i_1} + S_{i_2}^{-1} z_{i_2}}{S_{i_1}^{-1} + S_{i_2}^{-1}} \qquad (6.13)$$

where S_{i_s} is the covariance associated with measurement z_{i_s}.

The cost of the individual pairings Z_{i_1, i_2} was established and now it is nec-essary to determine the total cost of all pairs. Let Γ be the set of all feasible partitions, i.e. $\Gamma = \{\gamma\}$. The idea is to find the pairings or partition γ that maximizes $L(\gamma)/L(\gamma_0)$, where the likelihood $L(\gamma)$ of a partition is defined as

$$L(\gamma) = p(Z_1, Z_2|\gamma) = \prod_{Z_{i_1, i_2} \in \gamma} \Lambda(Z_{i_1, i_2}|X) \qquad (6.14)$$

The maximization of $L(\gamma)/L(\gamma_0)$ is equivalent to

$$\min_{\gamma \in \Gamma} J(\gamma) = \min_{\gamma \in \Gamma}[-\ln(L(\gamma))] \qquad (6.15)$$

which leads to

$$\min_{\gamma \in \Gamma} J(\gamma) = \min_{\gamma \in \Gamma} \sum_{Z_{i_1, i_2} \in \gamma} \left\{ \delta_{i_1, i_2} \ln\left(\frac{P_D^2 \phi}{(1 - P_D)|(2\pi)^d S|^{\frac{1}{2}}}\right) + \right.$$

$$\left. (1 - \delta_{i_1, i_2})\left[\frac{1}{4}(z_{i_1} - z_{i_2})' S^{-1}(z_{i_1} - z_{i_2})\right] \right\} \qquad (6.16)$$

assuming that the covariances S_{i_s} are equal to S.

The first term of the summation represents the cost of an occlusion in the left or right views, while the latter term is the cost of matching two features. Clearly, as the probability of occlusion $(1 - P_D)$ becomes small the cost of not matching a feature increases, as expected.

The problem with this approach is that it relies on the assumption that any two corresponding features (pixels) in the left and right images are normally distributed about their true value. The authors noted that changes in illumination conditions and differences in camera responses were the principal source of errors to their normal assumption. The changes in illumination and/or camera responses were modeled by constant multiplicative and additive factors, i.e.

$$I_L(x, y) = A I_R(x, y) + B \qquad (6.17)$$

In their model, the intensity histograms for the left and right images are approximatively the same except for the fixed offset B and the scaling term A (considering that the number of occluded points is small compared to the overall number of pixels). Estimation of the constants A and B was performed by first calculating the intensity histograms for both left and right image and then plotting the ten percentile points. A linear regression can be performed on these points, the slope and offset providing estimates for A and B, respectively. Applying this model they alter the intensities of the stereo pair and compensate these effects prior to the stereo matching. Instead of altering the original data, our solution proposes to model the noise distribution and to estimate the corresponding metric to be used in matching.

4.   Stereo Matching Experiments

The best way to measure the success of a stereo matching method is to compare the results against the ground truth, or range information measured using means other than stereo. Typically, the ground truth in stereo matching is generated manually. A set of reference points are defined in the images and then a person finds the correspondences for the stereo pair. Unfortunately, relatively little ground truth data is publicly available. Despite this fact, many attempts were made in the literature to create standard stereo sets and to compare different stereo algorithms using the stereo sets as benchmarks. One such study, the ARPA JISCT stereo evaluation [Bolles et al., 1993], compared the results of four stereo methods. However, since ground truth was not available, most of their statistics dealt with agreement between the results; not "method A is 80% accurate," but "methods A and B agree on 80% of the images." Thus they could neither evaluate stereo methods independently nor quantitatively characterize their performance. The study conclusion states in part that the "ground truth is expensive, but there is no substitute for assessing quantitative issues." In our experiments we used different standard stereo sets from the literature with ground truth provided by the authors.

4.1 Stereo Sets

The first stereo data sets we used in our experiments (Castle set and Tower set) were provided by the Calibrated Imaging Laboratory, Robotics Institute, Carnegie Mellon University. These datasets contain multiple images of static scenes with accurate information about object locations in 3D. The 3D locations are given in X-Y-Z coordinates with a simple text description (at best accurate to 0.3 mm) and the corresponding image coordinates (the ground truth) are provided for all eleven images taken for each scene. For each image there are 28 ground truth points in the Castle set and 18 points in the Tower set. An example of two stereo images from the Castle data set is given in Figure 6.6. Note that on the left image the ground truth points were superimposed on the image.

Figure 6.6. A stereo image pair from the Castle data set

In order to evaluate the performance of the stereo matching algorithms under difficult matching conditions we also used the Robots stereo pair [Lew et al., 1994] from University of Illinois at Urbana-Champaign. This stereo pair is more difficult due to varying levels of depth and occlusions (Figure 6.7). For this stereo pair, the ground truth consists of 1276 point pairs, given with one pixel accuracy.

In addition, we also used two stereo datasets, Flat and Suburb (Figure 6.8), which contain aerial views of a suburban region. These were taken from Stuttgart ISPRS Image Understanding datasets [Guelch, 1988]. These stereo sets were selected because they show the potential of a stereo matcher to perform automated terrain mapping. Moreover, a substantial number of ground truth points were given (53020 points for the Flat stereo pair and 52470 for the Suburb stereo pair).

4.2 Stereo Matching Results

The first experiments were done using the template based stereo algorithm introduced in Section 6.3.1. In each image we considered the templates around

Figure 6.7. Robots stereo pair

(a)   (b)

Figure 6.8. Left images from the Flat and Suburb stereo pairs; (a) Flat, (b) Suburb

points which were given by the ground truth. We wanted to find the model for the real noise distribution which gave the best accuracy in finding the corresponding templates in the other image. As a measure of performance we computed the accuracy of finding the corresponding points in the neighborhood of one pixel around the points provided by the test set. In searching for the corresponding pixel, we examined a band of height 7 pixels and width equal to the image dimension centered at the row coordinate of the pixel provided by the test set.

In this application we used a template size of $n = 25$, i.e. a 5×5 window around the central point. For all the stereo images we divided the ground truth points in two equal sized non-overlapping sets: the training set and the test set. The assignment of a particular point from the ground truth to one of these sets was done randomly. In order to compute the real noise distribution we placed templates around the training set points, and we created the normalized histogram of the differences between pixels in corresponding templates.

We present the real noise distribution corresponding to the Castle dataset in Figure 6.9. As one can see from Table 6.1 the Cauchy distribution had the best fit to the measured noise distribution relative to L_1 and L_2 for both Castle and Tower stereo sets.

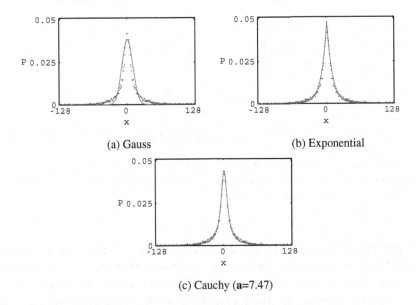

(a) Gauss   (b) Exponential

(c) Cauchy (**a=7.47**)

Figure 6.9.   Noise distribution in the stereo matcher using Castle data set

Table 6.1.   The approximation error for the corresponding point noise distribution in stereo matching using Castle and Tower stereo sets

Set	Gauss	Exponential	Cauchy
Castle	0.0486	0.0286	0.0246
Tower	0.049	0.045	0.043

As mentioned before, the Robots stereo pair is more difficult due to varying levels of depth and occlusions. This fact is illustrated in the shape of the real noise distribution (Figure 6.10). Note that the distribution in this case has wider spread and is less smooth. The Cauchy distribution is the best fit, followed by the Exponential and the Gaussian.

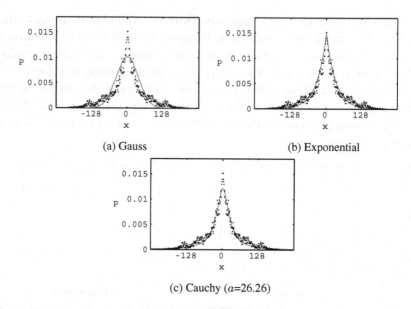

(a) Gauss   (b) Exponential

(c) Cauchy (a=26.26)

Figure 6.10.   Noise distribution for the Robots stereo pair compared with the best fit Gaussian (a) (approximation error is 0.0267), best fit Exponential (b) (approximation error is 0.0156), and best fit Cauchy (c) (approximation error is 0.0147)

A different behavior can be noted for the real noise distribution in the case of Flat and Suburb stereo pairs. In this case, the shape of the real noise distribution clearly resembles a Gaussian distribution. The tails are less prominent (Figure 6.11) and as a consequence the Exponential and the Cauchy distributions are worse approximations (see Table 6.2). In these conditions, one expects L_2 to have greater matching accuracy comparing with L_1 and L_c.

Table 6.2.   The approximation error for the corresponding point noise distribution in stereo matching using Flat and Suburb stereo pairs

Set	Gauss	Exponential	Cauchy
Flat	0.0356	0.0412	0.0446
Suburb	0.0217	0.0273	0.0312

The complete results for the template based matching are presented in Table 6.3. Note that the results are consistent with the matching between the real noise distribution and the model distributions. In the case where Cauchy distribution was the best fit (Castle, Tower, and Robots stereo sets), the results obtained with L_c are better than the ones obtained with L_1 and L_2. For all

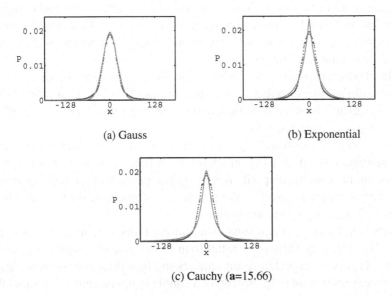

(a) Gauss

(b) Exponential

(c) Cauchy (**a=15.66**)

Figure 6.11. Noise distribution for the Suburb stereo pair compared with the best fit Gaussian (a) (approximation error is 0.0217), best fit Exponential (b) (approximation error is 0.0273), and best fit Cauchy (c) (approximation error is 0.0312)

these stereo sets, the Gaussian was the worst fit and consequently the results obtained with L_2 were the worst. On the other hand, in the case of Flat and Suburb stereo pairs, the Gaussian was the best fit and consequently the results obtained with L_2 were the best. Now, the worst results were obtained with L_c because the Cauchy distribution was the worst fit to the real noise distribution. For all the stereo sets, significant improvement in accuracy was obtained when the ML metric (see Section 2.6) was used.

Table 6.3. The accuracy of the stereo matcher (%) using template matching

Set	L_2	L_1	K	L_c	ML
Castle	91.05	92.43	92.12	93.71 **a=7.47**	94.52
Tower	91.11	93.32	92.84	94.26 **a=5.23**	95.07
Robots	71.19	73.35	75.34	76.79 **a=26.2**	78.54
Flat	78.39	77.50	77.22	75.92 **a=17.17**	83.67
Suburb	80.08	79.24	78.59	77.36 **a=15.66**	85.11

Note also the range in the accuracy values for all stereo sets. The best results were obtained for Castle and Tower stereo sets. For the other stereo pairs, there were more difficult matching conditions due to occlusions and complex background and therefore the matching accuracy is lower. However, for these stereo pairs (especially for Robots) the improvement in accuracy given by the ML metric is more significant.

In the next experiments, we investigated the influence of similarity noise using Fusiello's multiple windows stereo algorithm [Fusiello et al., 1997] (see Section 6.3.2) and the maximum likelihood stereo algorithm by Cox et al. [Cox et al., 1996] (see Section 6.3.3).

In the maximum likelihood algorithm, matching was done on the individual pixel intensity, instead of using an adaptive window as in the template based methods. In this case the disparity map gives the location of the corresponding pixels. The accuracy is given by the percentage of pixels in the test set which are matched correctly by the algorithm.

In Tables 6.4 and 6.5, the results using different distance measures are presented. The accuracy values are better than in the case of template based algorithm. This is an expected result since both algorithms use more sophisticated procedures in matching, instead of a simple template centered around the matching points.

Table 6.4. The accuracy of the stereo matcher using Fusiello's multiple window stereo algorithm

Set	L_2	L_1	K	L_c	ML
Castle	92.27	92.92	92.76	94.82 a=7.47	95.73
Tower	91.79	93.67	93.14	95.28 a=5.23	96.05
Robots	72.15	73.74	75.87	77.69 a=26.2	79.54
Flat	79.43	77.92	77.76	76.82 a=17.17	84.69
Suburb	81.14	79.67	79.14	78.28 a=15.66	86.15

The results are also consistent with the fitting between the real noise distribution and the model distributions. For all of the stereo sets, ML had the

Table 6.5. The accuracy of the stereo matcher using maximum likelihood stereo algorithm

Set	L_2	L_1	K	L_c	ML
Castle	93.45	94.72	94.53	95.72 a=7.47	96.37
Tower	93.18	95.07	94.74	96.18 a=5.23	97.04
Robots	74.81	76.76	78.15	82.51 a=26.2	84.38
Flat	81.19	80.67	80.15	79.23 a=17.17	86.07
Suburb	82.07	81.53	80.97	80.01 a=15.66	87.18

highest accuracy. Note the improvement in accuracy comparing with L_2 (SSD) which was used in the original algorithms. For the multiple window stereo algorithm, the ML beat L_2 by 3 to 7 percent. For the maximum likelihood algorithm the ML metric had improved accuracy over the L_2 of approximately 3 to 9 percent.

4.3 Summary

We implemented a template matching algorithm, an adaptive, multi-window algorithm by Fusiello et al. [Fusiello et al., 1997], and a maximum likelihood method using pixel intensities by Cox et al. [Cox et al., 1996]. Note that the SSD was used in the paper by Fusiello et al. [Fusiello et al., 1997] and in the work by Cox et al. [Cox et al., 1996]. Furthermore, we used international stereo data sets from Carnegie Mellon University(Castle and Tower), University of Illinois at Urbana-Champaign (Robots) and University of Stuttgart (Flat and Suburb).

From our experiments, it was clear that choosing the correct metric had significant impact on the accuracy. Specifically, among the L_2, L_1, Cauchy, and Kullback metrics, the accuracy varied up to 7%.

For the stereo pairs and the algorithms in our experiments, the maximum likelihood metric consistently outperformed all of the other metrics. Furthermore, it is optimal with respect to maximizing the probability of similarity. The breaking points occur when there is no ground truth, or when the ground truth is not representative.

There appear to be two methods of applying maximum likelihood toward improving the accuracy of matching algorithms in stereo matching. The first method recommends altering the images so that the measured noise distribution is closer to the Gaussian and then using the SSD. The second method is to find a metric which has a distribution which is close to the real noise distribution.

5. Motion Tracking Experiments

Automatic motion tracking has long been an important topic in computer vision. Recently facial motion analysis has captured the attention of many researchers as the interests for model based video compression and human-computer interaction grow [Tao and Huang, 1999][Black and Yacoob, 1995]. One important aspect in analyzing human facial movement is to automatically track moving feature points on human faces. The motion parameters of these feature points can be used to reconstruct the original motion (e.g., human expression synthesis [Tang and Huang, 1994]) or for further analysis (e.g., computerized lipreading [Bregler et al., 1993] and expression recognition [Black and Yacoob, 1995]).

There are two classical methods for tracking feature points, namely optical flow and block correlation (template matching). Optical flow tries to find the correspondence between two images by calculating the velocity (displacement vector) at which a point on the first image moves in the second image. Block correlation tracks a specific point by finding the maximum similarity between two pixel patterns of images containing this point. There are many different algorithms available for computing optical flow [Barron et al., 1994]. However, since the assumptions to calculate optical flow are not usually satisfied in real situations, particularly for human facial movements [Mase, 1991], the results of optical flow are often unreliable. Problems also occur with the block correlation method [Tang et al., 1994]. This method identifies an image pattern as a template and moves it over a specific search area in a second image. Correlations between the template and the second image are then calculated. The point at which the maximum correlation occurs is the tracking result. Obviously, the accuracy of this method is affected by the size of both the template and the search area. If the search area is too small, the points with bigger motion will be lost. In contrast, if the search area is too large search, the computation will be expensive and possibly an erroneous estimation of the position of the point will be found. When the small template is used, the local details are captured. On the other hand, when the template is large you lose all the local details and concentrate on more coarse (global) details.

We used a video sequence containing 19 images on a talking head in a static background [Tang et al., 1994]. An example of three images from this video sequence is given in Figure 6.12. For each image in this video sequence there are 14 points given as ground truth.

The motion tracking algorithm between the test frame and another frame performed template matching to find the best match in a 5×5 template around a central pixel. In searching for the corresponding pixel, we examined a region of width and height of 7 pixels centered at the position of the pixel in the test frame.

The idea of this experiment was to trace moving facial expressions. Therefore, the ground truth points were provided around the lips and eyes which are moving through the sequence. This movement causes the templates around the ground truth points to differ more when far-off frames are considered. This is illustrated in Figure 6.13.

Between the first frame and a later frame, the tracking error represents the average displacement (in pixels) between the ground truth and the corresponding pixels found by the matching algorithm. When consecutive frames are considered (frame difference = 1), the average displacement is low, however, when far-off frames are compared (frame difference = 3) the displacement error is significantly increased. Note that regardless of the frame difference, L_c had the least error and L_2 had the greatest error.

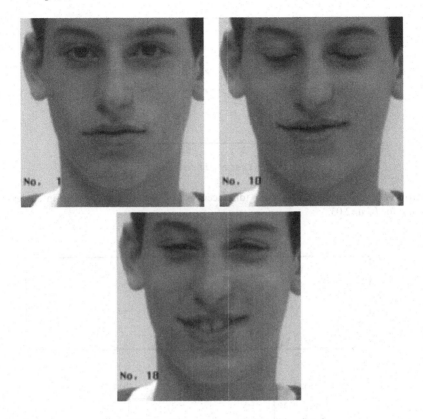

Figure 6.12. Video sequence of a talking head

In Figure 6.14 we display the fit between the real noise distribution and the three model distributions. The real noise distribution was calculated using templates around points in the training set (6 points for each frame) considering sequential frames. The best fit is the Cauchy distribution, and the Exponential distribution is a better match than the Gaussian distribution.

Since the Cauchy distribution was the best fit overall, it is expected that the accuracy is greater when using L_c than when using L_1 and L_2 (Table 6.6). For L_c, the greatest accuracy was obtained around the values of the parameter a which gave the best fit between the Cauchy distribution and the real distribution (Figure 6.15). The ML metric gave the best results overall.

In addition, we considered the situation of motion tracking between non-adjacent frames. In Table 6.6, the results are shown for tracking pixels between frames located at interframe distances of 1, 3, and 5.

Note that as the interframe distance increases, the accuracy decreases and the error increases. The ML metric had improved accuracy over the L_2 (which is typically used in matching) of approximately 5 to 9 percent.

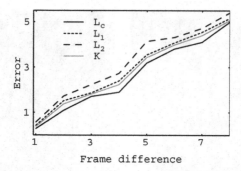

Figure 6.13. Average tracking error (displacement) of corresponding points in successive frames; for L_c a=2.03

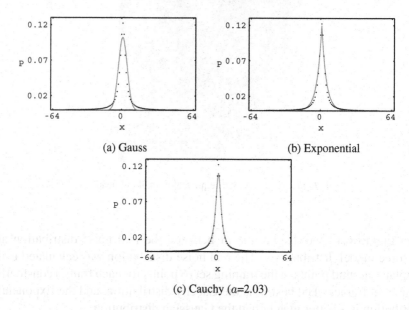

(a) Gauss   (b) Exponential

(c) Cauchy (a=2.03)

Figure 6.14. Noise distribution in the video sequence using sequential frames compared with the best fit Gaussian (a) (approximation error is 0.083), best fit Exponential (b) (approximation error is 0.069), and best fit Cauchy (c) (approximation error is 0.063)

6. Concluding Remarks

We examined two topic areas from computer vision which were stereo matching and motion tracking. In stereo matching we implemented a template based matching algorithm, an adaptive, multi-window algorithm by Fusiello et al. [Fusiello et al., 1997], and a maximum likelihood method using pixel intensities by Cox et al. [Cox et al., 1996]. In motion tracking, we implemented

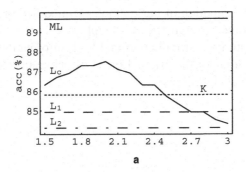

Figure 6.15. The accuracy of the matching process in the video sequence using sequential frames

Table 6.6. The accuracy (%) of the matching process in the video sequence

Interframe Distance	L_2	L_1	K	L_c	ML
1	84.11	84.91	85.74	87.43 (a=2.03)	89.67
3	74.23	75.36	76.03	78.15 (a=13.45)	81.25
5	65.98	67.79	68.56	70.14 (a=21.15)	74.19

a template based matching algorithm to track pixels on a moving object in a video sequence. We examined the tracking error and accuracy between adjacent and non-adjacent frames.

For most of our experiments, better accuracy was obtained when the Cauchy metric was substituted for the SSD, SAD, or Kullback relative information. The only exception occurred in stereo matching when the Flat and Suburb stereo pairs were used. In this case the similarity noise distribution exhibited a Gaussian shape. One of the possible explanation for this relies on the particularity of these stereo pairs. They consist of aerial images and therefore, the depth values in the scene are much lower than the distance from where the images were taken. In this conditions, the noise in the camera may be the main source of errors. As was shown in the work by Boie and Cox [Boie and Cox, 1992] the camera noise can be appropriately modeled as a Gaussian noise. However, also in this case the accuracy results were consistent with the fitting of the real noise distribution and the model distribution, in the sense that when a model distribution was the best fit then, the accuracy obtained with the corresponding metric was the best.

An important aspect was to use the original source code as was the case for the multi-window algorithm by Fusiello et al. [Fusiello et al., 1997] and for Cox' maximum likelihood stereo algorithm [Cox et al., 1996]. In order to have a reliable evaluation of our method we modified only the part of the code where the comparison metric was employed. In these conditions, using the ML metric estimated from the ground truth information we significantly improved the accuracy of the original methods. Note that the SSD (L_2) was used in both original algorithms.

Chapter 7

FACIAL EXPRESSION RECOGNITION

The most expressive way humans display emotions is through facial expressions. Humans detect and interpret faces and facial expressions in a scene with little or no effort. Still, development of an automated system that accomplishes this task is rather difficult. There are several related problems: detection of an image segment as a face, extraction of the facial expression information, and classification of the expression (e.g., in emotion categories). A system that performs these operations accurately and in real time would be a major step forward in achieving a human-like interaction between the man and machine.

In this chapter we present a system for classification of facial expressions from continuous video input. We introduce and test different Bayesian network classifiers for classifying expressions from video, focusing on changes in distribution assumptions and feature dependency structures. In particular we use Naive Bayes classifiers and change the distribution from Gaussian to Cauchy. Observing that the features independence assumption used by the Naive Bayes classifiers may be inappropriate we use Gaussian Tree-Augmented Naive Bayes (TAN) classifiers to learn the dependencies among different facial motion features. We also introduce a facial expression recognition from live video input using temporal cues. We exploit the existing methods and present an architecture of hidden Markov models (HMMs) for automatically segmenting and recognizing human facial expression from video sequences. The architecture automatically performs both segmentation and recognition of the facial expressions using a multi-level architecture composed of an HMM layer and a Markov model layer. We explore both person-dependent and person-independent recognition of expressions and compare the different methods using two databases.

1.   Introduction

In recent years there has been a growing interest in improving all aspects of the interaction between humans and computers. This emerging field has been a research interest for scientists from several different scholastic tracks, i.e., computer science, engineering, psychology, and neuroscience. These studies focus not only on improving computer interfaces, but also on improving the actions the computer takes based on feedback from the user. Feedback from the user has traditionally been given through the keyboard and mouse. Other devices have also been developed for more application specific interfaces, such as joysticks, trackballs, datagloves, and touch screens. The rapid advance of technology in recent years has made computers cheaper and more powerful, and has made the use of microphones and PC-cameras affordable and easily available. The microphones and cameras enable the computer to "see" and "hear," and to use this information to act. A good example of this is the "Smart-Kiosk" [Garg et al., 2000].

It is argued that to truly achieve effective human-computer intelligent interaction (HCII), there is a need for the computer to be able to interact naturally with the user, similar to the way human-human interaction takes place.

Human beings possess and express emotions in everyday interactions with others. Emotions are often reflected on the face, in hand and body gestures, and in the voice, to express our feelings or likings. While a precise, generally agreed upon definition of emotion does not exist, it is undeniable that emotions are an integral part of our existence. Facial expressions and vocal emotions are commonly used in everyday human-to-human communication, as one smiles to show greeting, frowns when confused, or raises one's voice when enraged. People do a great deal of inference from perceived facial expressions: "You *look* tired," or "You *seem* happy." The fact that we understand emotions and know how to react to other people's expressions greatly enriches the interaction. There is a growing amount of evidence showing that emotional skills are part of what is called "intelligence" [Salovey and Mayer, 1990; Goleman, 1995]. Computers today, on the other hand, are still quite "emotionally challenged." They neither recognize the user's emotions nor possess emotions of their own.

Psychologists and engineers alike have tried to analyze facial expressions in an attempt to understand and categorize these expressions. This knowledge can be for example used to teach computers to recognize human emotions from video images acquired from built-in cameras. In some applications, it may not be necessary for computers to recognize emotions. For example, the computer inside an automatic teller machine or an airplane probably does not need to recognize emotions. However, in applications where computers take on a social role such as an "instructor," "helper," or even "companion," it may enhance their functionality to be able to recognize users' emotions. In her book,

Picard [Picard, 1997] suggested several applications where it is beneficial for computers to recognize human emotions. For example, knowing the user's emotions, the computer can become a more effective tutor. Synthetic speech with emotions in the voice would sound more pleasing than a monotonous voice. Computer "agents" could learn the user's preferences through the users' emotions. Another application is to help the human users monitor their stress level. In clinical settings, recognizing a person's inability to express certain facial expressions may help diagnose early psychological disorders.

This chapter presents a real time automatic facial expression recognition system using video input developed at University of Illinois at Urbana-Champaign. We focus on the design of the classifiers used for performing the recognition following extraction of features using a real time face tracking system. We describe classification schemes in two types of settings: dynamic and 'static' classification.

The 'static' classifiers classify a frame in the video to one of the facial expression categories based on the tracking results of that frame. More specifically, we use Bayesian network classifiers and compare two different models: (1) Naive Bayes classifiers where the features are assumed to be either Gaussian or Cauchy distributed, and (2) Gaussian Tree-Augmented Naive (TAN) Bayes classifiers. The Gaussian Naive Bayes classifier is a standard classifier which has been used extensively in many classification problems. We propose changing the assumed distribution of the features from Gaussian to Cauchy because of the ability of Cauchy to account for heavy tail distributions. While Naive Bayes classifiers are often successful in practice, they use a very strict and often unrealistic assumption, that the features are independent given the class. We propose using the Gaussian TAN classifiers which have the advantage of modeling dependencies between the features without much added complexity compared to the Naive Bayes classifiers. TAN classifiers have an additional advantage in that the dependencies between the features, modeled as a tree structure, are efficiently learnt from data and the resultant tree structure is assured to maximize the likelihood function.

Dynamic classifiers take into account the temporal pattern in displaying facial expression. We first describe the hidden Markov model (HMM) based classifiers for facial expression recognition which have been previously used in recent works [Otsuka and Ohya, 1997a; Oliver et al., 1997; Lien, 1998]. We further advance this line of research and present a multi-level HMM classifier, combining the temporal information which allows not only to perform the classification of a video segment to the corresponding facial expression, as in the previous works on HMM based classifiers, but also to automatically segment an arbitrary long video sequence to the different expressions segments without resorting to heuristic methods of segmentation.

An important aspect is that while the static classifiers are easier to train and implement, the dynamic classifiers require more training samples and many more parameters to learn.

The rest of the chapter is organized as follows. Section 7.2 introduces the emotion recognition studies and presents the facial expression recognition state-of-the-art. In Section 7.3 we briefly describe the real-time face tracking system and the features extracted for classification of facial expressions. Section 7.4 describes the Bayesian network classifiers used for classifying frames in the video sequence to the different expressions. In Section 7.5 we describe HMM based classifiers for facial expression recognition from presegmented video sequences and introduce the multi-level HMM classifier for both recognizing facial expression sequences and automatically segmenting the video sequence. We perform experiments for all the described methods using two databases in Section 7.6. The first is a database of subjects displaying facial expressions collected by Chen [Chen, 2000]. The second is the Cohn-Kanade database [Kanade et al., 2000]. We have concluding remarks in Section 7.7.

2.   Emotion Recognition

There is little agreement about a definition of emotion and many theories of emotion have been proposed. Some of these could not be verified until recently when measurement of some physiological signals became available. In general, emotions are short-term, whereas moods are long-term, and temperaments or personalities are very long-term [Jenkins et al., 1998]. A particular mood may sustain for several days, and a temperament for months or years. Finally, emotional disorders can be so disabling that people affected are no longer able to lead normal lives.

Darwin [Darwin, 1890] held an ethological view of emotional expressions, arguing that the expressions from infancy and lower life forms exist in adult humans. Following the *Origin of Species* he wrote *The Expression of the Emotions in Man and Animals*. According to him, emotional expressions are closely related to survival. Thus in human interactions, these nonverbal expression are as important as the verbal interaction. James [James, 1890] viewed emotions not as *causes* but as *effects*. Situations arise around us which cause changes in physiological signals. According to James, "the bodily changes follow directly the perception of the exciting fact, and that our feeling of the same changes as they occur *is* the emotion." Carl Lange proposed a similar theory independently at around the same time. This is often referred to as the "James-Lange" theory of emotion. Cannon [Cannon, 1927], contrary to James, believed that emotions are first felt, then exhibited outwardly causing certain behaviors.

2.1 Judgment Studies

Despite these diverse theories, it is evident that people display expressions to various degrees. One frequently studied task is the judgment of emotions—how well can human observers tell the emotional expressions of others, in the voice, on the face, etc? Related questions are: Do these represent their true emotions? Can they be convincingly portrayed? How well can people conceal their emotions? In such tasks, researchers often use two different methods to describe the emotions.

One approach is to label the emotions in discrete categories, i.e., human judges must choose from a prescribed list of word labels, such as *joy, fear, love, surprise, sadness*, etc. One problem with this approach is that the stimuli may contain blended emotions. Also the choice of words may be too restrictive, or culturally dependent.

Another way is to have multiple dimensions or scales to describe emotions. Instead of choosing discrete labels, observers can indicate their impression of each stimulus on several continuous scales, for example, pleasant–unpleasant, attention–rejection, simple–complicated, etc. Two common scales are valence and arousal. Valence describes the pleasantness of the stimuli, with positive (or pleasant) on one end, and negative (or unpleasant) on the other. For example, *happiness* has a positive valence, while *disgust* has a negative valence. The other dimension is arousal or activation. For example, *sadness* has low arousal, whereas *surprise* has high arousal level. The different emotional labels could be plotted at various positions on a two-dimensional plane spanned by these two axes to construct a 2D emotion model [Lang, 1995]. Scholsberg [Schlosberg, 1954] suggested a three-dimensional model in which he had *attention–rejection* in addition to the above two.

Another interesting topic is how the researchers managed to obtain data for observation. Some people used posers, including professional actors and non-actors. Others attempted to induce emotional reactions by some clever means. For example, Ekman showed stress-inducing film of nasal surgery in order to get the disgusted look on the viewers' faces. Some experimenter even dumped water on the subjects or fired blank shots to induce surprise, while others used clumsy technicians who made rude remarks to arouse fear and anger [Hilgard et al., 1971]. Obviously, some of these are not practical ways of acquiring data. After studying acted and natural expressions, Ekman concluded that expressions can be convincingly portrayed [Ekman, 1982].

2.2 Review of Facial Expression Recognition

Since the early 1970s, Paul Ekman and his colleagues have performed extensive studies of human facial expressions [Ekman, 1994]. They found evidence to support universality in facial expressions. These "universal facial expressions" are those representing happiness, sadness, anger, fear, surprise, and disgust. They studied facial expressions in different cultures, including preliterate cultures, and found much commonality in the expression and recognition of emotions on the face. However, they observed differences in expressions as well, and proposed that facial expressions are governed by "display rules" in different social contexts. For example, Japanese subjects and American subjects showed similar facial expressions while viewing the same stimulus film. However, in the presence of authorities, the Japanese viewers were more reluctant to show their real expressions. Babies seem to exhibit a wide range of facial expressions without being taught, thus suggesting that these expressions are innate [Izard, 1994].

Ekman and Friesen [Ekman and Friesen, 1978] developed the Facial Action Coding System (FACS) to code facial expressions where movements on the face are described by a set of action units (AUs). Each AU has some related muscular basis. Figure 7.1 shows some of the key facial muscles on the face [Faigin, 1990]. The muscle movements (contractions) produce facial expressions. For example, the *corrugator* is also known as the "frowning muscle," *zygomatic major* is responsible for smiling, and *lavator labii superioris* produces "sneering." Table 7.1 lists some example action units. Each facial expression may be described by a combination of AUs. This system of coding facial expressions is done manually by following a set prescribed rules. The inputs are still images of facial expressions, often at the peak of the expression. This process is very time-consuming.

Table 7.1.   Some example action units [Ekman and Friesen, 1978].

AU number	FACS name	Muscular basis
1	Inner brow raiser	Frontalis, pars medialis
2	Outer brow raiser	Frontalis, pars lateralis
5	Upper lid raiser	Levator palpebrae superioris
11	Nasolabial furrow	Zygomatic minor
12	Lip corner puller	Zygomatic major
20	Lip stretcher	Risorious

Ekman's work inspired many researchers to analyze facial expressions by means of image and video processing. By tracking facial features and measuring the amount of facial movement, they attempt to categorize different facial expressions. Recent work on facial expression analysis and recognition [Mase, 1991; Ueki et al., 1994; Lanitis et al., 1995; Black and Yacoob, 1995; Rosenblum et al., 1996; Essa and Pentland, 1997; Otsuka and Ohya, 1997a; Donato et al., 1999; Lien, 1998; Nefian and Hayes, 1999; Martinez, 1999; Oliver et al., 2000] has used these "basic expressions" or a subset of them. In [Pantic and

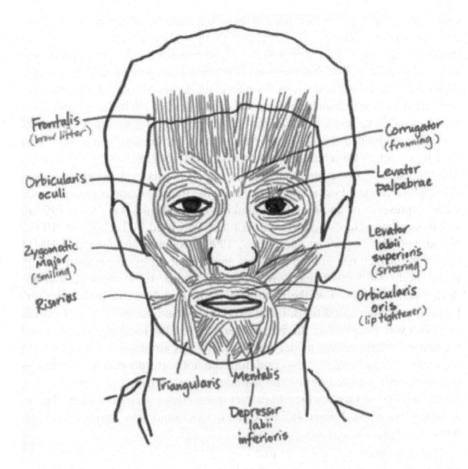

Figure 7.1. Some key facial muscles (adapted from [Faigin, 1990]).

Rothkrantz, 2000], Pantic and Rothkrantz provide an in depth review of many of the research done in automatic facial expression recognition in recent years.

The work in computer-assisted quantification of facial expressions did not start until the 1990s. Mase [Mase, 1991] used optical flow (OF) to recognize facial expressions. He was one of the first to use image processing techniques to recognize facial expressions. Lanitis et al. [Lanitis et al., 1995] used a flexible shape and appearance model for image coding, person identification, pose recovery, gender recognition, and facial expression recognition. Black and Yacoob [Black and Yacoob, 1995] used local parameterized models of image motion to recover non-rigid motion. Once recovered, these parameters were used as inputs to a rule-based classifier to recognize the six basic facial expressions. Yacoob and Davis [Yacoob and Davis, 1996] computed optical flow and used similar rules to classify the six facial expressions. Rosenblum, Yacoob, and Davis [Rosenblum et al., 1996] also computed optical flow of regions on the face, then applied a radial basis function network to classify expressions. Essa and Pentland [Essa and Pentland, 1997] used an optical flow region-based method to recognize expressions. Donato et al. [Donato et al., 1999] tested different features for recognizing facial AUs and inferring the facial expression in the frame. Otsuka and Ohya [Otsuka and Ohya, 1997a] first computed optical flow, then computed the 2D Fourier transform coefficients, which were used as feature vectors for a hidden Markov model (HMM) to classify expressions. The trained system was able to recognize one of the six expressions near real-time (about 10 Hz). Furthermore, they used the tracked motions to control the facial expression of an animated Kabuki system [Otsuka and Ohya, 1997b]. A similar approach, using different features, was used by Lien [Lien, 1998]. Nefian and Hayes [Nefian and Hayes, 1999] proposed an embedded HMM approach for face recognition that uses an efficient set of observation vectors based on the DCT coefficients. Martinez [Martinez, 1999] introduced an indexing approach based on the identification of frontal face images under different illumination conditions, facial expressions, and occlusions. A Bayesian approach was used to find the best match between the local observations and the learned local features model and an HMM was employed to achieve good recognition even when the new conditions did not correspond to the conditions previously encountered during the learning phase. Oliver et al. [Oliver et al., 2000] used lower face tracking to extract mouth shape features and used them as inputs to an HMM based facial expression recognition system (recognizing neutral, happy, sad, and an open mouth).

These methods are similar in that they first extract some features from the images, then these features are used as inputs into a classification system, and the outcome is one of the preselected emotion categories. They differ mainly in the features extracted from the video images and in the classifiers used to distinguish between the different emotions.

Another interesting aspect to point out is commonly confused categories in the six basic expressions. As reported by Ekman, *anger* and *disgust* are commonly confused in judgment studies. Also, *fear* and *surprise* are commonly confused. The reason why these confusions occur is because they share many similar facial actions [Ekman and Friesen, 1978]. *Surprise* is sometimes mistaken for *interest*, but not the other way around. In the computer recognition studies, some of these are observed [Black and Yacoob, 1995; Yacoob and Davis, 1996].

As mentioned in the Section 7.1, the classifiers used can either be 'static' classifiers or dynamic ones. Static classifiers use feature vectors related to a single frame to perform classification (e.g., Neural networks, Bayesian networks, linear discriminant analysis). Temporal classifiers try to capture the temporal pattern in the sequence of feature vectors related to each frame such as the HMM based methods of [Otsuka and Ohya, 1997a; Lien, 1998; Oliver et al., 2000].

3. Face Tracking and Feature Extraction

The real time facial expression recognition system (see Figure 7.2) is composed of a face tracking algorithm which outputs a vector of motion features of certain regions of the face. The features are used as inputs to a classifier. The face tracker is based on a system developed by Tao and Huang [Tao and Huang, 1998] called the Piecewise Bezier Volume Deformation (PBVD) tracker.

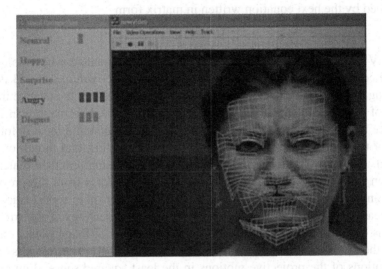

Figure 7.2. A snap shot of the realtime facial expression recognition system. On the right side is a wireframe model overlayed on a face being tracked. On the left side the correct expression, Angry, is detected (the bars show the relative probability of Angry compared to the other expressions). The example is from Cohn-Kanade database [Kanade et al., 2000].

This face tracker uses a model-based approach where an explicit 3D wireframe model of the face is constructed. In the first frame of the image sequence, landmark facial features such as the eye corners and mouth corners are selected interactively. The generic face model is then warped to fit the selected facial features. The face model consists of 16 surface patches embedded in Bezier volumes. The surface patches defined this way are guaranteed to be continuous and smooth. The shape of the mesh can be changed by changing the locations of the control points in the Bezier volume. Before describing the Bezier volume, we begin with the Bezier curve.

Given a set of $n+1$ control points $\mathbf{b}_0, \mathbf{b}_1, \ldots, \mathbf{b}_n$, the corresponding Bezier curve (or Bernstein-Bezier curve) is given by

$$\mathbf{x}(u) = \sum_{i=0}^{n} \mathbf{b}_i B_i^n(u) = \sum_{i=0}^{n} \mathbf{b}_i \binom{n}{i} u^i (1-u)^{n-i} \tag{7.1}$$

where the shape of the curve is controlled by the control points $\mathbf{b}_i$ and $u \in [0, 1]$. As the control points are moved, a new shape is obtained according to the Bernstein polynomials $B_i^n(u)$ in Equation (7.1). The displacement of a point on the curve can be described in terms of linear combinations of displacements of the control points.

The Bezier volume is a straight-forward extension of the Bezier curve and is defined by the next equation written in matrix form

$$\mathbf{V} = \mathbf{BD}, \tag{7.2}$$

where $\mathbf{V}$ is the displacement of the mesh nodes, $\mathbf{D}$ is a matrix whose columns are the control point displacement vectors of the Bezier volume, and $\mathbf{B}$ is the mapping in terms of Bernstein polynomials. In other words, the change in the shape of the face model can be described in terms of the deformations in $\mathbf{D}$.

Once the model is constructed and fitted, head motion and local deformations of the facial features such as the eyebrows, eyelids, and mouth can be tracked. First the 2D image motions are measured using template matching between frames at different resolutions. Image templates from the previous frame and from the very first frame are both used for more robust tracking. The measured 2D image motions are modeled as projections of the true 3D motions onto the image plane. From the 2D motions of many points on the mesh, the 3D motion can be estimated by solving an overdetermined system of equations of the projective motions in the least squared sense. Figure 7.3 shows four frames of tracking result with the meshes overlaid on the face.

The recovered motions are represented in terms of magnitudes of some predefined motion of various facial features. Each feature motion corresponds to a simple deformation on the face, defined in terms of the Bezier volume control parameters. We refer to these motions vectors as Motion-Units (MU's). Note that they are similar but not equivalent to Ekman's AU's and are numeric in nature, representing not only the activation of a facial region, but also the direction and intensity of the motion. The MU's used in the face tracker are shown in Figure 7.4 and are described in Table 7.2.

Each facial expression is modeled as a linear combination of the MU's:

$$\mathbf{V} = \mathbf{B} \left[\mathbf{D}_0 \mathbf{D}_1 \ldots \mathbf{D}_m \right] \begin{bmatrix} p_0 \\ p_1 \\ \vdots \\ p_m \end{bmatrix} = \mathbf{BDP} \tag{7.3}$$

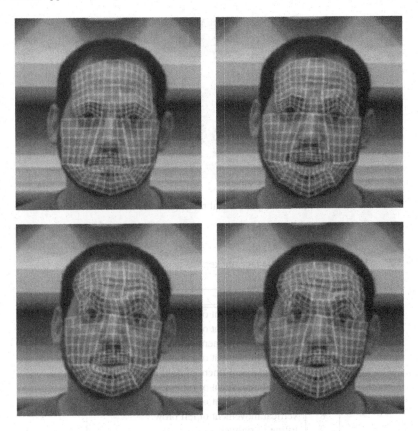

Figure 7.3. The wireframe model overlaid on a face being tracked

where each of the $\mathbf{D}_i$ corresponds to an MU, and the p_i are the corresponding magnitudes (or coefficients) of each deformation. The overall motion of the head and face is

$$\mathbf{R}(\mathbf{V}_0 + \mathbf{BDP}) + \mathbf{T} \qquad (7.4)$$

where $\mathbf{R}$ is the 3D rotation matrix, $\mathbf{T}$ is the 3D translation matrix, and $\mathbf{V}_0$ is the initial face model.

The MU's are used as the basic features for the classification scheme described in the next sections.

4. The Static Approach: Bayesian Network Classifiers

Bayesian networks can represent joint distributions in an intuitive and efficient way; as such, Bayesian networks are naturally suited for classification. We can use a Bayesian network to compute the posterior probability of a set of

Figure 7.4. The facial motion measurements

Table 7.2. Motion units used in the face tracker.

MU	Description
1	vertical movement of the center of upper lip
2	vertical movement of the center of lower lip
3	horizontal movement of left mouth corner
4	vertical movement of left mouth corner
5	horizontal movement of right mouth corner
6	vertical movement of right mouth corner
7	vertical movement of right brow
8	vertical movement of left brow
9	lifting of right cheek
10	lifting of left cheek
11	blinking of right eye
12	blinking of left eye

labels given the observable *features*, and then we classify the features with the most probable label.

A few conventions are adopted throughout. The goal here is to label an incoming vector of *features* (MUs) **X**. Each instantiation of **X** is a *record*. We assume that there exists a *class variable* C; the values of C are the *labels*, one of the facial expressions. The classifier receives a record x and generates a label $\hat{c}(\mathbf{x})$. An optimal classification rule can be obtained from the exact distribution $p(C, \mathbf{X})$. However, if we do not know this distribution, we have to learn it from expert knowledge or data.

For recognizing facial expression using the features extracted from the face tracking system, we consider probabilistic classifiers that represent the a-posteriori probability of the class given the features, $p(C, \mathbf{X})$, using Bayesian networks [Pearl, 1988]. A Bayesian network is composed of a directed acyclic graph in which every node is associated with a variable X_i and with a conditional distribution $p(X_i|\Pi_i)$, where Π_i denotes the parents of X_i in the graph. The directed acyclic graph is the *structure*, and the distributions $p(X_i|\Pi_i)$ represent the *parameters* of the network.

Typically, Bayesian network classifiers are learned with a fixed structure – the paradigmatic example is the Naive Bayes classifier. More flexible learning methods allow Bayesian network classifiers to be selected from a small subset of possible structures – for example, the Tree-Augmented-Naive-Bayes structures [Friedman et al., 1997]. After a structure is selected, the parameters of the classifier are usually learned using maximum likelihood estimation.

Given a Bayesian network classifier with parameter set Θ, the optimal classification rule under the maximum likelihood (ML) framework to classify an observed feature vector of n dimensions, $\mathbf{X} \in R^n$, to one of $|C|$ class labels, $c \in \{1, ..., |C|\}$, is given as:

$$\hat{c} = \underset{c}{argmax}\ P(\mathbf{X}|c; \Theta) \qquad (7.5)$$

There are two design decisions when building Bayesian network classifiers. The first is to choose the structure of the network, which will determine the dependencies among the variables in the graph. The second is to determine the distribution of the features. The features can be discrete, in which case the distributions are probability mass functions. The features can also be continuous, in which case one typically has to choose a distribution, with the most common being the Gaussian distribution. Both these design decisions determine the parameter set Θ which defines the distribution needed to compute the decision function in Equation (7.5)). Designing the Bayesian network classifiers for facial expression recognition is the focus of this section.

4.1   Continuous Naive-Bayes: Gaussian and Cauchy Naive Bayes Classifiers

Naive Bayes classifier is a probabilistic classifier in which the features are assumed independent given the class. Naive-Bayes classifiers have a very good record in many classification problems, although the independence assumption is usually violated in practice. The reason for the Naive-Bayes success as a classifier is attributed to the small number of parameters needed to be estimated. Recently, Garg and Roth [Garg and Roth, 2001] showed using information theoretic arguments additional reasons for the success of Naive-Bayes classifiers. An example of a Naive Bayes classifier is given in Figure 7.5.

If the features in $\mathbf{X}$ are assumed to be independent of each other conditioned upon the class label c (the Naive Bayes framework), Eq. (7.5) reduces to:

$$\hat{c} = \underset{c}{argmax} \prod_{i=1}^{n} P(x_i|c; \Theta) \qquad (7.6)$$

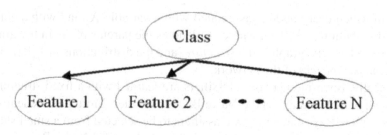

Figure 7.5. An example of a Naive Bayes classifier.

Now the problem is how to model $P(x_i|c; \Theta)$, which is the probability of fea-
ture x_i given the class label. In practice, the common assumption is that we
have a Gaussian distribution and the ML can be used to obtain the estimate
of the parameters (mean and variance). However, we showed that the Gaussian assumption is often invalid and we proposed the Cauchy distribution as an
alternative model. This model is referred to as *Cauchy Naive Bayes*.

The difficulty of this model is in estimating the parameters of the Cauchy
distribution. For this we used the procedure presented in Section 2.6.1.

The Naive-Bayes classifier was successful in many applications mainly due
to its simplicity. Also, this type of classifier is working well even if there is not
too much training data. However, the strong independence assumption may
seem unreasonable in some cases. Therefore, when sufficient training data is
available we want to learn and to use the dependencies present in the data.

4.2   Beyond the Naive-Bayes Assumption: Finding Dependencies among Features Using a Gaussian TAN Classifier

The goal of this section is to provide a way to search for a structure that
captures the dependencies among the features. Of course, to attempt to find
all the dependencies is an NP-complete problem. So, we restrict ourselves to
a smaller class of structures called the Tree-Augmented-Naive Bayes (TAN)
classifiers. TAN classifiers have been introduced by Friedman et al. [Friedman
et al., 1997] and are represented as Bayesian networks. The joint probability
distribution is factored to a collection of conditional probability distributions
of each node in the graph.

In the TAN classifier structure the class node has no parents and each feature
has as parents the class node and at most one other feature, such that the result
is a tree structure for the features (see Figure 7.6). Friedman et al. [Friedman
et al., 1997] proposed using the TAN model as a classifier, to enhance the
performance over the simple Naive-Bayes classifier. TAN models are more
complicated than the Naive-Bayes, but are not fully connected graphs. The

existence of an efficient algorithm to compute the best TAN model makes it a good candidate in the search for a better structure over the simple NB.

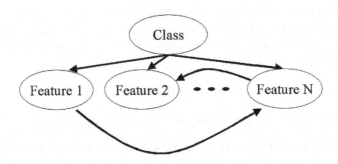

Figure 7.6. An example of a TAN classifier.

Learning the TAN classifier is more complicated. In this case, we do not fix the structure of the Bayesian network, but we try to find the TAN structure that maximizes the likelihood function given the training data out of all possible TAN structures.

In general, searching for the best structure has no efficient solution, however, searching for the best TAN structure does have one. The method is using the modified Chow-Liu algorithm [Chow and Liu, 1968] for constructing tree augmented Bayesian networks [Friedman et al., 1997]. The algorithm finds the tree structure among the features that maximizes the likelihood of the data by computation of the pairwise class conditional mutual information among the features and building a maximum weighted spanning tree using the pairwise mutual information as the weights of the arcs in the tree. The problem of finding a maximum weighted spanning is defined as finding the set of arcs connecting the features such that the resultant graph is a tree and the sum of the weights of the arcs is maximized. There have been several algorithms proposed for building a maximum weighted spanning tree [Cormen et al., 1990] and in our implementation we use the Kruskal algorithm described in Box 7.1.

The five steps of the TAN algorithm are described in Box 7.2. This procedure ensures to find the TAN model that maximizes the likelihood of the data we have. The algorithm is computed in polynomial time ($O(n^2 log N)$, with N being the number of instances and n the number of features).

The learning algorithm for the TAN classifier as proposed by Friedman et al. [Friedman et al., 1997] relies on computations of the class conditional mutual information of discrete features. In our problem the features are continuous, and computation of the mutual information for a general distribution is very complicated. However, if we assume that the features are Gaussian, computation of the conditional mutual information is feasible and is given by (see

Box 7.1 (Kruskal's Maximum Weighted Spanning Tree Algorithm)

Consider an undirected graph with n vertices and m edges, where each edge (u, v) connecting the vertices u and v, has an associated positive weight $w_{(u,v)}$. To construct the maximum weighted spanning tree graph follow the following steps:

1 Create an empty set of edges called *spanningTree*.

2 For each vertex v in the graph, create a set containing v.

3 Sort all edges in the graph using the weights in the edges from highest to lowest.

4 In order of the sorted edges, for each edge (u, v) if the set that contains u is different from the set that contains v:

   ■ Put the edge (u, v) in *spanningTree*

   ■ Make u and v belong to the same set (union of sets).

5 *spanningTree* contains all the edges in the maximum weighted spanning tree.

Box 7.2 (TAN learning algorithm)

1 Compute the class conditional pair-wise mutual information between each pair of features, (X_i, X_j) for all $i, j \in \{1, ..., n\}$,

$$I_P(X_i, X_j|C) = \sum_{X_i, X_j, C} P(x_i, x_j, c) \log \frac{P(x_i, x_j|c)}{P(x_i|c)P(x_j|c)}, i \neq j.$$

2 Build a complete undirected graph in which each vertex is a variable, and the weight of each edge is the mutual information computed in Step 1.

3 Build a maximum weighted spanning tree (MWST) (see Box 7.1).

4 Transform the undirected MWST of Step 3 to a directed graph by choosing a root node and pointing the arrows of all edges away from the root.

5 Make the class node the parent of all the feature nodes in the directed graph of Step 4.

Box 7.3 for details):

$$I(X_i, X_j | C) = -\frac{1}{2} \sum_{c=1}^{|C|} P(C = c) \log(1 - \rho_{(ij)|c}^2), \qquad (7.7)$$

where $\rho_{(ij)|c}$ is the correlation coefficient between X_i and X_j given the class label c. We replace the expression for the mutual information in Step 1 of the TAN algorithm with the expression in Equation (7.7), to find the maximum likelihood Gaussian-TAN classifier.

The full joint distribution of the Gaussian-TAN model can be written as:

$$p(c, x_1, x_2, ..., x_n) = p(c) \prod_{i=1}^{n} p(x_i | \Pi_i, c), \qquad (7.8)$$

where Π_i is the feature that is the additional parent of feature x_i. Π_i is empty for the root feature in the directed tree graph of Step 4 in the Kruskal's algorithm.

Using the Gaussian assumption, the probability density functions (pdf's) of the distribution in the product above are:

$$p(X_i = x_i | \Pi_i, C = c) = N_c(\mu_{x_i} + a \cdot \Pi_i, \sigma_{x_i}^2 \cdot (1 - \rho^2)), \qquad (7.9)$$

where $N_c(\mu, \sigma^2)$ refers to the Gaussian distribution with mean and variance given that the class is c, $\mu_{x_i}, \sigma_{x_i}^2$ are the mean and variance of the feature x_i,

$$\rho = \frac{COV(x_i, \Pi_i)}{\sigma_{x_i} \sigma_{\Pi_i}}$$

is the correlation coefficient between x_i and Π_i, and

$$a = \frac{COV(x_i, \Pi_i)}{\sigma_{\Pi_i}^2}.$$

For further details on the derivation of the parameters see Box 7.3.

After learning the structure, the Gaussian-TAN classifier's added complexity compared to the Naive Bayes classifier is small; there are $|C| \cdot (n - 1)$ extra parameters to estimate (the covariances between features and their parents). For learning the structure, all pairwise mutual information are estimated using the estimates for the covariances.

5. The Dynamic Approach: Expression Recognition Using Multi-level HMMs

As discussed in Section 7.1, the second approach to perform classification of video sequences to facial expression is the dynamic approach. The dynamic

Box 7.3 (Gaussian-TAN Parameters Computation)

The mutual information between continuous random variables, X, Y is given as:

$$I(X,Y) = \int \int p(x,y) \log \left(\frac{p(x,y)}{p(x)p(y)} \right) dxdy = H(x) + H(y) - H(x,y)$$

where $H(\cdot)$ is the differential entropy, analogous to the entropy of discrete variables, defined as:

$$H(Z) = - \int p(z) \log p(z) dz. \tag{7.10}$$

Here $p(z)$ is the probability density function of Z and the integral is over all dimensions in z.

For a Gaussian random vector Z of N dimensions with covariance matrix Σ, by inserting the Gaussian pdf to Eq. (7.10) and taking the integral, we get that the differential entropy of Z is:

$$H(Z) = \frac{1}{2} \log \left((2\pi e)^N |\Sigma| \right) \tag{7.11}$$

where $|\Sigma|$ is the determinant of Σ.

Suppose now that X and Y are jointly Gaussian. Then,

$$p(X,Y) \sim N \left(\begin{bmatrix} \mu_X \\ \mu_Y \end{bmatrix}, \Sigma_{XY} \right) \tag{7.12}$$

where Σ_{XY} is the covariance matrix given as:

$$\Sigma_{XY} = \begin{bmatrix} \sigma_X^2 & COV(X,Y) \\ COV(X,Y) & \sigma_Y^2 \end{bmatrix}. \tag{7.13}$$

Using Eqs. (7.11) and (7.10) we get that the mutual information of X and Y is given by:

$$I(X,Y) = -\frac{1}{2} \log \left(\frac{\sigma_X^2 \sigma_Y^2}{\sigma_X^2 \sigma_Y^2 - COV(X,Y)^2} \right)$$

$$= -\frac{1}{2} \log \left(\frac{1}{1 - \frac{COV(X,Y)^2}{\sigma_X^2 \sigma_Y^2}} \right) = -\frac{1}{2} \log \left(\frac{1}{1 - \rho_{XY}^2} \right) \tag{7.14}$$

where $\rho_{XY} = \frac{COV(X,Y)^2}{\sigma_X^2 \sigma_Y^2}$ is the correlation coefficient between X and Y.

In the TAN classifiers, the class is the parent of all features, and the features are Gaussian given a class label. Thus all the results above apply with an understanding that the distributions are conditioned on the class label (which is omitted for clarity). The class conditional mutual information between the pair X and Y is derived as follows:

$$
\begin{aligned}
I(X, Y | C) &= \sum_{c=1}^{|C|} \int \int p(x, y, c) \log \left(\frac{p(x, y | c)}{p(x | c) p(y | c)} \right) dx dy \\
&= \sum_{c=1}^{|C|} \int \int p(c) p(x, y | c) \log \left(\frac{p(x, y | c)}{p(x | c) p(y | c)} \right) \\
&= \sum_{c=1}^{|C|} p(c) I(X, Y | C = c) \\
&= -\frac{1}{2} \sum_{c=1}^{|C|} p(c) \log \left(\frac{1}{1 - \rho_{XY|c}^2} \right)
\end{aligned}
\tag{7.15}
$$

After finding the TAN structure, suppose that we find that feature X is the parent of Y. Given the class label, X and Y are jointly Gaussian with mean vector and covariance as defined in Eqs. (7.12) and (7.13) (again omitting the conditioning on the class variable for clarity). Since X is the parent of Y, we are interested in finding the parameters of the conditional distribution $p(Y | X)$ as a function of the parameters of the joint distribution. Because X and Y are jointly Gaussian, $Y | X$ is also Gaussian. Using $p(X, Y) = p(X) p(Y | X)$ and the Gaussian pdf, after some manipulations we get:

$$
\begin{aligned}
p(Y | X) &= \frac{p(X, Y)}{p(X)} \\
&= \frac{1}{(2\pi \sigma_Y^2 (1 - \rho_{XY}^2))^{1/2}} \exp \left(-\frac{(y - \mu_Y - ax)^2}{2\sigma_Y^2 (1 - \rho_{XY}^2)} \right) \\
&= N \left(\mu_Y + ax, \sigma_Y^2 (1 - \rho_{XY}^2) \right)
\end{aligned}
\tag{7.16}
$$

where $a = \frac{COV(X,Y)}{\sigma_X^2}$.

approach uses classifiers that can use temporal information to discriminate different expressions. The logic behind using the temporal information is that expressions have a unique temporal pattern. When recognizing expressions from video, using the temporal information can lead to more robust and accurate classification results compared to methods that are 'static'.

The method we present automatically segments the video to the different facial expression sequences, using a multi-level HMM structure. The first level of the architecture is comprised of independent HMMs related to the different emotions. This level of HMMs is very similar to the one used in [Lien, 1998], [Oliver et al., 1997], and [Otsuka and Ohya, 1997a] who used the likelihood of a given sequence in a ML classifier to classify a given video sequence. Instead of classifying using the output of each HMM, we use the state sequence of the HMMs as the input of the higher level Markov model. This is meant to segment the video sequence, which is the main problem facing the previous works using HMM's for expression recognition. Moreover, this also increases the discrimination between the classes since it tries to find not only the probability of each the sequence displaying one emotion, but also the probability of the sequence displaying one emotion and not displaying all the other emotions at the same time.

5.1   Hidden Markov Models

Hidden Markov models have been widely used for many classification and modeling problems. Perhaps the most common application of HMM is in speech recognition [Rabiner and Juang, 1983]. One of the main advantages of HMMs is their ability to model nonstationary signals or events. Dynamic programming methods allow one to align the signals so as to account for the non stationarity. However, the main disadvantage of this approach is that it is very time-consuming since all of the stored sequences are used to find the best match. The HMM finds an implicit time warping in a probabilistic parametric fashion. It uses the transition probabilities between the hidden states and learns the conditional probabilities of the observations given the state of the model. In the case of emotion expression, the signal is the measurements of the facial motion. This signal is non stationary in nature, since an expression can be displayed at varying rates, with varying intensities even for the same individual.

An HMM is given by the following set of parameters:

$$
\begin{aligned}
\lambda &= (A, B, \pi) \\
a_{ij} &= P(q_{t+1} = S_j | q_t = S_i), 1 \le i, j \le N \\
B &= \{b_j(O_t)\} = P(O_t | q_t = S_j), 1 \le j \le N \\
\pi_j &= P(q_1 = S_j)
\end{aligned}
$$

where A is the state transition probability matrix, B is the observation probability distribution, and π is the initial state distribution. The number of states of the HMM is given by N. It should be noted that the observations (O_t) can be either discrete or continuous, and can be vectors. In the discrete case, B becomes a matrix of probability entries (Conditional Probability Table), and in the continuous case, B will be given by the parameters of the probability distribution function of the observations (normally chosen to be the Gaussian distribution or a mixture of Gaussians). Given an HMM there are three basic problems that are of interest. The first is how to efficiently compute the probability of the observations given the model. This problem is related to classification in the sense that it gives a measure of how well a certain model describes an observation sequence. The second is how to find the corresponding state sequence in some optimal way, given a set of observations and the model. This will become an important part of the algorithm to recognize the expressions from live input and will be described later in this paper. The third is how to learn the parameters of the model λ given the set of observations so as to maximize the probability of observations given the model. This problem relates to the learning phase of the HMMs which describe each facial expression sequence. A comprehensive tutorial on HMMs is given by Rabiner [Rabiner, 1989].

5.2   Expression Recognition Using Emotion-Specific HMMs

Since the display of a certain facial expression in video is represented by a temporal sequence of facial motions it is natural to model each expression using an HMM trained for that particular type of expression. There will be six such HMMs, one for each expression: {*happy(1), angry(2), surprise(3), disgust(4), fear(5), sad(6)*}. There are several choices of model structure that can be used. The two main models are the left-to-right model and the ergodic model. In the left-to-right model, the probability of going back to the previous state is set to zero, and therefore the model will always start from a certain state and end up in an 'exiting' state. In the ergodic model every state can be reached from any other state in a finite number of time steps. In [Otsuka and Ohya, 1997a], Otsuka and Ohya used left-to-right models with three states to model each type of facial expression. The advantage of using this model lies in the fact that it seems natural to model a sequential event with a model that also starts from a fixed starting state and always reaches an end state. It also involves fewer parameters and therefore is easier to train. However, it reduces the degrees of freedom the model has to try to account for the observation sequence. There has been no study to indicate that the facial expression sequence is indeed modeled well by the left-to-right model. On the other hand, using the ergodic HMM allows more freedom for the model to account for the observation sequences, and in fact, for an infinite amount of training data it can be shown that the ergodic model will reduce to the left-to-right model, if that is indeed the true model. In this work both types of models were tested with various numbers of states in an attempt to study the best structure that can model facial expressions.

The observation vector O_t for the HMM represents continuous motion of the facial action units. Therefore, B is represented by the probability density functions (pdf) of the observation vector at time t given the state of the model. The Gaussian distribution is chosen to represent these pdf's, i.e.,

$$B = \{b_i(O_t)\} \sim N(\mu_j, \Sigma_j), 1 \le j \le N \qquad (7.17)$$

where μ_j and Σ_j are the mean vector and full covariance matrix, respectively.

The parameters of the model of emotion-expression specific HMM are learned using the well-known Baum-Welch reestimation formulas (see [Levinson et al., 1983] for details of the algorithm). For learning, hand labeled sequences of each of the facial expressions are used as ground truth sequences, and the Baum algorithm is used to derive the maximum likelihood (ML) estimation of the model parameters (λ).

Parameter learning is followed by the construction of a ML classifier. Given an observation sequence O_t, where $t \in (1, T)$, the probability of the observation given each of the six models $P(O_t|\lambda_j)$ is computed using the forward-backward procedure [Rabiner, 1989]. The sequence is classified as the emotion corresponding to the model that yielded the highest probability, i.e.,

$$c^* = \underset{1 \le c \le 6}{argmax}[P(O|\lambda_c)] \qquad (7.18)$$

5.3   Automatic Segmentation and Recognition of Emotions Using Multi-level HMM.

The main problem with the approach taken in the previous section is that it works on isolated facial expression sequences or on pre-segmented sequences of the expressions from the video. In reality, this segmentation is not available, and therefore there is a need to find an automatic way of segmenting the sequences. Concatenation of the HMMs representing phonemes in conjunction with the use of grammar has been used in many systems for continuous speech recognition. Dynamic programming for continuous speech has also been proposed in different researches. It is not very straightforward to try and apply these methods to the emotion recognition problem since there is no clear notion of language in displaying emotions. Otsuka and Ohya [Otsuka and Ohya, 1997a] used a heuristic method based on changes in the motion of several regions of the face to decide that an expression sequence is beginning and ending. After detecting the boundaries, the sequence is classified to one of the emotions using the emotion-specific HMM. This method is prone to errors because of the sensitivity of the classifier to the segmentation result. Although the result of the HMMs are independent of each other, if we assume that they model realistically the motion of the facial features related to each emotion, the combination of the state sequence of the six HMMs together can provide very useful information and enhance the discrimination between the different classes. Since we will use a left-to-right model (with return), the changing of the state sequence can have a physical attribute attached to it (such as opening and closing of mouth when smiling), and therefore there we can gain useful information from looking at the state sequence and using it to discriminate between the emotions at each point in time.

To solve the segmentation problem and enhance the discrimination between the classes, a different kind of architecture is needed. Figure (7.7) shows the architecture for automatic segmentation and recognition of the displayed expression at each time instance. The motion features are continuously used as input to the six emotion-specific HMMs. The state sequence of each of the HMMs is decoded and used as the observation vector for the high level Markov model. The high-level Markov model consists of seven states, one for each of the six emotions and one for *neutral*. The *neutral* state is necessary as for the large portion of time, there is no display of emotion on a person's face. In this implementation of the system, the transitions between emotions are imposed to pass through the *neutral* state since our training data consists of facial expression sequences that always go through the *neutral* state.

It is possible (although less likely) for a person to go from one expression to another without passing through a neutral expression, as has been reported in [Otsuka and Ohya, 1997a]. Handling such cases is done by slightly modifying the high level HMM of Figure 7.7. We simply have to set the transition probabilities of passing from all states to all states to values higher than zero (which appears as arcs between the different states of the expressions in the high-level HMM).

The recognition of the expression is done by decoding the state that the high-level Markov model is in at each point in time since the state represents the displayed emotion.

The training procedure of the system is as follows:

- Train the emotion-specific HMMs using a hand segmented sequence as described in the previous section.

- Feed all six HMMs with the continuous (labeled) facial expression sequence. Each expression sequence contains several instances of each facial expression with *neutral* instances separating the emotions.

- Obtain the state sequence of each HMM to form the six-dimensional observation vector of the higher-level Markov model, i.e., $O_t^h = [q_t^{(1)}, ..., q_t^{(6)}]^T$,

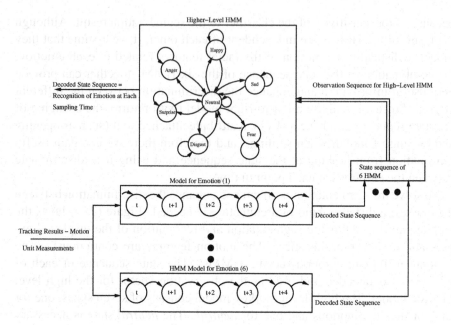

Figure 7.7. Multilevel HMM architecture for automatic segmentation and recognition of emotion.

where $q_t^{(i)}$ is the state of the ith emotion-specific HMM. The decoding of the state sequence is done using the Viterbi algorithm [Rabiner, 1989].

■ Learn the probability observation matrix for each state of the high-level Markov model using $P(q_j^{(i)}|S_k) = \{$expected frequency of model i being in state j given that the true state was $k\}$, and

$$B^{(h)} = \{b_k(O_t^h)\} = \left\{ \prod_{i=1}^{6}(P(q_j^{(i)}|S_k) \right\} \tag{7.19}$$

where $j \in (1, Number\ of\ States\ for\ Lower\ Level\ HMM)$.

■ Compute the transition probability $A = \{a_{kl}\}$ of the high-level HMM using the frequency of transiting from each of the six emotion classes to the *neutral* state in the training sequences and from the *neutral* state to the other emotion states. For notation, the *neutral* state is numbered 7 and the other states are numbered as in the previous section. All the transition probabilities could also be set using expert knowledge, and not necessarily from training data.

■ Set the initial probability of the high level Markov model to be 1 for the *neutral* state and 0 for all other states. This forces the model to always start at the *neutral* state and assumes that a person will display a *neutral* expression in the beginning of any video sequence. This assumption is made just for simplicity of the testing.

The steps followed during the testing phase are very similar to the ones followed during training. The face tracking sequence is used as input into the lower-level HMMs and a decoded state sequence is obtained using the Viterbi algorithm. The decoded lower-level state sequence O_t^h is used as input to the higher-level HMM and the observation probabilities are computed using Eq. (7.19). Note that in this way of computing the probability, it is assumed that the state sequences of the lower-level HMMs are independent given the true labeling of the sequence. This assumption is reasonable since the HMMs are trained independently and on different training sequences. In addition, without this assumption, the size of B will be enormous, since it will have to account for all possible combinations of states of the six lower-level HMMs, and it would require a huge amount of training data.

Using the Viterbi algorithm again for the high level Markov model, a most likely state sequence is produced. The state that the HMM was in at time t corresponds to the expressed emotion in the video sequence at time t. To make the classification result robust to undesired fast changes, a smoothing of the state sequence is done by preserving the actual classification result if the HMM did not stay in a particular state for more than T times, where T can vary between 1 and 15 samples (assuming a 30-Hz sampling rate). The introduction of the smoothing factor T will cause a delay in the decision of the system, but of no more than T sample times.

6. Experiments

In order to test the algorithms described in the previous sections we use two different databases, a database collected by Chen [Chen, 2000] and the Cohn-Kanade [Kanade et al., 2000] AU code facial expression database.

The first is a database of subjects that were instructed to display facial expressions corresponding to the six types of emotions. The data collection method is described in detail in [Chen, 2000]. All the tests of the algorithms are performed on a set of five people, each one displaying six sequences of each one of the six emotions, and always coming back to a neutral state between each emotion sequence. The restriction of coming back to the neutral state after each emotion was imposed for the sake of simplicity in labeling the sequence. However, as mentioned in the previous section the system is also able to deal with the situation where a person can go from one expression to another without passing through a neutral expression.

Each video sequence was used as the input to the face tracking algorithm described in Section 7.3. The sampling rate was 30 Hz, and a typical emotion sequence is about 70 samples long (~2s). Figure 7.8 shows one frame of each emotion for each subject.

The data was collected in an open recording scenario, where the person was asked to display the expression corresponding to the emotion being induced. This is of course not the ideal way of collecting emotion data. The ideal way would be using a hidden recording, inducing the emotion through events in the normal environment of the subject, not in a studio. The main problem with collecting the data this way is the impracticality of it and the ethical issue of hidden recording.

We use this database in two types of experiments. First we performed person dependent experiments, in which part of the data for each subject was used as training data, and another part as test data. Second, we performed person independent experiments, in which we used the data of all but one person as training data, and tested on the person that was left out.

For the TAN classifiers we used the dependencies shown in Figure 7.9, learned using the algorithm described in Section 7.4.2. The arrows are from parents to children MUs. From the tree structure we see that the TAN learning algorithm produced a structure in which the bottom half of the face is almost disjoint from the top portion, except for a weak link between MU 4 and MU 11.

For the HMM-based models, several states were tried (3-12) and both the ergodic and left-to-right with return were tested. The results presented below are of the best configuration (an ergodic model using 11 states), determined using cross-validation over the training set.

The Cohn-Kanade database [Kanade et al., 2000] consists of expression sequences of subjects, starting from a Neutral expression and ending in the peak of the facial expression. There are 104 subjects in the database. Because for some of the subjects, not all of the six facial expressions sequences were available to us, we used a subset of 53 subjects, for which at least four of the sequences were available. For each person there are on average 8 frames for each expression, which makes insufficient data to perform person dependent tests. Also, the fact that each sequence ends in the peak of the facial expression makes the use of our dynamic multi-level HMM classifier impractical since in this case each sequence counts for an incomplete temporal pattern. In these conditions, we only used this database for performing person independent tests using the static Bayesian network classifiers.

A summary of both databases is presented in Table 7.3.

For the frame based methods (NB-Gaussian, NB-Cauchy, and TAN), we measure the accuracy with respect to the classification result of each frame, where each frame in the video sequence was manually labeled to one of the expressions (including neutral). This manual labeling can introduce some 'noise' in the classification because the boundary between Neutral and the expression

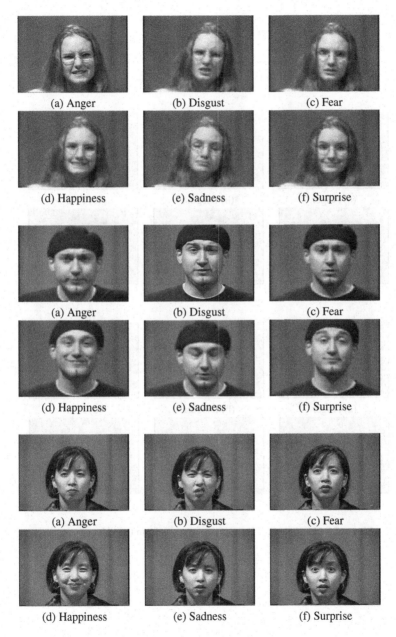

Figure 7.8. Examples of images from the video sequences.

(a) Anger   (b) Disgust   (c) Fear

(d) Happiness   (e) Sadness   (f) Surprise

(a) Anger   (b) Disgust   (c) Fear

(d) Happiness   (e) Sadness   (f) Surprise

Figure 7.8 (continued).   Examples of images from the video sequences.

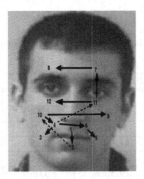

Figure 7.9. The learned TAN structure for the facial features. Dashed lines represent links that are relatively weaker than the others.

of a sequence is not necessarily optimal, and frames near this boundary might cause confusion between the expression and the Neutral. A different labeling scheme is to label only some of the frames that are around the peak of the expression leaving many frames in between unlabeled. We did not take this approach because a real-time classification system would not have this information available to it. The accuracy for the temporal based methods is measured with respect to the misclassification rate of an expression sequence, not with respect to each frame.

6.1 Results Using the Chen Database

6.1.1 Person-Dependent Tests

A person-dependent test is first tried. Tables 7.4 and 7.5 show the recognition rate of each subject and the average recognition rate of the classifiers. The fact that subject 5 was poorly classified can be attributed to the inaccurate tracking result and lack of sufficient variability in displaying the emotions. It can also be seen that the multilevel HMM achieves similar recognition rate (and improves it in some cases) compared to the emotion-specific HMM, even though the input is unsegmented continuous video.

Table 7.3. Summary of the databases

Database	Subjects	Sequences per expression	Sequences per subject per expression	average frames per expression
Chen DB	5	30	6	70
Cohn-Kanade DB	53	53	1	8

Table 7.4. Person-dependent facial expression recognition accuracies using frame based methods.

Subject	NB-Gaussian	NB-Cauchy	TAN
1	80.97%	81.69%	85.94%
2	87.09%	84.54%	89.39%
3	82.5%	83.05%	86.58%
4	77.18%	79.25%	82.84%
5	69.06%	71.74%	71.78%
Average	79.36%	80.05%	83.31%

Table 7.5. Person-dependent facial expression recognition rates using the emotion-specific HMM and multilevel HMM.

Subject	Single HMM	Multilevel HMM
1	82.86%	80%
2	91.43%	85.71%
3	80.56%	80.56%
4	83.33%	88.89%
5	54.29%	77.14%
Average	78.49%	82.46%

The NB-Cauchy assumption does not give a significant improvement in recognition rate comparing with the NB-Gaussian assumption mainly due to the fact that in this case there are not many outliers in the data (we train and test with sequences of the same person in the same environment). This may not be the case in a natural setting experiment. Note that only in the case of subject 2 the Gaussian assumption gave better results than the Cauchy assumption. This result can be attributed to the fact that this subject shows the expressions in a more consistent way over time and this counts fewer outliers in the recorded data. It is also important to observe that taking into account the dependencies in the features (the TAN model) gives significantly improved results. In average the best results are obtained by TAN followed by the NB-Cauchy and NB-Gaussian.

The confusion matrix for the TAN classifier is presented in Table 7.6. The analysis of the confusion between different emotions shows that most of the confusion of the classes is with the Neutral class. This can be attributed to the arbitrary labeling of each frame in the expression sequence. The first and last few frames of each sequence are very close to the Neutral expression and thus are more prone to become confused with it. We also see that most expression do not confuse with Happy.

Table 7.6. Person-dependent confusion matrix using the TAN classifier

Emotion	Neutral	Happy	Anger	Disgust	Fear	Sad	Surprise
Neutral	<u>79.58</u>	1.21	3.88	2.71	3.68	5.61	3.29
Happy	1.06	<u>87.55</u>	0.71	3.99	2.21	1.71	2.74
Anger	5.18	0	<u>85.92</u>	4.14	3.27	1.17	0.30
Disgust	2.48	0.19	1.50	<u>83.23</u>	3.68	7.13	1.77
Fear	4.66	0	4.21	2.28	<u>83.68</u>	2.13	3.00
Sad	13.61	0.23	1.85	2.61	0.70	<u>80.97</u>	0
Surprise	5.17	0.80	0.52	2.45	7.73	1.08	<u>82.22</u>

The confusion matrices for the HMM based classifiers (described in details in [Cohen, 2000]) show similar results, with *happiness* achieving near 100%, and *surprise* approximately 90%.

6.1.2   Person-Independent Tests

In the previous section it was seen that a good recognition rate was achieved when the training sequences were taken from the same subject as the test sequences. A more challenging application is to create a system which is person-independent. In this case the variation of the data is more significant and we expect that using a Cauchy-based classifier we will obtain significantly better results.

For this test all of the sequences of one subject are used as the test sequences and the sequences of the remaining four subjects are used as training sequences. This test is repeated five times, each time leaving a different person out (leave one out cross validation). Table 7.7 shows the recognition rate of the test for all classifiers. In this case the recognition rates are lower compared with the person-dependent results. This means that the confusions between subjects are larger than those within the same subject.

Table 7.7. Recognition rate for person-independent test.

Classifier	NB-Gaussian	NB-Cauchy	TAN	Single HMM	Multilevel HMM
Recognition rate	60.23%	64.77%	66.53%	55.71%	58.63%

In this case the TAN classifier provides the best results. It is important to observe that the Cauchy assumption also yields a larger improvement compared to the Gaussian classifier, due to the capability of the Cauchy distribution to handle outliers. One of the reasons for the misclassifications is the fact that the subjects are very different from each other (three females, two males, and different ethnic backgrounds); hence, they display their emotion differently. Although it appears to contradict the universality of the facial expressions as studied by Ekman and Friesen [Ekman and Friesen, 1978], the results show that for practical automatic emotion recognition, consideration of gender and race play a role in the training of the system.

Table 7.8 shows the confusion matrix for the the TAN classifier. We see that Happy, Fear, and Surprise are detected with high accuracy, and other expressions are greatly confused mostly with Neutral. Here the differences in the intensity of the expressions among the different subjects played a significant role in the confusion among the different expressions.

Table 7.8.   Person-independent average confusion matrix using the TAN classifier

Emotion	Neutral	Happy	Anger	Disgust	Fear	Sad	Surprise
Neutral	<u>76.95</u>	0.46	3.39	3.78	7.35	6.53	1.50
Happy	3.21	<u>77.34</u>	2.77	9.94	0	2.75	3.97
Anger	14.33	0.89	<u>62.98</u>	10.60	1.51	9.51	0.14
Disgust	6.63	8.99	7.44	<u>52.48</u>	2.20	10.90	11.32
Fear	10.06	0	3.53	0.52	<u>73.67</u>	3.41	8.77
Sad	13.98	7.93	5.47	10.66	13.98	<u>41.26</u>	6.69
Surprise	4.97	6.83	0.32	7.41	3.95	5.38	<u>71.11</u>

6.2   Results Using the Cohn-Kanade Database

For this test we first divided the database in 5 sets which contain the sequences corresponding to 10 or 11 subjects (three sets with 11 subjects, two sets with 10 subjects). We used the sequences from a set as test sequences and the remaining sequences were used as training sequences. This test was repeated five times, each time leaving a different set out (leave one out cross validation). Table 7.9 shows the recognition rate of the test for all classifiers. Note that the results obtained with this database are much better than the ones obtained with the Chen database. This is because in this case we have more training data. For training we had available the data from more than 40 different persons. Therefore, the learnt model is more accurate and can achieve better classification rates when using the test data.

In average the best results were obtained using the TAN followed by NB-Cauchy and NB-Gaussian which is consistent with the results obtained with the Chen database.

Table 7.9. Recognition rate for Cohn-Kanade database.

Classifier	NB-Gaussian	NB-Cauchy	TAN
Recognition rate	67.03%	68.14%	73.22%

The confusion matrix for the TAN classifier is presented in Table 7.10. In this case, Surprise was detected with over 93% accuracy and Happy with over 86% accuracy. The other expressions are greatly confused with each other.

Emotion	Neutral	Happy	Anger	Disgust	Fear	Sad	Surprise
Neutral	78.59	1.03	3.51	8.18	1.85	5.78	1.03
Happy	0	86.22	4.91	5.65	3.19	0	0
Anger	2.04	4.76	66.46	14.28	5.21	6.09	1.14
Disgust	3.40	1.13	10.90	62.27	10.90	9.09	2.27
Fear	1.19	13.57	7.38	7.61	63.80	3.80	1.90
Sad	5.55	1.58	13.25	11.19	3.96	61.26	3.17
Surprise	0	0	0	0	2.02	4.04	93.93

Table 7.10. Person-independent average confusion matrix using the TAN classifier

7. Summary and Discussion

In this chapter we presented several methods for expression recognition from video. The intention was to perform an extensive evaluation of different methods using static and dynamic classification.

In the case of static classifiers the idea was to classify each frame of a video to one of the facial expressions categories based on the tracking results of that frame. The classification in this case was done using Bayesian networks classifiers. We showed that there are two design decisions for building such classifiers: (1) determining the distribution of the features and (2) choosing the structure of the network which determines the dependencies among the features.

We first presented Naive Bayes classifiers which assumed that the features are independent given the class. The common assumption is that we have Gaussian distribution for the features but we showed that in practice using the Cauchy distribution we obtained improved classification results. The problem with the Naive Bayes approach is that the independence assumption is not justified in this case because the facial motion measurements are highly correlated when humans display emotions. Therefore, the next effort was in developing another classifier that took into account these dependencies among features. We used the TAN classifier and showed a method to search for the optimal TAN structure when the features were assumed to be Gaussian. We showed that after learning the structure from data, the Gaussian-TAN classifier added only small complexity to the Naive Bayes approach and improved significantly the classification results.

A legitimate question here is, "Is it always possible to learn the TAN structure from the data and use it in classification?" Provided that there is sufficient training data, the TAN structure indeed can be extracted and used in classification. However, when the data is insufficient the learnt structure is unreliable and the use of the Naive Bayes classifier is recommended. Note also that in the Naive Bayes approach one can use a better distribution assumption than the Gaussian (e.g. Cauchy) while in TAN this would be extremely difficult.

In the case of dynamic classifiers the temporal information was used to discriminate different expressions. The idea is that expressions have a unique temporal pattern and recognizing these patterns can lead to improved classification results. We introduced the multi-level HMM architecture and compared it to the straight forward Emotion-specific HMM. We showed that comparable results can be achieved with this architecture, although it does not rely on any pre-segmentation of the video stream.

When one should use a dynamic classifier versus a static classifier? This is a difficult question to ask. It seems, both from intuition and from the results, that dynamic classifiers are more suited for systems that are person dependent due to their higher sensitivity not only to changes in appearance of expressions among different individuals, but also to the differences in temporal patterns. Static classifiers are easier to train and implement, but when used on a continuous video sequence, they can be unreliable especially for frames that are not at the peak of an expression. Another important aspect is that the dynamic classifiers are more complex, therefore they require more training samples and many more parameters to learn compared with the static approach. A hybrid of classifiers using expression dynamics and static classification is the topic of future research.

An important problem in the facial expression analysis field is the lack of agreed upon benchmark datasets and methods for evaluating performance. A well-defined and commonly used database is a necessary prerequisite to compare the performances of different methods in an objective manner. The Cohn-Kanade database is a step in this direction, although there is still a need for an agreement on how to measure performance: frame based classification, sequence based classification and even the number and names of the classes. The large deviations in the reported performance of different methods surveyed by Pantic and Rothkrantz [Pantic and Rothkrantz, 2000] demonstrate the need to resolve these issues. As a consequence, it is hard to compare our results with the one reported in the literature and assert superiority or inferiority of our methods over others.

Are these recognition rates sufficient for real world use? We think that it depends upon the particular application. In the case of image and video retrieval from large databases, the current recognition rates could aid in finding the right image or video by giving additional options for the queries. Moreover, the integration of multiple modalities such as voice analysis and context would be expected to improve the recognition rates and eventually improve the computer's understanding of human emotional states. Voice and gestures are widely believed to play an important role as well [Chen, 2000; De Silva et al., 1997], and physiological states such as heart beat and skin conductivity are being suggested [Cacioppo and Tassinary, 1990]. People also use context as an indicator of the emotional state of a person.

References

Abramowitz, A. and Stegun, I.A. (1972). *Handbook of Mathematical Functions with Formulas, Graphs, and Mathematical Tables*. Dover Publications.

Aggarwal, J.K. and Nandhakumar, N. (1988). On the computation of motion from sequences of images - A review. *Proceedings of IEEE*, 76(8):917–933.

Aigrain, P. (1987). Organizing image banks for visual access: Model and techniques. *International Meeting for Optical Publishing and Storage*, pages 257–270.

Akaike, H. (1973). Information theory and an extension of the maximum likelihood principle. *2nd International Symposium on Information Theory*, pages 267–281.

Aloimonos, Y. (1988). Visual shape computation. *Proceedings of IEEE*, 76(8):899–916.

Amini, A.A., Tehrani, S., and Weymouth, T.E. (1988). Using dynamic programming for minimizing the energy of active contours in the presence of hard constraints. *International Conference on Computer Vision*, pages 95–99.

Attneave, F. (1954). Some informational aspects of visual perception. *Psychological Review*, 61:183–193.

Barnard, S. and Fischler, M. (1982). Computational stereo. *ACM Computing Surveys*, 14(4):553–572.

Barnard, S. and Fischler, M. (1987). Stereo vision. *Encyclopedia of Artificial Intelligence, New York: John Wiley*, pages 422–438.

Barron, J.L., Fleet, D.J., and Beauchemin, S.S. (1994). Performance of optical flow techniques. *International Journal of Computer Vision*, 12(1):43–77.

Beck, J., Sutter, A., and Ivry, A. (1987). Spatial frequency channels and perceptual grouping in texture segregation. *Computer Vision, Graphics, and Image Processing*, 37:299–325.

Bergen, J.R. and Adelson, E.H. (1988). Early vision and texture perception. *Nature*, 333:363–364.

Berman, A. and Sapiro, L.G. (1997). Efficient image retrieval with multiple distance measures. *SPIE, Storage and Retrieval for Image/Video Databases*, 3022:12–21.

Bhat, D.N. and Nayar, S.K. (1998). Ordinal measures for image correspondence. *IEEE Transactions on Pattern Analysis and Machine Intelligence*, 20(4):415–423.

Black, M.J. (September 1992). *Robust Incremental Optical Flow*. PhD thesis, Yale University.

Black, M.J. and Yacoob, Y. (1995). Tracking and recognizing rigid and non-rigid facial motions using local parametric models of image motion. *International Conference on Computer Vision*, pages 374–381.

Boie, R. and Cox, I. (1992). An analysis of camera noise. *IEEE Transactions on Pattern Analysis and Machine Intelligence*, 14(6):671–674.

Bolles, R.C., Baker, H.H., and Hannah, M.J. (1993). The JISCT stereo evaluation. *ARPA Image Understanding Workshop*, pages 263–274.

Boufama, B. and Mohr, R. (1995). Epipole and fundamental matrix estimation using visual parallax. *International Conference on Computer Vision*, pages 1030–1036.

Bovik, A., Clarke, M., and Geisler, W. (1990). Multichannel texture analysis using localized spatial filters. *IEEE Transactions on Pattern Analysis and Machine Intelligence*, 12(1):55–73.

Box, G.E.P. (1953). Non-normality and test on variances. *Biometrika*, 40:318–335.

Boyle, E., Anderson, A.H., and Newlands, A. (1994). The effects of visibility on dialog in a cooperative problem solving task. *Language and speech*, 37(1):1–20.

Boynton, R.M. (1990). Human color perception. *Science of Vision, Leibovic, K.N., ed.*, pages 211–253.

Bregler, C., Manke, S., Hild, H., and Waibel, A. (1993). Improving connected letter recognition by lipreading. In *IEEE International Conference on Acoustics, Speech, and Signal Processing*, pages 557–560.

Brodatz, P. (1966). *Textures: A Photographic Album for Artists and Designers*. Dover Publications.

Cacioppo, J.T. and Tassinary, L.G. (1990). Inferring psychological significance from physiological signals. *American Psychologist*, 45:16–28.

Caelli, T., Julesz, B., and Gilbert, E. (1978). On perceptual analyzers underlying visual texture discrimination: Part II. *Biological Cybernetics*, 29(4):201–214.

Campbell, F.W. and Robson, J.G. (1968). Application of Fourier analysis to the visibility of gratings. *Journal of Physiology*, 197:551–566.

Cannon, W. B. (1927). The James-Lange theory of emotion: A critical examination and an alternative theory. *American Journal of Psychology*, 39:106–124.

Chang, N.S. and Fu, K.S. (1980). Query by pictorial example. *IEEE Transactions on Software Engineering*, 6(6):519–524.

Chang, T. and Kuo, C. (1993). Texture analysis and classification with tree-structured wavelet transform. *IEEE Transactions on Image Processing*, 2(4):429–441.

Chaudhuri, B., Sarkar, N., and Kundu, P. (1993). Improved fractal geometry based texture segmentation technique. *Proceedings of IEE*, 140:233–241.

Chen, L.S. (2000). *Joint processing of audio-visual information for the recognition of emotional expressions in human-computer interaction*. PhD thesis, University of Illinois at Urbana-Champaign, Dept. of Electrical Engineering.

Chen, S., Keller, J., and Crownover, R. (1990). Shape from fractal geometry. *Artificial Intelligence*, 43:199–218.

Chow, C.K. and Liu, C.N. (1968). Approximating discrete probability distribution with dependence trees. *IEEE Transactions on Information Theory*, 14:462–467.

Clark, M. and Bovik, A. (1987). Texture segmentation using Gabor modulation/demodulation. *Pattern Recognition Letters*, 6:261–267.

Cohen, I. (2000). Automatic facial expression recognition from video sequences using temporal information. In *MS Thesis*, University of Illinois at Urbana-Champaign, Dept. of Electrical Engineering.

Cohen, I., Sebe, N., Garg, A., and Huang, T.S. (2003). Facial expression recognition from video sequences: Temporal and static modeling. *to appear in Computer Vision and Image Understanding*.

Cohen, I., Sebe, N., Garg, A., Lew, M.S., and Huang, T.S. (2002). Facial expression recognition from video sequences. *IEEE International Conference on Multimedia and Expo*, II:121–124.

Cohen, L. (1991). On active contour models and balloons. *Computer Vision, Graphics, and Image Processing: Image Understanding*, 53:211–218.

Cohen, L. and Cohen, I. (1993). Finite-element methods for active contours models and balloons for 2-D and 3-D images. *IEEE Transactions on Pattern Analysis and Machine Intelligence*, 15:1131–1147.

Comaniciu, D., Meer, P., Xu, K., and Tyler, D. (1999). Performance improvement through low rank corrections. In *IEEE Workshop on Content-based Access of Image and Video Libraries*, pages 50–54.

Cormen, T.H., Leiserson, C.E., and Rivest, R.L. (1990). *Introduction to algorithms*. MIT Press, Cambridge, MA.

Cornsweet, T. N., editor (1970). *Visual Perception*. Academic Press.

Cox, I., Hingorani, S., and Rao, S. (1996). A maximum likelihood stereo algorithm. *Computer Vision and Image Understanding*, 63(3):542–567.

Darwin, C. (1890). *The Expression of the Emotions in Man and Animals*. John Murray, London, 2nd edition.

Daugman, J. (1980). Two-dimensional spectral analysis of cortical receptive profile. *Vision Research*, 20:847–856.

Daugman, J. (1985). Uncertainty relation for resolution in space, spatial frequency and orientation optimized by two-dimensional visual cortical filters. *Journal of the Optical Society of America*, A 4:221–231.

Daugman, J. (1989). Entropy reduction and decorrelation in visual coding by oriented neural receptive fields. *IEEE Transactions on Biomedical Engineering*, 36(1):107–114.

Davis, L. (1977). Understanding shape: Angles and sides. *IEEE Transactions on Computers*, 26:236–242.

De Silva, L.C., Miyasato, T., and Natatsu, R. (1997). Facial emotion recognition using multimodal information. In *IEEE Int. Conf. on Information, Communications and Signal Processing (ICICS'97)*, pages 397–401.

De Valois, R.L., Albrecht, D.G., and Thorell, L.G. (1982). Spatial-frequency selectivity of cells in macaque visual cortex. *Vision Research*, 22:545–559.

Del Bimbo, A. (1999). *Visual Information Retrieval*. Morgan Kaufmann.

Del Bimbo, A. and Pala, P. (1997). Visual image retrieval by elastic matching of user sketches. *IEEE Transactions on Pattern Analysis and Machine Intelligence*, 19(2):121–132.

Devroye, L., Gyorfi, L., and Lugosi, G. (1996). *A Probabilistic Theory of Pattern Recognition*. Springer.

Dhond, U.R. and Aggarwal, J.K. (1989). Structure from stereo - A review. *IEEE Transactions on Systems, Man, and Cybernetics*, 19(6):1489–1510.

Donato, G., Bartlett, M.S., Hager, J.C., Ekman, P., and Sejnowski, T.J. (1999). Classifying facial actions. *IEEE Transactions on Pattern Analysis and Machine Intelligence*, 21(10):974–989.

Durikovic, R., Kaneda, K., and Yamashita, H. (1995). Dynamic contour: A texture approach and contour operations. *The Visual Computer*, 11:277–289.

Ekman, P., editor (1982). *Emotion in the Human Face*. Cambridge University Press, New York, NY, 2nd edition.

Ekman, P. (1994). Strong evidence for universals in facial expressions: A reply to Russell's mistaken critique. *Psychological Bulletin*, 115(2):268–287.

Ekman, P. and Friesen, W.V. (1978). *Facial Action Coding System: Investigator's Guide*. Consulting Psychologists Press, Palo Alto, CA.

Essa, I.A. and Pentland, A.P. (1997). Coding, analysis, interpretation, and recognition of facial expressions. *IEEE Transactions on Pattern Analysis and Machine Intelligence*, 19(7):757–763.

Faigin, G. (1990). *The Artist's Complete Guide To Facial Expression*. Watson-Guptill Publications, New York, NY.

Faugeras, O. (1993). *Three-Dimensional Computer Vision*. MIT Press.

Ferwerda, J.G. (1987). *The World of 3-D - A Practical Guide to Stereo Photography*. 3-D Book Productions.

Fischler, M.A. and Wolf, H.C. (1994). Locating perceptually salient points on planar curves. *IEEE Transactions on Pattern Analysis and Machine Intelligence*, 16(2):113–129.

Flicker, M., Sawhney, H., Niblack, W., Ashley, J., Huang, Q., Dom, B., Gorkani, M., Hafner, J., Lee, D., Petkovic, D., Steele, D., and Yanker, P. (1995). Query by image and video content: The QBIC system. *IEEE Computer*, 28(9):23–32.

Fridlund, A.J. (1991). Evolution and facial action in reflex, social motive, and paralanguage. *Biological Psychology*, 32:2–100.

Friedman, N., Geiger, D., and Goldszmidt, M. (1997). Bayesian network classifiers. *Machine Learning*, 29(2):131–163.

Frisby, J.P. and Pollard, S.B. (1991). Computational issues in solving the stereo correspondence problem. *Computational Models of Visual Processing, M.S. Landy and J.A. Movshon, eds.*, pages 331–357.

Fukunaga, K. (1972). *Introduction to Statistical Pattern Recognition*. Academic Press.

Fusiello, A., Roberto, V., and Trucco, E. (1997). Efficient stereo with multiple windowing. *IEEE Conference on Computer Vision and Pattern Recognition*, pages 858–863.

Fusiello, A., Roberto, V., and Trucco, E. (2000). Symmetric stereo with multiple windowing. *International Journal of Pattern Recognition and Artificial Intelligence*, 14(8):1053–1066.

Garg, A., Pavlovic, V., Rehg, J., and Huang, T.S. (2000). Audio–visual speaker detection using dynamic Bayesian networks. In *International Conference on Automatic Face and Gesture Recognition*, pages 374–471.

Garg, A. and Roth, D. (2001). Understanding probabilistic classifiers. In *European Conference on Machine Learning*, pages 179–191.

Gevers, T. and Smeulders, A. (1999). Color-based object recognition. *Pattern Recognition*, 32(3):453–464.

Gevers, T. and Smeulders, A. (2000). PicToSeek: Combining color and shape invariant features for image retrieval. *IEEE Transactions on Image Processing*, 20(1):102–119.

Gibson, J.J. (1950). *The perception of the visual world*. Houghton.

Goethe, J.W. (1840). *Farbenlehre*. Princeton University Press (reprinted 1988).

Goleman, D. (1995). *Emotional Intelligence*. Bantam Books, New York.

Gombrich, H.E. (1960). *Art and Illusion*. Phaidon Press.

Gorkani, M. and Picard, R. (1994). Texture orientation for sorting photos 'at a glance'. *International Conference on Pattern Recognition*, pages 459–464.

Granrath, D. (1981). The role of human visual models in image processing. *Proceedings of IEEE*, 69:552–561.

Green, R. (1976). Outlier-prone and outlier-resistant distributions. *Journal of the American Statistical Association*, 71(354):502–505.

Grimson, W. (1985). Computational experiments with a feature based stereo algorithm. *IEEE Transactions on Pattern Analysis and Machine Intelligence*, 7:17–34.

Gudivada, V.N. and Raghavan, V. (1995). Design and evaluation of algorithms for image retrieval by spatial similarity. *ACM Transactions on Information Systems*, 13(2):115–144.

Guelch, E. (1988). Results of test on image matching of ISPRS WG III/4. *International Archives of Photogrammetry and Remote Sensing*, 27(3):254–271.

Guillemin, V. and Pollack, A. (1974). *Differential topology*. Prentice Hall.

Gupta, A., Santini, S., and Jain, R. (1997). In search of information in visual media. *Communications of the ACM*, 12:34–42.

Gupta, S. and Prince, J. (1996). Stochastic models for DIV-CURL optical flow methods. *IEEE Signal Processing Letters*, 3(2):32–35.

Haas, G., Bain, L., and Antle, C. (1970). Inferences for the Cauchy distribution based on maximum likelihood estimators. *Biometrika*, 57(2):403–408.

Hafner, J., Sawhney, H., Equitz, W., Flicker, M., and Niblack, W. (1995). Efficient color histogram indexing for quadratic form distance functions. *IEEE Transactions on Pattern Analysis and Machine Intelligence*, 17(7):729–736.

Hampel, F.R., Ronchetti, E.M., Rousseeuw, P.J., and Stahel, W.A. (1986). *Robust Statistic: The Approach Based on Influence Functions*. John Wiley and Sons, New York.

Haralick, R. and Shapiro, L. (1993). *Computer and Robot Vision II*. Addison-Wesley.

Haralick, R.M. (1979). Statistical and structural approaches to texture. *Proceedings of IEEE*, 67:786–804.

Haralick, R.M., Shanmugam, K., and Dinstein, I. (1973). Textural features for image classification. *IEEE Transactions on Systems, Man, and Cybernetics*, 3(6):610–621.

Harwood, D., Ojala, T., Pietikainen, M., Kelman, S., and Davis, L. (1995). Texture classification by center-symmetric auto-correlation using Kullback discrimination of distributions. *Pattern Recognition Letters*, 16:1–10.

Hawkins, D.M. (1980). *Identification of Outliers*. Chapman and Hall.

Hebb, D.O. (1949). *The organization of behavior*. John Wiley.

Heisenberg, W. (1967). *Goethe's View of Nature and the World of Science and Technology*. Harper & Row (reprinted 1974).

Helmholtz, H. von (1962, P.C. Southall trans. and ed.). *Treatise on Physiological Optics*. Dover, New York.

Hilgard, E., Atkinson, R.C., and Hilgard, R.L. (1971). *Introduction to Psychology*. Harcourt Brace Jovanovich, New York, NY, 5th edition.

Hoff, W. and Ahuja, N. (1989). Surfaces from stereo: Integrating feature matching, disparity estimation, and contour detection. *IEEE Transactions on Pattern Analysis and Machine Intelligence*, 11(2):121–136.

Hoffman, D.D. and Richards, W.A. (1984). Parts of recognition. *Cognition*, 18:65–96.

Horaud, R. and Brady, M. (1988). On the geometric interpretation of image contours. *Artificial Intelligence*, 37:333–353.

Horn, B. and Schunck, B. (1981). Determining optical flow. *Artificial Intelligence*, 17:185–203.

Hu, M.K. (1962). Visual pattern recognition by moment invariants. *IRA Transactions on Information Theory*, 17-8(2):179–187.

Huang, J., Ravi Kumar, S., Mitra, M., Zhu, W., and Zabih, R. (1997). Image indexing using color correlogram. *IEEE Conference on Computer Vision and Pattern Recognition*, pages 762–768.

Huber, P.J. (1981). *Robust Statistics*. John Wiley and Sons, New York.

Huijsmans, D.P., Poles, S., and Lew, M.S. (1996). 2D pixel trigrams for content-based image retrieval. In *1st International Workshop on Image Databases and Multimedia Search*, pages 139–145.

Hunt, R.W.G. (1989). *Measuring Color*. Halsted Press, New York.

Ittelson, W.H. (1960). *Visual Space Perception*. Springer.

Izard, C.E. (1994). Innate and universal facial expressions: Evidence from developmental and cross-cultural research. *Psychological Bulletin*, 115(2):288–299.

Jain, A. (1989). *Fundamentals of digital image processing*. Prentice Hall.

Jain, A., Zhong, Y., and Lakshmanan, S. (1996). Object matching using deformable template. *IEEE Transactions on Pattern Analysis and Machine Intelligence*, 18:267–278.

Jain, A.K. and Vailaya, A (1996). Image retrieval using color and shape. *Pattern Recognition*, 29(8):1233–1244.

James, W. (1890). *The Principles of Psychology*. Henry Holt, New York, NY.

Jenkin, M.R. and Jepson, A.D. (1994). Recovering local surface structure through local phase difference measurements. *Computer Vision, Graphics, and Image Processing: Image Understanding*, 59(1):72–93.

Jenkins, J. M., Oatley, K., and Stein, N. L., editors (1998). *Human Emotions: A Reader*. Blackwell Publishers, Malden, MA.

Jones, D.G. and Malik, J. (1992). Computational framework for determining stereo correspondence from a set of linear spatial filters. *Image and Vision Computing*, 10:699–708.

Julesz, B. (1971). *Foundations of Cyclopean Perception*. University of Chicago Press.

Julesz, B. (1975). Experiments in the visual perception of texture. *Scientific American*, 232:34–43.

Julesz, B. (1981a). Textons, the elements of texture perception and their interactions. *Nature*, 290:91–97.

Julesz, B. (1981b). A theory of preattentive texture discrimination based on first-order statistics of textons. *Biological Cybernetics*, 41(2):131–138.

Julesz, B. (1995). *Dialogues on Perception*. MIT Press.

Julesz, B., Gilbert, E.N., Shepp, L.A., and Frisch, H.L. (1973). Inability of humans to discriminate between visual textures that agree in second-order statistics. *Perception*, 2:391–405.

Kailath, K. (1967). The divergence and Bhattachayya distance measures in signal selection. *IEEE Transactions on Communication Technology*, 15:52–60.

Kanade, T., Cohn, J., and Tian, Y. (2000). Comprehensive database for facial expression analysis.

Kanade, T. and Okutomi, M. (1994). A stereo matching algorithm with an adaptive window: Theory and experiment. *IEEE Transactions on Pattern Analysis and Machine Intelligence*, 16(9):920–932.

Kanade, T., Okutomi, M., and Nakahara, T. (1992). A multi-baseline stereo method. *ARPA Image Understanding Workshop*, pages 409–426.

Kass, M., Witkin, A., and Terzopoulos, D. (1988). Snakes: Active contour models. *International Journal of Computer Vision*, 1(4):321–331.

Kato, K. (1992). Database architecture for content-based image retrieval. *SPIE - Conference on Image Storage and Retrieval Systems*, 1662:112–123.

Katzir, N., Lindenbaum, M., and Porat, M. (1994). Curve segmentation under partial occlusion. *IEEE Transactions on Pattern Analysis and Machine Intelligence*, 16:513–519.

Kelly, P.M., Cannon, T.M., and Barros, J.E. (1996). Efficiency issues related to probability density function comparison. *SPIE - Storage and Retrieval for Image and Video Databases*, 2670(4):42–49.

Kelly, P.M., Cannon, T.M., and Hush, D.R. (1995). Query by image example: The CANDID approach. *SPIE - Storage and Retrieval for Image and Video Databases*, 2420:238–248.

Kendall, M.G. and Buckland, W.R. (1981). *A Dictionary of Statistical Terms*. Oliver and Boyd, Edinburgh, 4th ed.

Koenderink, J. (1984). The structure of images. *Biological Cybernetics*, 50:363–370.

Koenderink, J. and Van Doorn, A. (1986). Dynamic shape. *Biological Cybernetics*, 53:383–396.

Kullback, S. (1968). *Information Theory and Statistics*. Dover Publications.

Kundu, A. and Chen, J-L. (1992). Texture classification using QMF bank-based subband decomposition. *Computer Vision, Graphics, and Image Processing: Graphical Models and Image Processing*, 54(5):369–384.

Lang, P. (1995). The emotion probe: Studies of motivation and attention. *American Psychologist*, 50(5):372–385.

Lanitis, A., Taylor, C.J., and Cootes, T.F. (1995). A unified approach to coding and interpreting face images. In *International Conference on Computer Vision*, pages 368–373.

Laws, K.I. (1980). Textured energy measures. In *Image Understanding Workshop*, pages 47–51.

Layer, H. (1979). Stereoscopy: Where did it come from? Where will it lead? *Exposure*, 17(3):34–48.

Leroy, B., Herlin, I., and Cohen, L. (1996). Multi-resolution algorithms for active contour models. In *International Conference on Analysis and Optimization of Systems*, pages 58–65.

Levinson, S.E., Rabiner, L.R., and Sondhi, M.M. (1983). An introduction to the application of the theory of probabilistic functions of a Markov process to automatic speech recognition. *The Bell Lab System Technical Journal*, 62(4):1035–1072.

Lew, M., Huang, T., and Wong, K. (1994). Learning and feature selection in stereo matching. *IEEE Transactions on Pattern Analysis and Machine Intelligence*, 16(9):869–882.

Lew, M. and Sebe, N. (2000). Visual websearching using iconic queries. *IEEE Conference on Computer Vision and Pattern Recognition*, 2:788–789.

Lew, M., Sebe, N., and Huang, T.S. (2000). Improving visual matching. *IEEE Conference on Computer Vision and Pattern Recognition*, 2:58–65.

Leymarie, F. and Levine, M. (1993). Tracking deformable objects in the plane using an active contour model. *IEEE Transactions on Pattern Analysis and Machine Intelligence*, 15(6):617–634.

Leyton, M. (1987). Symmetry-curvature duality. *Computer Vision, Graphics, and Image Processing*, 38:327–341.

Leyton, M. (1989). Inferring causal history from shape. *Cognitive Science*, 13:357–387.

Lien, J. (1998). *Automatic recognition of facial expressions using hidden Markov models and estimation of expression intensity*. PhD thesis, Carnegie Mellon University.

Little, J.J. and Gillet, W.E. (1990). Direct evidence for occlusions in stereo and motion. *Image and Vision Computing*, 8(4):328–340.

Liu, F. and Picard, R. (1996). Periodicity, directionality, and randomness: Wold features for image modeling and retrieval. *IEEE Transactions on Pattern Analysis and Machine Intelligence*, 18(7):722–733.

Loncaric, S. (1998). A survey of shape analysis techniques. *Pattern Recognition*, 31(8):983–1001.

Loupias, E., Sebe, N., Bres, S., and Jolion, J-M. (2000). Wavelet-based salient points for image retrieval. In *IEEE International Conference on Image Processing*, volume 2, pages 518–521.

Lowe, D. G. (1985). *Perceptual organization and visual recognition*. Kluwer Academic.

Lowe, D. G. (1987). Three-dimensional object recognition from single two-dimensional images. *Artificial Intelligence*, 31:355–395.

Luo, W. and Maitre, H. (1990). Using surface model to correct and fit disparity data in stereo vision. *International Conference on Pattern Recognition*, 1:60–64.

Ma, W.Y. and Manjunath, B.S. (1995). A comparison of wavelet transform features for texture image annotation. *IEEE International Conference on Image Processing*, 2:256–259.

Ma, W.Y. and Manjunath, B.S. (1996). Texture features and learning similarity. *IEEE Conf. on Computer Vision and Pattern Recognition*, pages 425–430.

Ma, W.Y. and Manjunath, B.S. (1998). A texture thesaurus for browsing large aerial photographs. *Journal of the American Society for Information Science*, 49(7):633–648.

Maimone, M.W. (1996). *Characterizing Stereo Matching Problems using Local Spatial Frequency*. PhD thesis, Carnegie Mellon University.

Malik, J. and Rosenholtz, R. (1997). Computing local surface orientation and shape from texture for curved surfaces. *International Journal of Computer Vision*, 23(2):149–168.

Marr, D. (1976). Early processing of visual information. *Proc. Royal Society Lond.*, B275:483–519.

Marr, D. (1982). *Vision*. Freeman.

Marr, D. and Hildreth, E. (1980). Theory of edge detection. *Proc. Royal Society Lond.*, B207:187–217.

Marr, D. and Poggio, T. (1979). A computational theory of human stereo vision. *Proc. Royal Society Lond.*, B204:301–328.

Marshall, S. (1989). Review of shape coding techniques. *Image and Vision Computing*, 7(4):281–294.

Martinez, A (1999). Face image retrieval using HMMs. In *IEEE Workshop on Content-based Access of Images and Video Libraries*, pages 35–39.

Mase, K. (1991). Recognition of facial expression from optical flow. *IEICE Transactions*, E74(10):3474–3483.

Matthies, L.H. (1989). *Dynamic Stereo Vision*. PhD thesis, Carnegie Mellon University.

McInerney, T. and Terzopoulos, D. (1995). A dynamic finite element surface model for segmentation and tracking in multidimensional medical images with applications to cardiac 4d image analysis. *Computerized Medical Imaging and Graphics*, 19(1):69–83.

Mehrabian, A. (1968). Communication without words. *Psychology Today*, 2(4):53–56.

Mori, K.I., Kidode, M., and Asada, H. (1973). An iterative prediction and correction method for automatic stereo comparison. *Computer Graphics and Image Processing*, 2(3/4):393–401.

Morse, P.M. and Feshbach, H. (1953). *Methods of Theoretical Physics*. McGraw-Hill, New York.

Munsell, A.H. (1905). *A Color Notation*. Munsell Color, Baltimore (reprinted 1976).

Murase, H. and Nayar, S. (1995). Visual learning and recognition of 3D objects from appearance. *International Journal of Computer Vision*, 14(1):5–24.

Nefian, A. and Hayes, M. (1999). Face recognition using an embedded HMM. In *IEEE Conf. on Audio and Video-based Biometric Person Authentication*, pages 19–24.

Newton, I. (1704). *Optics*. Dover, New York (reprinted 1952).

Nieman, H. (1990). *Pattern Analysis and Understanding*. Springer Series in Information Sciences, Springer Verlag.

Ogle, V. and Stonebracker, M. (1995). Chabot: Retrieval from a relational database of images. *IEEE Computer*, 28(9):40–48.

Ohanian, P. and Dubes, R. (1992). Performance evaluation for four classes of textural features. *Pattern Recognition*, 25:819–833.

Ojala, T., Pietikainen, M., and Harwood, D. (1996). A comparative study of texture measures with classification based on feature distribution. *Pattern Recognition*, 29:51–59.

Oliver, N., Pentland, A., and Berard, F. (2000). LAFTER: A real-time face and lips tracker with facial expression recognition. *Pattern Recognition*, 33:1369–1382.

Oliver, N., Pentland, A.P., and Berard, F. (1997). LAFTER: Lips and face real time tracker. In *IEEE Conference on Computer Vision and Pattern Recognition*, pages 123–129.

Otsuka, T. and Ohya, J. (1997a). Recognizing multiple persons' facial expressions using HMM based on automatic extraction of significant frames from image sequences. In *IEEE International Conference on Image Processing*, pages 546–549.

Otsuka, T. and Ohya, J. (1997b). A study of transformation of facial expressions based on expression recognition from temporal image sequences. Technical report, Institute of Electronic, Information, and Communications Engineers (IEICE).

Pantic, M. and Rothkrantz, L.J.M. (2000). Automatic analysis of facial expressions: The state of the art. *IEEE Transactions on Pattern Analysis and Machine Intelligence*, 22(12):1424–1445.

Pearl, J. (1988). *Probabilistic Reasoning in Intelligent Systems: Networks of Plausible Inference*. Morgan Kaufmann, San Mateo, California.

Pentland, A. (1984). Fractal-based description of natural scenes. *IEEE Transactions on Pattern Analysis and Machine Intelligence*, 6:661–674.

Pentland, A. (1986). Perceptual organization and the representation of natural form. *Artificial Intelligence*, 28:293–331.

Pentland, A., Picard, R., and Sclaroff, S. (1996). Photobook: Content-based manipulation of image databases. *International Journal of Computer Vision*, 18:233–254.

Picard, R., Kabir, T., and Liu, F. (1993). Real-time recognition with the entire brodatz texture database. *IEEE Conference on Computer Vision and Pattern Recognition*, pages 638–639.

Picard, R. and Minka, T. (1995). Vision texture for annotation. *Multimedia Systems*, 3(1):3–14.

Picard, R.W. (1997). *Affective Computing*. MIT Press, Cambridge, MA.

Posner, M.I. (1989). *Foundations of Cognitive Science*. MIT Press.

Price, K. (1986). Anything you can do, I can do better (No you can't)... *Computer Vision, Graphics, and Image Processing*, 36:387–391.

Rabiner, L.R. (1989). A tutorial on hidden Markov models and selected applications in speech processing. *Proceedings of IEEE*, 77(2):257–286.

Rabiner, L.R. and Juang, B. (1983). *Fundamentals of Speech Recognition*. Prentice Hall.

Ramsey, M., Chen, H., Zhu, B., and Schatz, B. (1999). A collection of visual thesauri for browsing large collections of geographic images. *Journal of the American Society of Information Science*, 50(9):826–834.

Reed, T. and Du Buf, J. (1993). A review of recent texture segmentation and feature extraction techniques. *Computer Vision, Graphics, and Image Processing*, 57(3):359–373.

Rey, W. (1983). *Introduction to Robust and Quasi-Robust Statistical Methods*. Springer-Verlag.

Richards, W. and Polit, A. (1974). Texture matching. *Kybernetic*, 16:155–162.

Rissanen, J. (1978). Modeling by shortest data description. *Automatica*, 14:465–471.

Rosenblum, M., Yacoob, Y., and Davis, L.S. (1996). Human expression recognition from motion using a radial basis function network architecture. *IEEE Transactions on Neural Network*, 7(5):1121–1138.

Rousseeuw, P.J. and Leroy, A.M. (1987). *Robust Regression and Outlier Detection*. John Wiley and Sons, New York.

Russell, J.A. (1994). Is there universal recognition of emotion from facial expression? *Psychological Bulletin*, 115(1):102–141.

Salovey, P. and Mayer, J.D. (1990). Emotional intelligence. *Imagination, Cognition, and Personality*, 9(3):185–211.

Sanger, T.D. (1988). Stereo disparity computation using Gabor filters. *Biological Cybernetics*, 59:405–418.

Sawhney, H.S. and Hafner, J.L. (1994). Efficient color histogram indexing. In *IEEE International Conference on Image Processing*, volume 2, pages 66–70.

Schlosberg, H. (1954). Three dimensions of emotion. *Psychological Review*, 61:81–88.

Sclaroff, S. and Pentland, A. (1995). Modal matching for correspondence and recognition. *IEEE Transactions on Pattern Analysis and Machine Intelligence*, 17(6):545–561.

Sebe, N., Cohen, I., Garg, A., Lew, M.S., and Huang, T.S. (2002). Emotion recognition using a Cauchy naive Bayes classifier. *International Conference on Pattern Recognition*, I:17–20.

Sebe, N. and Lew, M.S. (1999a). Multi-scale sub-image search. *ACM Multimedia*, 2:79–82.

Sebe, N. and Lew, M.S. (1999b). Robust color indexing. *ACM Multimedia*, 1:239–242.

Sebe, N. and Lew, M.S. (2000a). Color based retrieval and recognition. *IEEE International Conference on Multimedia and Expo*, pages 311–314.

Sebe, N. and Lew, M.S. (2000b). A maximum likelihood investigation into color indexing. *Visual Interface*, pages 101–106.

Sebe, N. and Lew, M.S. (2000c). A maximum likelihood investigation into texture classification. *Asian Conference on Computer Vision*, pages 1094–1099.

Sebe, N. and Lew, M.S. (2000d). Wavelet-based texture classification. *International Conference on Pattern Recognition*, 3:959–962.

Sebe, N. and Lew, M.S. (2001a). Color-based retrieval. *Pattern Recognition Letters*, 22(2):223–230.

Sebe, N. and Lew, M.S. (2001b). Texture features for content-based retrieval. *Principles of Visual Information Retrieval, M.S. Lew, ed.*, pages 51–85.

Sebe, N., Lew, M.S., and Huijsmans, D.P. (1998). Which ranking metric is optimal? with applications in image retrieval and stereo matching. *International Conference on Pattern Recognition*, pages 265–271.

Sebe, N., Lew, M.S., and Huijsmans, D.P. (2000a). Toward improved ranking metrics. *IEEE Transactions on Pattern Analysis and Machine Intelligence*, 22(10):1132–1141.

Sebe, N., Tian, Q., Loupias, E., Lew, M.S., and Huang, T.S. (2000b). Color indexing using wavelet-based salient points. In *IEEE Workshop on Content-based Access of Image and Video Libraries*, pages 15–19.

Slama (ed.), C.C. (1980). *Manual of Photogrammetry*. American Society of Photogrammetry and Remote Sensing.

Smeulders, A., Worring, M., Santini, S., Gupta, A., and Jain, R. (2000). Content based image retrieval at the end of the early years. *IEEE Transactions on Pattern Analysis and Machine Intelligence*, 22(12):1349–1380.

Smith, A.R. (1978). Color gamut transform pairs. *Computer Graphics*, 12(3):12–19.

Smith, J.R. (February 1997). *Integrated Spatial and Feature Image Systems: Retrieval, Compression, and Analysis*. PhD thesis, Columbia University.

Smith, J.R. and Chang, S.-F. (1994). Transform features for texture classification and discrimination in large image databases. *IEEE International Conference on Image Processing*, 3:407–411.

Smith, J.R. and Chang, S.F. (1996). VisualSEEk: A fully automated content-based image query system. *ACM Multimedia*, pages 87–93.

Stephenson, G.M., Ayling, K., and Rutter, D.R. (1976). The role of visual communication in social exchange. *British Journal of Social Clinical Psychology*, 15:113–120.

Stevens, S. (1974). *Patterns in nature*. Atlantic-Little Brown Books.

Stokely, E M. and Wu, S.Y. (1992). Surface parametrization and curvature measurement of arbitrary 3-D objects: Five practical methods. *IEEE Transactions on Pattern Analysis and Machine Intelligence*, 14:833–840.

Stricker, A. and Orengo, M. (1995). Similarity of color images. *SPIE - Storage and Retrieval for Image and Video Databases III*, 2420:381–392.

Stricker, M. and Dimai, A. (1997). Spectral covariance and fuzzy regions for image indexing. *Machine Vision and Applications*, 10(2):66–73.

Swain, M.J. and Ballard, D.H. (1991). Color indexing. *International Journal of Computer Vision*, 7(1):11–32.

Tamura, H., Mori, S., and Yamawaki, Y. (1978). Textural features corresponding to visual perception. *IEEE Transactions on Systems, Man, and Cybernetics*, 8:460–473.

Tang, L. and Huang, T.S. (1994). Analysis-based facial expression synthesis. In *IEEE International Conference on Image Processing*, volume 3, pages 98–102.

Tang, L., Kong, Y., Chen, L.S., Lansing, C.R., and Huang, T.S. (1994). Performance evaluation of a facial feature tracking algorithm. *NSF/ARPA Workshop: Performance vs. Methodology in Computer Vision*, pages 218–229.

Tao, H. and Huang, T.S. (1998). Connected vibrations: A modal analysis approach to non-rigid motion tracking. In *IEEE Conference on Computer Vision and Pattern Recognition*, pages 735–740.

Tao, H. and Huang, T.S. (1999). Explanation-based facial motion tracking using a piecewise bezier volume deformation model. *IEEE Conference on Computer Vision and Pattern Recognition*, pages 611–617.

Tek, H. and Kimia, B. (1995). Image segmentation by reaction-diffusion bubbles. In *International Conference on Computer Vision*, pages 156–162.

Terzopoulos, D. and Fleischer, K. (1988). Deformable models. *The Visual Computer*, 4:306–331.

Terzopoulos, D. and Szeliski, R. (1992). Tracking with Kalman snakes. *Active Vision, A. Blake and A. Yuille, eds.*, pages 2–20.

Thucydides (1972). *History of the Peloponnesian War, 428 BC*. New York, NY: Penguin Books, (in [Rey, 1983]).

Tuceryan, M. and Jain, A.K. (1998). Texture analysis. *Handbook of Pattern Recognition and Computer Vision, C.H. Chen, L.F. Pau, P.S.P. Wang, eds.*, pages 207–248.

Turner, M. (1986). Texture discrimination by Gabor functions. *Biological Cybernetics*, 55:71–82.

Tversky, A. (1977). Features of similarity. *Psychological Review*, 84(4):327–352.

Tversky, A. and Krantz, D.H. (1977). The dimensional representation and the metric structure of similarity data. *Journal of Mathematical Psychology*, 7:572–597.

Ueki, N., Morishima, S., Yamada, H., and Harashima, H. (1994). Expression analysis/synthesis system based on emotion space constructed by multilayered neural network. *Systems and Computers in Japan*, 25(13):95–103.

Unser, M. (1986). Sum and difference histograms for texture classification. *IEEE Transactions on Pattern Analysis and Machine Intelligence*, 8(1):118–125.

Van Gool, L., Dewaele, P., and Oosterlinck, A. (1985). Texture analysis. *Computer Vision, Graphics, and Image Processing*, 29(3):336–357.

Vasconcelos, N. and Lippman, A. (2000). A unifying view of image similarity. *International Conference on Pattern Recognition*, 1:38–41.

Voorhees, H. and Poggio, T. (1988). Computing texture boundaries in images. *Nature*, 333:364–367.

Wallach, M. (1958). On psychological similarity. *Psychological Review*, 65(2):103–116.

Watson, G.S. (1958). On Chi-square goodness-of-fit tests for continuous distributions. *Journal of the Royal Statistical Society*, 20(1):44–72.

Whittaker, E.T. and Robinson, G. (1967). *Normal Frequency Distribution, Ch. 8 in The Calculus of Observations: A Treatise on Numerical Mathematics*. Dover Publications.

Williams, D.J. and Shah, M. (1992). A fast algorithm for active contours and curvature estimation. *Computer Vision, Graphics, and Image Processing: Image Understanding*, 55:14–26.

Wuescher, D.M. and Boyer, K.L. (1991). Robust contour decomposition using a constant curvature criterion. *IEEE Transactions on Pattern Analysis and Machine Intelligence*, 13:41–51.

Wyszecki, G. and Stiles, W.S. (1982). *Color Science: Concepts and Methods, Quantitative Data and Formulae*. John Wiley and Sons, New York.

Xu, C. and Prince, J.L. (1997). Gradient vector flow: A new external force for snakes. *IEEE Conference on Computer Vision and Pattern Recognition*, pages 66–71.

Yacoob, Y. and Davis, L.S. (1996). Recognizing human facial expressions from long image sequences using optical flow. *IEEE Transactions on Pattern Analysis and Machine Intelligence*, 18(6):636–642.

Young, T.Y. and Calvert, T.W. (1974). *Classification, Estimation, and Pattern Recognition*. Elsevier.

Yukich, J.E. (1989). Optimal matching and empirical measures. *Proceedings of the American Mathematical Society*, 107(4):1051–1059.

Zhang, R., Tsai, P-S. Cryer, J., and Shah, M. (1999). Shape from shading: A survey. *IEEE Transactions on Pattern Analysis and Machine Intelligence*, 21(8):690–706.

Zusne, L., editor (1970). *Visual Perception of Forms*. Academic Press.

Index